T0248098

# Praise for Kenny Albert and *A Mic for All Seasons*

"I have been blessed to be a part of several great teams, an undefeated college team at Syracuse in 1987, and three Super Bowl championship teams with the Dallas Cowboys. One of the most meaningful compliments I will pay to somebody is that they are a great teammate because I know how important those people are to building championship teams. The same is true outside of the world of football and sports in general. Great companies, great charities, great organizations have great teammates as a part of their teams. Kenny Albert is a great teammate in the booth. He is passionate about every sport he broadcasts. His preparation is unmatched, he knows the rules better than I do—and I played the game—and he creates the likable and friendly vibe that comes across during the broadcast. And he always has that special nugget ready to go when the time is right! One of the things my family and friends love to do is to pop into the booth and watch the broadcast from behind the scenes and see the working relationship between the booth and the production truck. Kenny Albert takes you behind the curtain on gameday during all the different sporting events he has called throughout his amazing career. He has had a Hall of Fame broadcast career and now you will get a chance to share in all these fantastic stories."

—Daryl Johnston, FOX Sports broadcaster/former Dallas Cowboys fullback

"Inside you will learn he was born prematurely, and I am sure there was a 3" x 5" card with the number of days nearby somewhere. His journey to the top was earned, a student of all sports and sports broadcasting, riding the minor league buses, and making the best of the spontaneous curves he was thrown. (You gotta read about 'em!) The best thing about this autobiography? More seasons in all sports ahead!"

—Mike "Doc" Emrick, Hall of Fame hockey broadcaster

"Kenny's dad, Marv, was the inspiration for so many of us growing up in the New York City area who fell in love with sportscasting. One of his books was the reason I ended up attending his alma mater, Syracuse University. There my career took off in part because of the many people I met on campus who had the same inspiration and desire. That makes the joy of getting to be a peer and pal of Kenny's even more satisfying. A few can call multiple sports; no one can do it with the ease and comfort that Kenny does. He can follow the puck for a radio listener during a frantic 3-on-3 NHL overtime just as comfortably as he shares an anecdote while a batter has stepped out of the box during a televised MLB game. His range is matched by his preparation for the job and the ease with which he collaborates with his analysts. I hope the next generation of sportscasters is inspired by this book on sportscasting authored by an Albert. The Albert family has provided the soundtrack for generations of American sports fans. The older generation inspired me and many others, and now Kenny has taken the baton and sprinted to his own level of greatness. He is the most versatile, respected, and prepared announcer in our industry. You will enjoy his stories of life in the booth and on the road!"

—Mike Tirico, NBC Sports broadcaster

"After covering many sports for many years and covering them well, my friend Kenny Albert has stories from the booth that will both entertain and educate any fan about what it's like behind the scenes and what it takes to be one of the country's top announcing talents. Enjoy!"

—Joe Buck, ESPN broadcaster

"Kenny Albert is quickly becoming an icon of sports broadcasting, the consummate professional. I know firsthand the tireless work Kenny pours into everything he does. This book is destined to be a bestseller and a must-have for every sports fan's bookshelf."

—Tim Green, author, lawyer, broadcaster, former NFL linebacker

"Kenny has a unique ability to be all-in on the game he is calling and have every story and insight ready to roll. Then 20 hours later, Kenny is in another booth, in another state for another sport, and he is just as engaged and knowledgeable. The audience always wins when Kenny has the mic. He makes big events bigger."

—Sam Flood, NBC Sports executive producer

"I have had the pleasure and honor to work with some of the biggest and best names to call NHL hockey games. Kenny Albert is as professional, prepared, passionate, energizing, and loyal as anyone I have ever worked with. Whether it was working a regular-season game in the NHL, or an Olympic game in Sochi, or a Game Seven in an NHL playoff series, you always knew that Kenny would be ready to bring it at an amazingly high level. He always found a way to inform the viewer in a respectful and fun way. He is a true professional."

—Pierre McGuire, *NHL on NBC* analyst

"The natural tendency to attach Kenny Albert's achievements as an heir to the Albert Sportscasting Dynasty—born with a silver microphone at his mouth—would be woefully inaccurate. Kenny has worked since childhood to become what he is: an inexhaustible, versatile, well-prepared, professional communicator of sports on radio and TV. He paid his dues, starting from the bottom, to become the reliable, modest, and trusted lead voice of any and every assignment."

—Phil Mushnick, *New York Post* sports columnist

"I loved and admired my pal's broadcasting since he started at three years of age. The book is a hat trick of devotion to his family and craft."

—Richard Lewis, actor/comedian

"My MC sound emerged from the father, but many bars have come from the son. Kenny Albert calling play-by-play rings in our Knicks and Rangers veins."

—Chuck D, musician

"Kenny has enjoyed a front-row seat to A-list events almost since the womb, and his photographic memory of snapshots and stories, personalities, and performances is expertly shared in these pages. With the same enthusiasm, passion, and attention to detail that makes him America's most versatile sportscaster, Kenny Albert takes you behind the camera, behind the scenes, and behind the stories of his splendid sporting life. Enjoy the journey! I already can't wait for the sequel."

—John Giannone, MSG Networks sportscaster

"It's said that, 'Your reach should exceed your grasp.' Kenny Albert showed how true that is simply by plugging—and play-by-playing—away! Kenny is a latter-day Foster Hewitt, and that's the highest compliment I can give a hockey warbler. Hewitt, who invented: 'He shoots, he scores,' was my first favorite hockey play-by-play guy. Kenny is my now favorite. This wonderful—and highly instructive—book tells you how he got to be the best; that is 'The Maven of the Microphone.'"

—Stan "The Maven" Fischler, author/broadcaster

"During my grade-school days, when I first became interested in being a play-by-play broadcaster, I would turn down the sound of a baseball or basketball game that was on TV and announce it on my tape recorder. When Kenny decided he wanted to become a play-by-play broadcaster, he would do the same...but to my dismay, I was told it was usually a game that I was actually broadcasting. On a serious note, when Kenny was a youngster, he accompanied me on many of my road trips and would often keep statistics for me. I could tell that he had an amazing photographic, encyclopedic memory. After listening to many of his practice tapes broadcasting games off the TV, it was obvious as to where he was headed. In effect, I've been a firsthand witness to his growth into a terrific sportscaster. Aside from what he's accomplished on the air, it's been his low-key and humble personality that makes me so proud that he's my son."

—Marv Albert, Hall of Fame broadcaster

"I know it's a cliché, but Kenny truly is a pro's pro. I don't know anyone who works harder preparing for a broadcast. It doesn't matter if he's doing a local Rangers radio game or a FOX national football broadcast; he treats them all the same. In a business filled with major egos—after almost 30 years at FOX—Kenny is still the same classy guy we hired in 1994."

—Ed Goren, former FOX Sports president

"Kenny Albert is a great teammate, an extremely hard worker, and incredibly easy to work with. He makes us all better, and his viewers and listeners benefit. Most importantly, he is a friend!"

—Keith Jones, *NHL on NBC/NHL on TNT* analyst

"When we were together in the AHL, I always knew that Kenny was destined for bigger things. It was his sense of purpose and professionalism that was his strength. He always wanted to call games and he worked at his craft daily. From the notes to the research, he was trying to get better. It was impressive to watch. He would connect the dots on some facts or stats that would make you wonder where and how he got it. And when it was game time, he seamlessly integrated it into the broadcast while painting the game with his words and voice as if you were watching it live. That is his gift! He's the best, always humble and respectful. It was a pleasure working [and rooming] with him."

—Barry Trotz, Stanley Cup-winning head coach

"I have worked with Kenny for over a decade. And in addition to being one of the kindest humans you will ever meet, I have never met someone who knows every detail of every sport. He can give you almost any date, event, or milestone in seconds. His ability to combine all of his skill sets so seamlessly—in addition to growing up immersed in his craft—makes his story that much more compelling and interesting."

—Jill Martin, Emmy Award-winning television personality, fashion expert, and author

"In our biz it would be impossible to be more versatile, well-prepared, and well-liked than Kenny Albert—the ultimate hat trick. Plus, he's never missed a morning skate."

—Steve Levy, ESPN broadcaster

"I have the 'pleasure' every year of trying to interweave our Knicks and Rangers play-by-play needs with Kenny's other multiple broadcasting commitments. Kenny is 'Mr. Planes, Trains, and Automobiles.' Sometimes I have to pull him back from an assignment he swears he can make because the travel from one night to the next just seems too complicated. It's the only time I ever see any ego in Kenny, who is the nicest, most cooperative guy on the planet. When I say, 'I just think Edmonton to Miami might be taking too much of a chance with distance, weather, etc.' Kenny almost always answers, 'I'll do what you want, but I know I can make it.' And you know what, he's probably right...in fact he could probably find a way to do a high school volleyball game on the way and still make it on time!"

—Kevin Meininger, MSG Networks senior coordinating producer

"The indefatigable Kenny Albert gives you a firsthand, inside look at his incredible career. The infectious enthusiasm that he has for his job will come through on each page and give the reader some understanding of the pleasure it has been to work with him for many years."

—Jeff Filippi, former MSG Networks executive producer

"The ultimate professional and team player who always puts the broadcast and those that he works with ahead of himself while keeping up a standard that makes him one of the greatest play-by-play broadcasters of our generation, Kenny Albert sets a wonderful example of how all of us should treat every member of the broadcast crew. Those traits are just a few of the reasons why general managers, coaches, players, and team personnel gravitate to him. Kenny has always made people he works with better, and because of that, I will be eternally grateful. What a friend."

—Joe Micheletti, MSG Networks/NBC broadcaster

"I call Kenny 'The Voice.' Living in New York, I've witnessed any number of 'score, score, score' Rangers calls at a rockin' MSG, Carmelo game-winners, and, of course, so many amazing Giants calls. In particular, Manning to Victor Cruz against the Jets for 99 yards and straight into salsa time…or Manning to OBJ on the wide-receiver screen, then the bomb to Saquon for six! Not easy when your father is an all-time legend. But Kenny has done it on sheer skill and talent in market No. 1."

—Constantine Maroulis, Broadway star, *American Idol* icon

"Kenny Albert—my broadcast partner for 18 seasons and counting—is the consummate professional whose work ethic and preparation are unparalleled. Having watched him call a diverse spectrum of sports, he makes all of his analysts better at their job, and that certainly holds true for me. I have found his writing to be on par with his on-air work—very entertaining and a pleasure to absorb. Kenny is one of the best people in sports broadcasting with a lot to tell; his story is a great read and one that I highly recommend."

—Dave Maloney, New York Rangers captain, MSG Networks broadcaster

"Kenny has one of the best, most distinctive voices in sports broadcasting. To be honest, that and the fact his father is the incomparable Marv Albert, basically was how I knew Kenny prior to being paired with him in 2017. But I tell you what: he is legendary himself. Easily the busiest man in the business—he never seems to not be working. For this reason, I like to think I helped bring out the looser, more laid-back side of the man—like making him find his karaoke voice one Thanksgiving weekend in Miami. But the serious side of Kenny is what makes him truly great. His professionalism and the pride he puts into perfecting his craft are impressive. I always appreciated how these traits served to counterbalance me. He has a way of putting his analyst at ease because he is so buttoned-up and on top of things. With Kenny you never had to worry about a broadcast going off the rails. I was always confident that, no matter what I or anyone else said or did, Kenny could save us from ourselves. I count myself incredibly fortunate to have had the opportunity to work alongside him for three years in the broadcast booth and to share a friendship with him for life!"

—Rondé Barber, Pro Football Hall of Famer

"Kenny is truly one of the best ever! His mind is astounding. His information recall is second to none, and I've tested this. He has worked some of the greatest athletic events over the last few decades in so many different sports. His stories are endlessly entertaining. As great as he is on the mic, he is far and away a better person and friend, and I feel so fortunate to have worked alongside him for so many years."

—AJ Mleczko, U.S. Olympic women's hockey gold medalist, NBC Sports/ESPN broadcaster

"Kenny is a world-class storyteller, but unlike others he does it in real time, never missing a moment but never making it about himself. His stories about those moments captured in this book are priceless. Kenny's impact on FOX Sports started on Day One of our existence. He is the embodiment of teamwork and all that is good about sports. He has made everyone at FOX Sports better."

—Eric Shanks, FOX Sports president

"I remember when Kenny Albert was born. I was only 14, but when his arrival was chronicled in the newspapers, I thought to myself, *Well, this gives me about 21 years to land a good job in broadcasting because after that, Kenny will have them all!* I really wasn't wrong and I couldn't be happier to be right. Kenny deserves every bit of his success not only because he is so good at what he does, but also because you won't finder a kinder, finer person. I'm proud to say that he worked for me many years ago, and even then, before he graduated from college, his path was clear. Bravo on all that he has achieved…but leave a little something for the rest of us."

—Howie Rose, New York Mets broadcaster

"Ever meet someone through the mail? That's old school! In 1984 I was a 17-year-old U.S. Olympic hockey player who received a letter from a young fan—16-year-old Kenny Albert. I sent back a team picture signed by yours truly. We now share a TV booth for the *NHL on TNT* some 39 years later! He's an outstanding partner. I'm proud to know him in and out of the booth."

—Eddie Olczyk, *NHL on NBC/NHL on TNT* broadcaster

"Kenny Albert is not only one of the most versatile play-by-play announcers in broadcasting today, but he's also one of the most versatile of all time. I am constantly blown away by how he has mastered so many different sports. It's a product of his amazing talent and also his incredible work ethic. Add in his character, and Kenny represents the very best of our business."

—Mike Breen, MSG Networks/ESPN broadcaster

# A MIC
## for All
# SEASONS

My Three Decades Announcing
the NFL, NHL, NBA, MLB, and Olympics

## Kenny Albert

TRIUMPH
BOOKS

Library of Congress Cataloging-in-Publication Data

Names: Albert, Kenny, author.
Title: A mic for all seasons: my three decades announcing the NFL, NHL,
   NBA, MLB, and Olympics / Kenny Albert.
Description: Chicago: Triumph Books, [2023] |
Identifiers: LCCN 2023010892 | ISBN 9781637272176 (cloth)
Subjects: LCSH: Albert, Kenny | Sportscasters—United
   States—Biography. | BISAC: BIOGRAPHY & AUTOBIOGRAPHY / Sports |
   LANGUAGE ARTS & DISCIPLINES / Communication Studies
Classification: LCC GV742.42.A43 A3 2023 | DDC 796.092
   [B]—dc23/eng/20230425
LC record available at https://lccn.loc.gov/2023010892

This book is available in quantity at special discounts for your group or organization. For further information, contact:

**Triumph Books LLC**
814 North Franklin Street
Chicago, Illinois 60610
(312) 337-0747
www.triumphbooks.com

Printed in U.S.A.
ISBN: 978-1-63727-217-6
Design by Patricia Frey
Photos courtesy of Kenny Albert

*To Barbara, Amanda, and Sydney—*
*the best hat trick I could have ever hoped for!*

# Contents

# Foreword

When I was a young boy growing up, my father, Walter, would always tell me that through sports I was going to see the world, make great friends, and meet some of the nicest people ever. As a 35-year-old player for the New York Rangers late in my career, one of the best people I would meet would be Kenny Albert.

When I signed as a free agent with the Rangers in the summer of 1996, Kenny was about to begin his second season as a member of the team's outstanding broadcast crew, along with Sam Rosen, John Davidson, and Sal Messina. All three of them have subsequently been named recipients of the Foster Hewitt Memorial Award in recognition of their outstanding contributions to their profession and the game during their careers in hockey broadcasting.

During road trips with the Blueshirts, we spent countless hours together on team charter flights across North America. The coaches and management usually sat in the front section of the plane, the broadcasters and training staff in the middle area, and the players in the back. It has been well documented that I do not love flying, especially when turbulence starts rocking the airplane. Given that I played more than 900 road games during my pro hockey career, air travel was a necessary evil. To alleviate my fears, I would often wander to the front of the Rangers' plane and chat with the pilot, whom I nicknamed "The Red Baron." I would also spend a lot of time with the broadcasters, schmoozing about not only hockey, but also other sports, a variety of subjects, and life in general. I frequently noticed Kenny poring through materials while preparing for his NFL telecasts, and we would discuss the various teams, players, and matchups. Chatting about football (as well as basketball and baseball) seemed to make the flights go faster.

I'm not sure he realized how comfortable sitting beside him on those flights made me feel. He was a true New Yorker who loved everything about the Big Apple.

Kenny and his wife, Barbara, were on hand at the party following my final NHL game on April 18, 1999. In recent years I have enjoyed becoming his colleague on TNT and have joined him in the broadcast booth on a few occasions. Kenny and his partners, Eddie Olczyk and Keith Jones, do such a great job, and I have loved every minute of the time I have spent with them.

Now that I am a member of the Turner Sports family, I have an even greater understanding and appreciation of everything it takes to prepare for a broadcast. To see Kenny have the knowledge he does for the NHL—as well as the NFL, NBA, and MLB—speaks volumes to how dedicated, prepared, and knowledgeable he is at his craft.

In the quarter century since Kenny and I traveled together on Rangers flights, he has been at the microphone for iconic sporting events—from Olympic hockey to playoff football and baseball to the Stanley Cup Final. His professional journey began in 1990, when he called minor league hockey games while traveling from city to city on the team bus. Some trips took as long as 10 hours—a far cry from the charter flights with first-class seats and all the food you can eat that we enjoyed together during my three seasons with the Rangers. I'm sure you will love reading all about Kenny's upbringing; his college years (including scoring the first goal in NYU club history, a record he reminds me that will never be broken); his entertaining stories about the games he has called; color analysts he has worked with; and a few travel tales as well. Having had the good fortune to hear firsthand how much he loves New York, his job, his country, as well as his family and his friends, I'm sure you will love this book, too.

—*Wayne Gretzky*

# Foreword

Kenny Albert is one of the greatest announcers of all time. His work in basketball, hockey, football, baseball, boxing—to name several sports—is simply unprecedented. Who can call all of those sports at the highest level? Nobody but Kenny.

I take pride in the fact that I have worked on the air with so many of the Alberts, including his father and uncles. I fondly remember Kenny when he was young and keeping stats for Marv at the Garden. I also recall never hearing him talk. He would never say *anything*. Then one day I learned he was starting to call hockey games in Baltimore, and he was off to the races. He found his voice.

I deeply admire his work as his broadcast partner; he is sagacious, enlightening, informative, and easy to listen to. As a sports fan, I continue to be in awe of his work whether he is calling basketball, football, hockey, or baseball. I really don't know which sport I enjoy hearing him call more.

When people ask me what separates Kenny from the others, it's his preparation and tenacious work ethic (like his father always had) that has catapulted him to the top of the business. He is in-depth in what he studies and brings up nuggets of information that others wouldn't even think about. In time, Kenny is going to get the recognition he so deserves.

Marv always used to tell me, "Never say anything on the air you can't authenticate." Kenny lives by those words during each and every broadcast.

Off the air, he is a terrific person; I thought Mike Breen was the most unselfish person I met, someone with absolutely no ego, but Kenny is right there with him. He is always humble with kind words to share and remains a true team player. Quite simply, Kenny is the quintessential guy who carries himself with dignity and good manners. That is Kenny; he is just himself.

In this book fans can expect unprecedented insight from one of the most versatile announcers ever, who also happens to be loved and adored—on and off the air.

—*Walt "Clyde" Frazier*

# Introduction
## They Call This Work?

I have never worked a day in my life. Sure, I spend countless hours every day preparing for broadcasts and have been away from my family for thousands of days and nights over the last three decades. But I am one of the very fortunate ones. I have called sporting events professionally since 1990 (and as an amateur since the age of five) and have loved every minute of it. Despite all of the hard work and preparation that goes into each broadcast, as well as all the time on the road, it never feels like work. I enjoy the prep, the travel, the people I work with, and, of course, the actual games.

Play-by-play has been my passion ever since the day my parents gifted me a tape recorder for my fifth birthday. The journey has allowed me to call more than 3,000 games in the four major North American professional sports from historic venues such as Madison Square Garden, Fenway Park, Wrigley Field, Lambeau Field, and Wembley Stadium, as well as eight Olympic Games around the globe. I've also called numerous high school and college sports, WNBA games, Olympic hockey, track and field, volleyball, baseball, hosted horse racing shows, filed radio reports from golf and tennis tournaments, and even handled the public-address duties at a dog show and a robotics competition. I called Super Bowl XLVI to an international audience; 10 Stanley Cup Finals; classic NFL, MLB, and NBA postseason games; All-Star Games in three different sports; several college football bowl games; and championship prize fights in Las Vegas. I even played myself—in the role of a sportscaster (surprise!)—in two movies: *Game Day* (starring Richard Lewis) and *Juwanna Mann* (starring Vivica A. Fox).

I have been so fortunate to be involved in countless memorable moments and events throughout the last three decades. From the 1994 Stanley Cup Final to NFL Divisional Playoff games to the Jose Bautista home run and subsequent bat flip in the 2015 Divisional Playoff Game to the U.S. women's hockey Olympic gold-medal winning shootout in Pyeongchang, South Korea, in 2018 to the 2021 Stanley Cup Final on NBC and 2023 Stanley Cup Final on TNT.

I have called events involving some of the greatest athletes in history: Tom Brady, Peyton Manning, Brett Favre, Aaron Rodgers, Drew Brees, Wayne Gretzky, Mario Lemieux, Michael Jordan, LeBron James, Ken Griffey Jr., Randy Johnson, Derek Jeter, Usain Bolt, Manny Pacquiao. The list goes on and on.

In what other profession could I have been congratulated by Gretzky after scoring a goal in a charity game at Madison Square Garden, drawn the unlucky straw and sat directly behind 7'7" Gheorge Muresan on a Washington Bullets charter flight (yes, he reclined his seat), listened in awe as Pat Summerall—in his legendary cadence—ordered the "Kick Ass Chili" at a restaurant in Beverly Hills, played basketball with Magic Johnson, competed in Ping-Pong matches against Baseball Hall of Famer John Smoltz and Heisman Trophy winner Matt Leinart (I won), and played doubles tennis opposite Terry Bradshaw? During my college years, I even scored the first goal in the history of the NYU hockey club.

I am extremely proud to say that I am the only play-by-play broadcaster who has called NFL, NHL, NBA, and MLB games on a full-time basis in the 21st century. I began my NHL broadcasting career in 1992 after filling in on New York Islanders radio broadcasts. I called my first NFL game for FOX Sports in September 1994. After working several Major League Baseball games from 1994 through 1996, I started calling the sport on a regular basis in 1997. My first NBA broadcasts were as a fill-in with the Washington Bullets between 1993 and 1995. Over the last decade-plus, I have called approximately 20 New York Knicks games per season on MSG Networks. During a 19-day stretch in September/October 2019, I worked five different sports (my usual four in addition to boxing). Sports might just be the best form of reality television. When I step into the broadcast booth, there's a pretty good chance I will witness something never seen previously.

My partners in the broadcast booth have included all-time greats—including myriad Hall of Famers and champions in their respective sports: Gretzky, Bradshaw, Troy Aikman, Joe Namath, Howie Long, Joe Theismann, Anthony Muñoz, Rondé and Tiki Barber, Walt "Clyde" Frazier, Patrick Ewing, Tim McCarver, Jim Palmer, Keith Hernandez, Lou Piniella, Joe Girardi, Denis Potvin, Eddie Olczyk, "Sugar" Ray Leonard, and countless others. I might just hold the all-time record for most teammates in the broadcast booth—more than 225! And I have enjoyed working with each and every one of them.

I received one of the highest honors of my career in March 2020 when—for the second time in five years—I was named one of five finalists for a national Sports Emmy in the play-by-play category. The other finalists were Al Michaels, Jim Nantz, Mike Emrick, and Mike Breen—all giants in the industry. The announcement came two weeks after the postponement of the NHL and NBA seasons due to the spread of COVID-19; I slept in my own bed for 146 consecutive nights. To say the period of inactivity with no games to call, flights to catch, or hotel rooms to check into was bizarre and surreal would be an understatement. During a typical year, I do play-by-play for more than 150 sporting events in four different sports in cities all across North America and overseas. I have memorized the flight schedules of most major airlines and have mastered the art of maneuvering through TSA checkpoints with ease. In my world, years aren't measured by hours, days, weeks, and months but by preseason, regular season, postseason, and offseason. I have lived a charmed life.

A special thank you to my wife Barbara and daughters Amanda and Sydney. They have been poking and prodding me to write a book for many years. I never seemed to have the time; it took a worldwide pandemic to allow me to start writing several chapters. I continued during the spring and summer of 2022 on airplanes, in my home office, and my favorite spot—our backyard.

Professional sports have played a major role in my personal life (as they did for my parents). If not for several unlikely circumstances and coincidences—including the New York Rangers advancing to the Stanley Cup Final in 1994 and *losing* Game Five of the series—Barbara and I would not have met. We were introduced by Jerry Coleman, who attended college with Barbara and then became a friend and colleague of mine in Baltimore shortly thereafter. A generation earlier, my parents met due to a confluence of events at a New York Mets game.

I look forward to taking you on the journey from my premature birth in 1968 through my high school and college years…then over three decades in the broadcast booth. Thanks for reading, and I hope you enjoy.

# A MIC
## for All
# SEASONS

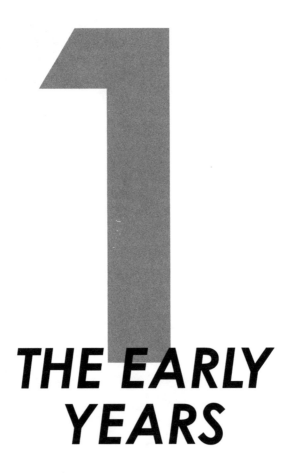

# THE EARLY
# YEARS

Although I was born on February 2, 1968, one of the most important dates that affected my life was October 17, 1960. Four days after Bill Mazeroski's walk-off home run in Game Seven of the World Series to defeat Casey Stengel's New York Yankees, a National League franchise was formally awarded to a group headed by Mrs. Joan Payson. Seven months later, the team's name was announced. Managed by Stengel, the New York Mets would spend their first two seasons (1962 and 1963) at the Polo Grounds in upper Manhattan, the former home of the baseball Giants before they moved to San Francisco following a sixth-place finish in 1957.

WABC 770 AM carried the Mets games on radio during the 1962 and 1963 seasons. The expansion Mets finished with a record of 40–120, the most losses by any Major League Baseball team in one season during the 20th century. Prior to the team's third campaign, the radio rights shifted to WHN 1050 AM. The pregame and postgame shows would be handled by 22-year-old Marv Albert.

In April 1964, a brand-new ballpark—Shea Stadium—opened in Flushing, Queens; it was named after the lawyer who was instrumental in bringing National League baseball back to New York. The Mets hired "usherettes," female hostesses who welcomed fans after they entered through the turnstiles and escorted them to their seats. A 19-year-old college student from Little Neck, Queens, named Benita Caress traveled via bus and subway (against her father's wishes) to attend tryouts. She was never officially hired but showed up anyway at the first home game, took a uniform, and started working.

Prior to the second-ever night game at Shea on May 8, 1964, Marv interviewed various stadium employees on his show. His childhood friend Arthur Friedman, who became the longtime statistician for both the Mets and

New York Rangers, wandered into the stands and selected Benita to head to the radio booth with him for an interview. And that is how my parents met. If not for the Giants and Dodgers moving west, Payson, William Shea, Friedman, and the shift in Mets radio rights, I would not be here today. They got married in August 1965 on the day after my mother's 21st birthday.

A few years later, WHN became the radio home of the New York Knicks and Rangers. After filling in on broadcasts during prior seasons, my father became the full-time radio voice of the Rangers in 1965–66 and the New York Knicks in 1967–68. (The 2022–23 season was the 57th consecutive season during which an Albert called Rangers games on the radio.)

Given that my mother's due date was May 5, 1968, there was no chance that my father was expecting to be paged at LaGuardia Airport after a flight from Montreal on the morning of Friday, February 2. The night before, he called the Montreal Canadiens' 5–2 victory against the Blueshirts at the Montreal Forum. He initially did not believe the news that my mother had gone into labor three months early and went from the airport to their apartment on West 55th Street in Manhattan. After entering an empty apartment, the news sunk in; he hurried to Lenox Hill Hospital and arrived a few hours after I was born at 11:50 AM (at one pound, 15 ounces) three months premature (at the 26-week point of the term). I was the first born of twin boys; my brother did not survive. Due to the lack of technology at the time, my mother had no idea that she was carrying two babies. My weight eventually dropped to one pound, eight ounces; I was an underdog for the first few months of my life and spent 10 weeks in an incubator.

Because my parents were unsure whether I would survive, they opted to not name me immediately. The word "baby" was typed into the first name box on my birth certificate and was later crossed out and replaced with a hand-written "Kenneth." When I was young, my parents told me that they selected my name by leafing through the NHL Guide and Record Book (instead of a traditional baby name book). My mother has said that I was named after Ken Hodge, though it could have also been either Ken Schinkel or Ken Wharram—the two others named Ken who played in the NHL during the 1967–68 season. I finally went home on April 12, 1968 (the day Rangers great Adam Graves was born) at 71 days old while weighing five pounds, five ounces.

A miracle baby, I was the first person in my family born with the surname Albert. My father and his brothers went through their childhood in Brooklyn with the last name Aufrichtig. After my father graduated from Lincoln High School and was headed to Syracuse University, it was apparent that he was going to advance in the broadcasting world. So, his parents (my grandparents) Max and Alida changed their last name to Albert, which rolled off the tongue smoother than Aufrichtig. They wanted to stick with the first letter A to stay near the top of the alphabet and selected the name after flipping through the phone book. So, my first and last names came from an NHL Guide and Record Book and the White Pages. Max owned a grocery store called Aufrichtig Brothers—along with his brother—in the Brighton Beach section of Brooklyn. I have a photo of myself "working" there at the age of six, stamping stickers with the price onto various items.

We lived on 55th Street and 6th Avenue during the first two-and-a-half years of my life; my mother took me for frequent walks in my stroller to Central Park. One day, as I was accompanying her to the laundry room in our apartment building, my hand got stuck in the elevator. After a quick trip to the hospital, we returned home, and I stuck my hand in the laundry detergent that she had left in the hallway—and ate it. Back to the emergency room we went, as there was never a dull moment with me! I suffered through myriad medical issues during my first three years: mumps, hernia, pneumonia, a cyst on my forehead, tonsils removed at age three. On a more positive note, one of my earliest memories is attending the taping of the children's television program *Wonderama*. My mother and I sat in the studio audience.

In 1971 we moved to a two-story house in Woodmere on the south shore of Long Island, where I attended nursery school, summer camp, and kindergarten. Around the age of five, I received a tape recorder from my parents and started to announce games in my bedroom—both off the television and fictional sporting events that I imagined. I was hooked. I knew then that I wanted to be a play-by-play broadcaster. My first appearance on a real radio station was around this same time, when I called into my father's sports talk show on WHN Radio; the producer knew it was me and put me through to ask a question live on air.

I still have a cassette tape of a sports, weather, and traffic report I recorded in my squeaky voice: "It's 68 degrees in Woodmere...there's bumper-to-bumper traffic on the Long Island Expressway." My other "talent" at a young age was playing the piano by ear. I took lessons but never really enjoyed reading music. To this day, if I am familiar with a song, I can play it on the piano (with one hand). Friends and family members are amazed when they see/hear my skills at the keyboard for the first time. My parents credit me with the moniker bestowed upon Phil Jackson of the Knicks in the early 1970s. I had an action figure named "Action Jackson" and as a young child I nicknamed the Knicks forward "Action Jackson." My father mentioned it during one of his radio broadcasts, and I received full credit.

In 1973 my parents arranged to be placed on a list to adopt a baby. I'll never forget when the phone call arrived that a baby was born in Allentown, Pennsylvania, and would be ours. A few days later, the three of us headed to Allentown to pick up two-day-old Jackie. I had been an only child for five years. One month after Jackie's birth, my mother became pregnant with twins. On April 5, my brother Brian and sister Denise were born in Manhattan. With four kids we outgrew the house in Woodmere and moved to Old House Lane in Sands Point (on Long Island's north shore) in August 1974; I started first grade at John J. Daly Elementary School a few weeks later.

I continued to announce games into the recorder at every opportunity. I transformed my new bedroom into a radio studio. My desk and television were set up at opposite ends of the bed. I compiled notebooks filled with rosters and statistics and called games off the TV into my cassette recorder. When my father invited his colleagues or—occasionally—a pro athlete to the house, I would hijack them into my bedroom to be interviewed. My subjects included Knicks analyst John Andariese, basketball Hall of Famers Julius Erving and Phil Jackson, hockey writer/broadcaster Stan Fischler, NHL goalie

Glenn "Chico" Resch, Rangers captain Dave Maloney (who would become my longtime broadcast partner), and New York Giants punter Dave Jennings. They all spent time getting interviewed on my fictitious radio station WKGA (Kenneth Gary Albert) modeled after my father's mock station as a youngster, WMPA (Marvin Philip Aufrichtig). Whenever my uncles Al and Steve (both longtime play-by-play broadcasters) visited our house on holidays or other special occasions, I enjoyed hearing stories about the various teams and networks they were employed by. During the conversations between my father and his brothers, I felt like I was listening to the first all-sports radio station and soaked it all in.

Growing up with three family members in the business had huge advantages. I accompanied my dad to hundreds of games throughout my childhood. I would watch him prepare for broadcasts, sit behind him in the broadcast booth, and then do the play-by-play in my head. During my teenage years, I frequently brought the recorder to Madison Square Garden, Shea Stadium, and Nassau Coliseum and called games—either from a somewhat empty section in the stands or in an auxiliary press box.

I loved attending games at MSG for as long as I could remember. I would usually sit with my mother—four rows behind the visitors' bench for Knicks games and Section 54 in the corner about 15 rows off the ice at Rangers games. When I was old enough, my father would allow me to sit behind him in the radio broadcast booth. He once let me sit in between him and analyst Sal Messina. I was doing play-by-play out loud. Apparently, my audio was seeping through their microphones, and by the second period, I was relegated back to my usual seat.

For my seventh birthday, I was gifted a trip to Washington, D.C., with my father. He was scheduled to broadcast the Rangers–Washington Capitals game on February 11, 1975. We took the train to D.C. and went sightseeing, including a photo-op in front of the exterior fence at the White House. It was my first trip to the Capital Centre in Landover, Maryland (where I would call games for the Capitals beginning in 1992 after the building was re-named U.S. Air Arena). The Capitals were in their inaugural NHL season and had a record of 4–45–5 heading into the encounter with the Rangers. They named ex-Blueshirt George "Red" Sullivan as their new head coach earlier in the day. The opening faceoff was delayed by nearly two hours. The Ice Capades had performed in Landover the night before, and there were issues with the paint on the ice. The radio statistician working with my father and Messina had an early flight the next morning. Due to the late start, he left after the second period. So, at the age of seven years and nine days, I made my debut keeping track of the goals and assists in the third period. The Capitals scored four goals in the third and defeated the Rangers 7–4. The first goal I ever wrote down as an official broadcast statistician was scored by Washington's Gord Brooks with assists from Yvon Labre and Ace Bailey. Labre became a Capitals team ambassador after his playing career (and the first Cap to have his number retired). He's a great guy; I knew him well during my time working in Washington. I met Bailey once. He was with his good pal Wayne Gretzky during a Rangers–Los Angeles Kings game at Staples Center in 2000, and they visited our radio booth together. Bailey tragically passed away while traveling on United Airlines flight 175 on September 11, 2001.

Around the age of five or six, I somehow became a rabid Vancouver Canucks fan. I'm not sure exactly why or how given that I lived 3,000 miles from British Columbia, and my father was one of the voices of the Rangers. My bedroom was painted in Canucks colors—initially green and blue and then red, yellow, and black when they changed their color scheme. I cut out Canucks box scores from the newspaper and put together scrapbooks with every Canucks photo and article I could find. I would wake up in the middle of the night and turn on 1010 WINS Radio at 15 or 45 minutes after the hour to hear the final score of a game played in the western time zone. During third grade (in January of 1977), I received the birthday present of a lifetime. My father was scheduled to broadcast two games in Vancouver: a Rangers game on January 23, followed by the NHL All-Star Game two days later.

The night before we were scheduled to fly, I tried on a suit, and my mother noticed a bump on my neck and suspected chicken pox. She drove me to the emergency room for confirmation. I was devastated. As a consolation prize, I accompanied my father to Vancouver two seasons later for a Rangers game and met legendary Canucks broadcaster Jim Robson for the first time. I would exchange letters with Robson for many years. He joked that the first time he received a letter from me—upon seeing an NBC logo on the envelope—he thought he was being offered a job. I was using the stationery my father brought home from the office. To this day, I keep in touch with Robson and am always thrilled to see him whenever I'm in Vancouver to call a game. He has been retired for many years but frequently attends games and visits the press box. And, by the way, I still haven't forgiven Harold Snepsts for his pass up the middle, which was intercepted by Mike Bossy of the New York Islanders, who turned it into the game-winning goal at 19:58 of overtime in Game One of the 1982 Stanley Cup Final, which left a 14 year old devastated by the Canucks defeat. Living on Long Island made it even worse. Most of my friends were Islanders fans who had already enjoyed back-to-back championship runs.

In August 1977 (at the age of nine), after completing my third summer at Shibley Day Camp in Roslyn, Long Island, my parents sent me away on my own for the first time to the five-day Pete Maravich Basketball Camp at Kutsher's Sports Academy in Monticello, New York. "Pistol Pete" had just completed his seventh NBA season and led the league in scoring at more than 31 points per game. His dazzling style on the court—dribbling the basketball between his legs, spinning the ball on his finger—made him one of the most popular athletes in the United States. Pete and his dad Press, who had been his head coach at LSU, didn't just lend their name to the camp. They worked closely with the young campers for the entire week and never left the premises. I was assigned the bottom bunk. During the middle of the first night, I was awoken by the crying of my roommate, who was on the floor in obvious pain after having fallen from the top bunk. A counselor came into our room and lifted him back onto his bed. If that happened in today's world, he would have immediately been taken to the hospital to be examined for a possible concussion but not in 1977.

In the morning my roommate woke up and told me his ankle hurt; he had no recollection of falling out of his bed the night before. For the rest of the week, he couldn't play basketball but was never more than a few feet from Pete Maravich, who took him under his wing. My roommate's name was Barry Baum. He later became a Knicks ballboy and has since gone on to a terrific career—first as a sportswriter with the *New York Post* and then as a public relations executive with the Brooklyn Nets and Milwaukee Bucks. On my 50th birthday—41 years after he fell out of the bed—Baum sent over a cake while I was broadcasting a Knicks–Bucks game in Milwaukee with Walt "Clyde" Frazier. Maravich, who died at the age of 40 in 1988, would be proud to know that two of his former campers have gone on to careers in the world of sports. I wrote a Letter to the Editor during my sophomore year at NYU, which was published in *The New York Times* after Maravich passed away:

"To The Sports Editor — The death of Pistol Pete Maravich brought back personal memories of a week with the National Basketball Association All-Star. My first experience away from home was in 1977 when, as a 9-year-old, I attended the Pistol Pete Basketball Camp in Monticello, N.Y. Big-time athletes often sell their names to sneaker companies, athletic-wear outlets or summer camps for huge sums of money, then don't put in any time. During the five-day camp, Maravich didn't step off the grounds once. He led every drill in the humid field house himself, instead of leaving it up to the teenage counselors. He proudly explained the schedule he imposed upon himself as a youngster: hours upon hours of basketball drills. Pete told us how he used to bring a ball to the movie theater and dribble it up and down the aisles; how he used to spin the ball on his fingers for hours until they bled. On the original camp schedule, activities such as swimming and tennis were listed. Maravich eliminated all sports not related to basketball. After dinner each night, when the campers played scrimmage games, Maravich stayed to help officiate, coach and score the games. The next year, when Pete came to Madison Square Garden as a member of the

```
New Orleans Jazz, at least 20 of us camp alumni wore our
yellow "Pistol Pete Basketball Camp" t-shirts and cheered
every one of his dazzling moves. After he retired as a
player, Maravich said that he would have traded all his
scoring records, awards and All-Star nominations for an
NBA championship. In my book, Pete Maravich will always
be a champion. KENNY ALBERT, New York"
```

My first day as a full-time, eight-week camper at Kutsher's Sports Academy was on June 29, 1979. It is also the day I met Rich Ackerman, a kid from Brooklyn who was also assigned to Olympic Village Bunk 9. We would become close friends, bunkmates for all six years I attended the camp and eventually roommates and broadcast partners for four years at New York University. Ackerman has enjoyed an outstanding radio career in Charlotte; Washington, D.C.; Chicago; and—for the last quarter of a century—at WFAN/CBS Sports Radio in New York. Our first counselor was Steve Carp, a Brooklyn native eight years our senior, who has gone on to a long career as a sportswriter in Las Vegas. To this day, Ackerman and I still keep in touch with Carp, as well as some of our other counselors in subsequent years— George Johnson, Dan Wiener, and Varadharajulu Gajapathy (known as "Gaja"). They were all authority figures but also became good friends.

During that summer of '79, I became the official scorekeeper for the very competitive weekly counselor basketball games played in the Clair F. Bee Fieldhouse. Red Auerbach was the camp director in the early 1970s and donated the old Boston Garden court to the Kutsher family. It is the same floor we (sacrilegiously) played floor hockey on—and scratched up—each and every day. Looking back, it was probably unfair to my bunkmates, but I received special privileges to stay out after curfew while I was keeping the scorebook. Another friend who I met at camp was Jesse Itzler, a terrific basketball player from Long Island. Itzler has gone on to a tremendous career as an entrepreneur, author, and rapper. He wrote and sang the Knicks theme song "Go New York Go" in 1992, was a cofounder of Marquis Jets, and is currently part of the Atlanta Hawks ownership group. Donna Geils (now Donna

Orender), a college basketball and pro star (with the New Jersey Gems), was a counselor at KSA during my early years. From 2005 through 2011, she was president of the WNBA. We have kept in touch through the years, and I am so happy for her success. Irwin Schtierman, another close friend from my KSA summers, later became the camp's associate director.

Every August the Maurice Stokes Memorial Basketball Classic took place in the fieldhouse. On the historic court where I played floor hockey, NBA stars past and present would come to our camp and participate in a charity basketball game in front of more than 5,000 fans. It was one of the marquee events in the Catskills each summer. I worked as a ball boy during my first four years at camp and then became the television statistician in 1983 and 1984 for broadcasters Gary Sussman and Dolph Schayes. I was always looking for ways to be involved in some fashion.

Numerous pro athletes and coaches visited KSA every summer to conduct clinics in their respective sport, including Erving, Rick Pitino, Ernie Grunfeld, Hubie Brown, Cotton Fitzsimmons, and Tiny Archibald from the world of basketball; Mookie Wilson and Pat Zachry from the Mets; players from the New York Cosmos of the North American Soccer League; and tennis pros.

Once on a rainy day, regular activities were canceled. I sat on the front steps of the camp's main building and played the *Sports Illustrated Baseball* board game with friends. I was using the 1969 Mets as my team, and Art Shamsky hit a home run. Thirty seconds later, the real Art Shamsky happened to walk by. He had come to KSA to run a baseball clinic. You couldn't make this stuff up.

During the summer of 1984, Pitino—then a Knicks assistant coach—discovered a seven-footer from Texas named Ron Cavenall while conducting a clinic at KSA. Pitino recommended Cavenall to the Knicks front office, and the rest was history. Cavenall played 53 games for the club during the 1984–85 season. A 17-year-old Dutchman named Rik Smits, who was entering his freshman year at Marist College and went on to enjoy a terrific 12-year career with the Indiana Pacers, and Joe Jones, the longtime head basketball coach at Columbia University and Boston University, were also KSA counselors during the summer of '84. The frequent counselor basketball games (for which I kept the scorebook) included Cavenall, Smits, Jones, KSA legend/sharpshooter Chris Cummings (a star at Centenary College of Louisiana who had a tryout with the Denver Nuggets), and Marc White (a longtime KSA counselor/coach and later the camp's owner) and were highly competitive.

A few summers into my tenure at KSA, I cofounded and edited a camp newspaper, *Kids and Kounselors* (yes, we spelled it with a K), thanks to the support of camp director Bob Trupin and head counselor Jerry Cohen. Along with bunkmate Gregg Gable, we wrote articles and compiled statistics from games and events around camp, typed the pages in the main office, and used the camp's mimeograph machine to make enough copies to distribute the next day.

The experience working on the camp newspaper steered me into writing for various publications at home. I wrote a few articles for the newspaper at John Philip Sousa Junior High School and had others published in the *Port Washington Mail and Reporter* (the secondary newspaper in town). In seventh grade I kept the scorebook for the girls' basketball team coached by my English teacher (and former Marist College basketball star) Steve Shackel. During ninth grade while still attending junior high school, I contacted Amy Pett, the editor at the *Port Washington News* (the town's main publication). She hired me to cover high school sports for $5 a week. It was my first paying job, and I thought I hit the jackpot. I covered various sports at Paul D. Schreiber High School—basketball, football, soccer, lacrosse, among many others. I developed relationships with the coaches, as well as athletic director Tom Romeo, before I was a student at Schreiber. The articles were due every Monday morning. So on Sunday nights, my mother would drive me to the small office on Main Street in Port Washington, and I would slide an envelope with my prose under the door. I was getting paid to write articles about high school sporting events, a harbinger of things to come. On occasion, I penned features on professional sports figures who lived on Long

Island, including pro soccer goalie Shep Messing and hockey broadcaster Bill Chadwick, which ran in all of the Anton Community Newspapers around Long Island.

When I began high school, I started to write for *The Schreiber Times* as well. I was always hanging around the gym and various sports fields at the school covering star athletes such as Rodney Dumpson, James Abercrombie, Barry Milhaven, Jennifer Marra, Nora Maguire, and Diane McLoughlin. Dan Biro was the longtime football coach at Schreiber (I always felt he bore a resemblance to Don Shula) and was also a favorite teacher of mine. Additionally, I gathered information and edited media guides and game programs for the boys and girls basketball teams coached by Herb Sondericker and Stephanie Joannon. I wrote letters to the opposing schools asking for rosters and then typed the information at home before bringing the pages to the athletic department secretary, Barbara Ochenkoski, to be mimeographed. The programs were then distributed to the fans prior to all home games. I also became the backup public-address announcer at the basketball games whenever John Broza, the chairman of the English department with a baritone voice, had other commitments. At Schreiber I took a television production class. A teacher named James Barchi was ahead of his time. He constructed a TV studio with state-of-the-art equipment. This was unheard of at the high school level in the mid-1980s.

I received a huge break in January 1984 midway through 10th grade. After we returned to school following the holiday recess, Mr. Romeo mentioned to me that a small cable television station, Cox Cable of Great Neck, would be coming to our gymnasium to film a girls basketball game. How they decided to come to Schreiber I will never know, but it turned into one of the most fortunate things to happen to me in my entire career. Their plan included a small production van, two cameras, and natural crowd sound with no announcers. The game was going to be televised on delayed tape a few days later. Romeo introduced me to the Cox producer, Roy Menton, who asked if I had interest in announcing the game. I jumped at the opportunity, and the rest is history. One of the technicians clipped a lavalier microphone onto my shirt, I sat three rows behind the Schreiber bench, and I did play-by-play. Anybody near me who did not notice the small microphone must have thought I was talking to myself.

I called Menton the next day and volunteered to do whatever he needed, wherever he needed me. Over the next two and a half years, I called play-by-play for close to one hundred games for Cox all over Long Island, including high school basketball, football, baseball, hockey, softball, soccer, lacrosse, as well as college basketball and football games at the United States Merchant Marine Academy in Kings Point, Long Island. I did not get paid, but I didn't care. I received invaluable experience. I felt I like I had a three-year head start on any other students who were interested in play-by-play but did not have an opportunity to practice their craft until college. As an added bonus, I brought friends, including Adam Holzer, Dalton Einhorn, Scott Marsel, and Howard Cheris, along to handle color commentary.

The outstanding USMMA Sports Information Director Dennis O'Donnell provided interesting tidbits and statistics and was a tremendous resource. The fact that I was calling Division III basketball and football games while still in high school was an amazing opportunity that I was so thankful for.

Menton moved on to Staten Island Cable, where I called Wagner College football games for him during my college years. In fact, a playoff game at Wagner (against Ithaca College) in 1988—with broadcast partner John Tassiello and Mitch Robinson—was the last football game I called prior to my first NFL telecast for FOX in 1994. I owe a debt of gratitude to Menton, whom I kept in touch with through the years prior to his passing in 2017. The last time I saw him was a few years before, when he invited me to work as a celebrity public-address announcer at a robotics competition at the Javits Center in Manhattan that one of his kids was involved in. I knew nothing about robotics, but Menton guided me along the way, just as he did in 1984 when he first hired me.

I was extremely busy during my high school years covering games for the *Port Washington News* and *The Schreiber Times*, calling games for Cox Cable, working as the backup public-address announcer at high school basketball games, editing school media guides and game programs, handling stats for my father at Rangers home games, and I also played club hockey. Somehow, I managed to find time to attend class and do my homework. I was the sports editor at *The Schreiber Times* in 11th and 12th grade. I initially wrote most of my *Port News* articles on an old-fashioned typewriter and then began to use the word processing program on early-day computers in Schreiber's English department. The first computer my parents bought for me was made by the Atari video game company. I recall it had a flat keyboard (the keys would often get stuck), but it got the job done. At one point, my mother explained that she did not want to spend more money on a next-level computer because she thought computers were a "fad" and would go away quickly. I still joke about it with her to this day. One of the writers on the staff of the high school newspaper was a friend since junior high school, Tom Gulitti, who has gone on to an outstanding career covering hockey for *The Bergen Record* and NHL.com. I take pride in the fact that I gave Gulitti his first writing assignment during our high school days.

When I was just 17, my father helped me secure an internship at National Hockey League headquarters in Manhattan with legendary public relations guru John Halligan, who had spent two decades working for the Rangers. Halligan was another major influence during my formative years in the working world. He had a fun and engaging personality and was highly respected by everyone in the world of hockey. On my first day, Halligan assigned me to work with Stu Hackel, who was the editor of *GOAL Magazine.*

I spent an enjoyable summer commuting to Manhattan via the Long Island Rail Road. During the first week, I kept imagining how much fun my friends were having at camp and wondered if I made the wrong decision by interning instead of returning to KSA. But it didn't take long to realize that it was the right move. Halligan and Hackel included me on various projects, and eventually Hackel allowed me to write a few articles for *GOAL.* I had a key to the league office and would meet Hackel there occasionally on weekends to help out. It was a different world in 1985. The NHL's New York office was much smaller than it is today; the staff consisted of no more than 30 people. These days, an intern would never have his or her own key. One afternoon, the longtime NHL receptionist, Lola Skaro, went to lunch and asked me to handle the switchboard until she returned. Unfortunately, when the daughter of NHL president John A. Ziegler Jr. called to speak to her father, I accidentally disconnected her as I attempted to transfer the call to his office. Thankfully, my internship was not terminated.

During the summer of 1986, I juggled two jobs: working part time at the NHL while adding public relations duties with the Staten Island Stallions of the United States Basketball League to my plate. Evan Pickman—the former head coach at the College of Staten Island and a scout for the Los Angeles Clippers—was one of the basketball coaches at KSA during several of my summers at camp. He was hired as the general manager of the Stallions and asked me to help with stats and PR. I was paid $50 per week plus expenses. (It was 100 miles round trip from my house on Long Island to the team office on Staten Island.) It was a blast! I was a jack-of-all-trades for the Stallions. I worked in the team office (on the second floor of a local printing press) writing press releases and compiling statistics, worked as the official scorer (and play-by-play typist) at home games, and traveled with the team via van to most away games (and flew with the team on a road trip to Florida). After home games I would fill out the postgame box score by hand and drive it back to the team office to fax it to the league office in Milford, Connecticut, followed by a 50-mile drive back home to Long Island. After road games I phoned in a game story and statistics to the *Staten Island Advance* newspaper.

During the two seasons of the team's existence (1986 and 1987), among the players to suit up for the Stallions were former Knicks—Ken "The Animal" Bannister, Eddie Lee Wilkins, and Eric Fernsten; Big East stalwarts Michael Graham, Kevin Williams, and Willie Glass; future NBA star John "Hot Rod" Williams; and Providence College point guard Billy Donovan, who played in 44 games under Pitino for the Knicks in 1987–88 before embarking on a terrific coaching career at both the collegiate and NBA levels. Opposing players included Muggsy Bogues, Manute Bol, Nancy Lieberman, and Mario Elie.

Prior to the 1986 season, Pickman had a number of meetings and negotiations with Phil Jackson—yes, *the* Phil Jackson—who was then coaching the CBA's Albany Patroons. They even drew up plays on napkins together at a diner following Patroons games. Jackson verbally accepted the Stallions' coaching job but changed his mind and decided to take a summer gig coaching in Puerto Rico for about $5,000 more than the Stallions had offered. Just five years later, Jackson led the Chicago Bulls to the first of his 11 championships as an NBA head coach. But in 1986, while still coaching in the minor leagues, every dollar mattered.

Hot Rod was a first-round pick by the Cleveland Cavaliers in 1985, but the start of his NBA career was delayed after he was arrested for suspicion of point shaving during his time at Tulane University. He was found not guilty but missed the entire 1985–86 NBA season. To condition himself back into basketball shape as well as get some games under his belt, he signed to play with the Stallions during the 1986 summer campaign. The week of my high school graduation (June 19), I was asked to pick Williams up at LaGuardia Airport on the way from Long Island to Staten Island. It was one of my first official duties with the club. At the minor league level—as I learned years later while working in the American Hockey League—everyone chips in no matter what the task. The budget of a USBL team was pretty tight, so a car service or limousine for Williams was out of the question. I have vivid memories of watching the 6'11", 23-year-old Louisiana native squeeze into the passenger seat of my blue Mazda 626. During the drive we heard a radio bulletin about the death of Maryland star Len Bias, who had been drafted by the Boston Celtics two days earlier. I looked to my right and noticed a tear trickling down Hot Rod's cheek.

I became friendly with Donovan during the 1987 USBL season. We were both Long Island natives and often sat together during van rides to away games. I had four tickets to Nassau Coliseum's closed-circuit telecast of a heavyweight championship prize fight between Gerry Cooney and Michael Spinks on June 15, 1987. I invited "Billy the Kid," and less than three months after we had watched him on TV during the Friars' improbable trip to the

Final Four, he joined me and my friends Holzer and Gulitti in the stands to watch the title bout.

As hard as it might be to fathom for millennials, cell phones and the Internet have not always existed. During my childhood and through my college years, there were only a few ways to find out scores of sporting events: watch the game on TV, listen on radio, tune in to sports updates every half hour, read the next day's newspaper or...call SportsPhone, a service based in the New York area. For 10 cents per call, fans could dial 976-1313 and hear a one-minute recording with all of the scores from around the country updated every ten minutes. Many prominent sportscasters got their start whizzing through the scores as SportsPhone employees, including Michael Kay, Howie Rose, Gary Cohen, and Al Trautwig. During my high school years, I was a frequent winner of the "Quickie Quiz." I would race home from school, then call at exactly 3:20 PM to hear the sports trivia question. If I knew the answer off the top of my head or found it while scurrying through a record book, I would quickly dial the hotline number. I won prizes including Dennis D'Agostino's *This Date in Mets History* and two tickets to a New Jersey Devils game.

When it was time to start applying to colleges, I may have been the only student in America with the following criteria: I wanted to attend school in an NHL city. (I couldn't fathom being away from pro hockey for four years.) I also only applied to schools where I would most likely have an opportunity to be on air right from the start. Due to the volume of students interested in broadcasting, I heard that it might take a few years at certain colleges with bigger programs.

I had initially considered Boston University, the University of Maryland, and George Washington University. But New York University—located in Greenwich Village—turned out to be the perfect choice. Ackerman mentioned that he had applied to NYU. Until then, I hadn't considered staying close to home for college. Soon thereafter, I was in the press box at Nassau Coliseum calling an Islanders game into my tape recorder. (I had a media credential thanks to my internship at the NHL office.) By chance, I met

C.J. Papa, a junior at NYU who was named the incoming sports director at student radio station WNYU. He told me all about the station and mentioned that amazingly—despite an enrollment of 40,000 students—only five or six joined the sports staff each year. I was sold! My father took me on a tour of NYU, where we visited former Knicks TV analyst Cal Ramsey, a star basketball player for the Violets in the 1950s who briefly played for the Knicks and then spent decades working both at Madison Square Garden and NYU as an assistant basketball coach and in alumni relations. NYU sports information director Bob Goldsholl, a longtime local television sportscaster, joined us and Ramsey for lunch.

C.J. Papa was right. During my freshman year, there were only a handful of us interested in calling basketball games. We all become close friends and rotated duties—play-by-play, color analyst, producer, engineer, statistician—throughout the season. Jason Wormser was a junior at the time; he became sports director the next year (and has enjoyed a career in television production at ESPN, FOX, and NFL Network). Going to college in New York allowed me to continue to keep stats on Knicks television and Rangers radio for four more years. Learning via osmosis while sitting next to some of the top broadcasters in the business was just as valuable as anything I learned in class (nothing against my professors, of course).

Calling NYU men's and women's basketball games was a lot of fun. We had top-notch Division III programs and played at a terrific facility, the Coles Sports Center. L. Jay Oliva, the NYU chancellor who would become school president in the 1990s, was a big proponent of collegiate athletics and was instrumental in forming the University Athletic Association in the mid-1980s. It had the feel of a big-time conference. Aside from NYU, the UAA included Emory University, the University of Rochester, Brandeis University, Case Western Reserve University, the University of Chicago, Washington University in St. Louis, and Carnegie Mellon University—all fine academic institutions. We were very fortunate to have the opportunity to travel to Atlanta, Rochester, Boston, Cleveland, Chicago, St. Louis, and Pittsburgh to call games for WNYU, which was very unusual at the

D-III level. The Violets even played one game per season at Madison Square Garden in the first game of a doubleheader, and we were there to call it. What a thrill for college broadcasters! One year, the nightcap was a St. John's–Georgetown matchup.

During a trip to Rochester, the phone jack in our broadcast booth didn't work. Fortunately, we were prepared for a potential emergency and carried a *really* long phone wire with us. In order to hook up the radio equipment, we ran the wire down a couple of flights of stairs into a working jack in a maintenance closet. During another game there was a problem with the equipment, and we wound up announcing the game into a phone while passing it back and forth. I did this during a Baltimore Skipjacks game in Binghamton a few years later with my partner Dave Starman. At one point, he handed the phone back to me and joked, "Here! It's for you."

One of the top players on the NYU men's basketball team was a guard from Brooklyn named Duane Martin. Ack and I became close friends with Martin. He was in a few of our classes, occasionally slept on the futon in our dorm room, and attended my surprise 21st birthday party at my house on Long Island. Martin has gone on to enjoy a terrific acting career on the West Coast. His first major role came in 1992 as a basketball player (no surprise) in *White Men Can't Jump*. Terry Tarpey was a senior during my freshman year; he broke the school's all-time scoring record in a game I covered for the university's weekly newspaper, *Washington Square News*.

In September of 1986 during my first month at NYU, I happened to notice a flier on the wall after leaving a class. A fellow student, Matthew Nafus, decided to start a club hockey team. I couldn't believe the fortunate timing. I played high school club hockey and also enjoyed participating in pick-up games at Sky Rink in Manhattan (on the 16th floor of an office building on 33rd Street between 9th and 10th Avenues) with several members of the hockey media. I attended the first meeting and told Nafus I was interested in not only playing, but also assisting with the administrative duties. I became involved in securing funds from NYU to supplement the cost of renting ice time for practices and games and also assisted in setting up transportation (vans provided by the school's athletic department) to road games in New Jersey, Long Island, Poughkeepsie, and even one trip to a tournament in Pittsburgh, for which we had to rent a full-sized bus.

Sky Rink became our home for practices and home games. Our inaugural game was in December 1986 against the College of Staten Island. It started around 10:00 or 11:00 PM. My parents and a few of my friends attended the game, but there were no spectator stands at Sky Rink. They all stood around the rink up against the boards and glass. Midway through the first period, the puck came to me at the top of the right faceoff circle, and my wrist shot somehow zigzagged through a maze of players and beat the screened goaltender for the first goal in the history of the NYU club hockey team! I didn't score many goals that season, but nobody can take away the first. My other personal highlight was a four-goal game in a 7–4 win against New Paltz in Bayonne, New Jersey, as a senior in January 1990.

Joining the hockey club allowed all of us to meet and become friendly with students from many different schools at NYU. Our best players were Gary Rothschild and Steve Spieczny. I didn't get to play on their line very often, but when I did, the puck always found its way onto my stick. We had a great group of guys, and I keep in touch with many of them to this day. For the first two seasons, I recruited Hackel (my boss at the NHL) as our volunteer head coach. He was a historian of the sport and enjoyed playing in adult hockey leagues. He jumped at the opportunity to coach the team (despite not drawing a salary) due to his love of the game.

NYU draws students from all across the world with a wide variety of interests. Another teammate was Jamie Walters, who went on to fame as an actor and singer (best known for a role on *Beverly Hills 90210*). Our team manager for a brief time was Caprice Crane, a Tisch School of the Arts student who grew up in Hollywood and was a huge Los Angeles Kings fan. Crane is the daughter of Tina Louise (Ginger on *Gilligan's Island*) and is a novelist, screenwriter, and TV writer/producer.

The team has come a long way in the three decades since it was just a vision in the mind of Nafus. I was so proud to hear that NYU won the

American Collegiate Hockey Association Division II national championship in both 2015 and 2017 under head coach Chris Cosentino.

Aside from calling games on WNYU and keeping stats at Madison Square Garden throughout my college years, I gained invaluable experience as the associate producer for *Mets Extra* during the 1987, 1988, and 1989 seasons (and for a few months in 1990). In 1987 Howie Rose was a 33-year-old sportscaster at WHN Radio who had also done some fill-in play-by-play for the Rangers. He had a long history with my family dating back to 1967. At the age of 13, Rose—a huge sports fan from Queens—was the founder of the Marv Albert Fan Club. He developed a relationship with my father by writing letters and calling to chat with him at his radio station and distributed newsletters to the fan club members. I first got to know Rose in 1984 when I was calling games for Cox Cable of Great Neck. Rose lived in the area and wanted to gain some television experience. He approached Menton about hosting a weekly sports talk show, during which he would interview various sports personalities living on Long Island. Highlights from games I broadcasted aired on the show, so I would often hang around the studio and assist with production tasks. Prior to the 1987 baseball season, Rose asked if I would be interested in working with him on the newly created Mets pregame and postgame shows that would air on WHN. Of course, I accepted.

Rose also mentioned that on July 1, 1987, the station would transition to an all-sports format and become WFAN. (I vividly recall bringing a boom box to the Staten Island Stallions office so I could listen to the very first moments of the first all-sports station in the United States, beginning with a sports update hosted by Suzyn Waldman.) In April, May, and September, I took either the Long Island Rail Road or the subway to Shea Stadium. During the summer months, I drove from Sands Point to Shea. I would hang around the field and Mets clubhouse while Rose taped the "Manager's Report" with Davey Johnson. After we ate dinner in the press room, Rose would start the show an hour before game time. I hunted down guests in the press box: usually a sportswriter, scout, or visiting team broadcaster. Jack

Buck and Harry Caray were frequent guests when their teams came into town, as well as Gene "Stick" Michael, Phil "The Vulture" Regan, and baseball writers including Red Foley, Marty Noble, Jack Lang, and George King. It was somewhat intimidating for this 18 or 19 year old to ask legendary broadcasters if they would take time from their preparation to head to our booth down the first-base line, but after a while, they all became familiar with Rose, his body of work, and the show.

I watched the games alongside Rose (we both kept meticulous scorebooks) and the radio engineer. In the eighth inning, I would head down to the Mets clubhouse, where a headset hung on the wall inside the front door. A few minutes after the game ended, I would check in with the engineer via the headset to make sure the connection was solid. From Doc Gooden to Darryl Strawberry to Ron Darling to the 25th man on the roster, legendary public relations director Jay Horwitz would then bring over a Mets player to chat with Rose for a few minutes, and I handed them the equipment after hundreds of Mets home games. Years later, I ran into backup catcher Barry Lyons at an airport, and we reminisced about the times he joined Rose as a postgame guest.

The postgame show was on until midnight, so Rose and I were among the last to leave the dark stadium. I would often walk alone to the dark LIRR or subway platform for the ride back into Manhattan. I hope my mother isn't reading this!

Aside from interviews with the manager and other guests, trivia questions, and a minor league report, Rose frequently took phone calls from listeners. Part of my job was to communicate with the WFAN studio producer, who answered the calls. In the early days of computer technology, we used a primitive version of instant messenger. A computer screen was set up in the booth at Shea, which was connected via a modem to the radio station six miles away in Astoria, Queens. The producer would type onto the screen "Joey from Massapequa" or "Bobby from the Bronx," which I would then write on an index card and relay to Rose. When Rose wanted to move on to the next caller, he would signal to me. I then typed a code word on the computer, and the producer would reply "ggggggggg" (with his finger pressed on the keyboard), which meant gone. This is how I met Eric Spitz, who remains one of my closest friends to this day. Spitz was one of the producers at WFAN, and we initially met by typing back and forth on the computer before we ever uttered a spoken word to each other. He has had a long, illustrious career in sports radio in various senior management positions at WFAN, Entercom, and SiriusXM. Spitz's roommate at the time was WFAN update anchor (and future ESPN star) Steve Levy.

When Eric married his wife Jennifer in November 1991, I left a Baltimore Skipjacks game in Portland, Maine, after the first period. (The teams played the night before as well, so I worked four of the six periods during the weekend series.) Another close friend, Dave Starman, took over for me during the last two periods. Starman used the first leg of my plane ticket to fly from LaGuardia to Portland and I used the other half. You could do that back in the day; the name on the ticket did not have to match the name of the passenger. Spitz arranged for another invited guest, a young WFAN producer at the time, to pick me up at LaGuardia and give me a ride to the wedding venue. We didn't know what each other looked like, and neither of us had a cell phone. But when I exited the airport, the producer was waiting in his car in the exact spot where Spitz told me he would be. And that is how I first met Ian Eagle, who has become one of the best play-by-play broadcasters of our generation.

I learned so much by watching Rose perform his craft. During our time together, he took time to listen to my broadcast tapes and even asked me to fill in for him on a Long Island University soccer match. Rose has gone on to have a tremendous career as the longtime play-by-play voice of the Mets on both television and radio. Two seasons after his iconic call of Stephane Matteau's double overtime goal to send the Rangers into the 1994 Stanley Cup Final—"Matteau! Matteau! Matteau! Stephane Matteau! And the Rangers have one more hill to climb baby, and it's Mount Vancouver!"—Rose became the TV voice of the Islanders for two decades. Showing how small a world it is, I replaced him on Rangers radio in 1995.

A huge perk of attending college in New York was hanging around press boxes and broadcast booths at MSG, Nassau Coliseum, and Shea Stadium and making connections. I befriended Joel Blumberg, a radio producer/engineer, who assigned me to attend press conferences at various local sporting events, including the U.S. Open. I would then feed the sound bites to various radio stations. I also assisted Blumberg on live radio shows from several NHL and NBA drafts. He was the producer for the Islanders Radio Network, and in 1988–89, the team signed a deal with WEVD Radio, whose studios happened to be located a few blocks from my dorm. Blumberg asked me to host several Islanders pregame and postgame shows from the studio. It was my first experience hosting professional broadcasts on air. During the summer of 1989, I sent a cassette tape with a sample of my play-by-play to Arthur Adler, the Islanders' vice president of broadcasting. I received a letter back informing me that I would be the team's back-up play-by-play radio broadcaster during the 1989–90 season should the need arise. So, as a 21-year-old college senior, I made my NHL debut calling an Islanders game in Winnipeg on Saturday, December 2, 1989, alongside color analyst Mike Farrell (a New York-area sportswriter). Earlier in the day, I received a telegram at my hotel from Spitz and Levy wishing me luck. The Islanders won the game 6–3. Brent Sutter scored the first NHL goal I called. Patrick Flatley, who worked with me as a color analyst on a Rangers–Toronto Maple Leafs game many years later, had assists.

I worked a few other Islanders games that season. My partner for home games was Bobby Nystrom, who had scored the Stanley Cup-winning goal for the Isles in May 1980. During our first broadcast, the clock stopped with 7:11 remaining in a period. "Bob, does 7:11 mean anything to you?" I asked. Nystrom's historic goal was scored at the 7:11 mark of overtime, and Nystrom chuckled at the mention. He always enjoyed whenever I referred to the goal. His seven-year-old son Eric sat behind us during some of the games in the Nassau Coliseum press box. Eric went on to enjoy a nine-year NHL career.

I now had actual NHL tapes to send out toward the end of my senior year at NYU to various minor league clubs as I searched for my first full-time job. I was contacted by the executives at Home Team Sports in Bethesda, Maryland, in February 1990 regarding a potential TV opening with the Capitals the following season. They flew me down and I called a practice game at the Capital Centre in Landover, Maryland, in March 1990 (against my once-beloved Canucks) along with former NHL goaltender Don Edwards. I did not expect to get hired at that point, but it was a great experience and was my initial connection with HTS executive producer Bill Brown, who would hire me two years later.

# 2
# A SKIPJACK
# OF ALL TRADES

**F**ollowing my graduation from NYU in May 1990, I had an audition for an anchor position at Sports News Network, a 24-hour cable channel based in Northern Virginia. One of my coanchors during the dry run was Bill Pidto, who went on to anchor ESPN's *SportsCenter* for many years and is now my colleague at MSG Network. Fortunately, I did not get hired. My passion was play-by-play, and I sent my demo tapes to teams in the NHL and various minor leagues. Around the same time, two friends had heard from others—WFAN's Steve Levy from New Haven Nighthawks broadcaster Dan Rusanowsky and hockey public relations executive Micah Buchdahl from Washington Capitals TV voice Jeff Rimer—that there was a radio opening with the American Hockey League's Baltimore Skipjacks. Levy, of course, has gone on to a terrific career at ESPN; Rusanowsky has been the radio voice of the San Jose Sharks since their inaugural 1991–92 season, and Rimer has enjoyed a long NHL play-by-play career as well.

I sent a portion of the New York Islanders–Winnipeg Jets game from the previous December to the Skipjacks, and the rest is history. When I phoned the team's office to confirm receipt of my tape, the voice on the other end was Doug MacLean, who had been the 'Jacks head coach. He became one of Washington's assistants for the 1990–91 season. (Five years later he would lead the upstart Florida Panthers to the Stanley Cup Final.) MacLean assured me that my tape would make it into the right hands.

I was asked to fly to Harrisburg, Pennsylvania, in early June 1990—just weeks after my college graduation—for an interview. I was met at the airport by Skipjacks owner Tom Ebright, who picked me up for the short ride to his summer home in Mt. Gretna, Pennsylvania, where team executives Alan Rakvin and Jim Riggs were waiting. I thought it went well, but I had no idea how many others they would be meeting with. Later that month, I traveled to Vancouver to co-host WEVD's NHL Draft coverage with Joel Blumberg. It turned out to be one of the strongest drafts in the league's history. The top five picks were Owen Nolan, Petr Nedved, Keith Primeau, Mike Ricci, and Jaromir Jagr. The New Jersey Devils chose Martin Brodeur with the 20th overall selection. I arrived in Vancouver earlier in the week, and several times each day, I would call my home answering machine to check for messages by inputting a code. (This was still during the pre-cell phone era.) Finally, late in the afternoon on Friday, June 15, 1990—the day before the draft—I received a message from the Skipjacks. The job was mine.

In my euphoria I jumped onto the hotel bed and bounced so high that I almost hit my head on the ceiling. I was told that my salary for the 1990–91 season would be $18,000 (plus per diem during road trips). I felt like I won the lottery. Looking back, I realize just how lucky I was to get hired by an American Hockey League team just one month after my college graduation… and in a major city. A week later, my mother and I searched for apartments in the Baltimore suburbs, and I was introduced (along with head coach Rob Laird) at a press conference at the Days Inn down the block from my new home, the Baltimore Arena. The next week, I loaded up all of my possessions into the same Mazda 626 that John "Hot Rod" Williams squeezed into four years earlier and headed south on I-95 to an apartment in Owings Mills, Maryland. It was the start of a wonderful journey that is still continuing three decades later.

My first summer in Baltimore crawled at a snail's pace. I could not wait for the actual games to begin. I worked in the team office every day from 9:00 AM to 5:00 PM. Among my duties were selling advertising, assisting with public relations and marketing, answering phones…basically whatever was needed. The major theme throughout the summer at the minor league level: sell, sell, sell. Sales was not my forte, but I tried my best. I closed three deals: with a sports bar in the Fells Point area of downtown Baltimore, a hotel gym, and a miniature golf/batting cage facility north of the city. For between $500 and $1,000, we threw in everything but an actual roster spot and seat on the bench. The packages included commercials on the radio, an advertisement on the boards or ice, an ad in the game program, tickets, player appearances, etc. I contacted several minor league baseball teams in the area, and the Double A Hagerstown Suns agreed to host a "Skipjacks Night," where I handed out flyers along with a few of my colleagues in an attempt to sell 'Jacks tickets for the upcoming season. That same summer, I attended a barbeque with other staff members and met our new assistant coach, Barry Trotz, for the first time. I was told that I would share a hotel room with Trotz on all road trips. At the minor league level, teams look to save money whenever possible. Some AHL teams assigned the team broadcaster to room with the bus driver. The Skipjacks decided it would be the radio guy (me) and assistant coach (Trotz).

During home preseason games in late September 1990, I did mock broadcasts from our booth. Before one of the games, a gentleman, whom I immediately recognized, came over to introduce himself. It was Gene Ubriaco, who had been the head coach of the Pittsburgh Penguins the prior season. Following his dismissal in the Steel City, he moved back to Baltimore, where he had coached previously with the Skipjacks and where his kids still attended school. Ubriaco, who grew up with Phil and Tony Esposito in Sault Ste. Marie, Ontario, volunteered to be my color analyst whenever needed. Since I didn't have an analyst and was scheduled to work alone, it seemed like a great deal. He worked at least half of the home games that season, as well as several others up I-83 in Hershey, Pennsylvania.

Prior to a preseason game in Hershey, I met Skipjacks goaltender Shawn Simpson. Simpson was the first goalie selected in the 1986 NHL Draft. He had played in 15 games with the Skipjacks during the previous season and also backed up one game for the Capitals. I had heard that "Simmer" had also done some radio work alongside my predecessor Mike Haynes for several games when he was the designated third goalie and did not dress. He expressed interest to me as well during our first meeting. Jim Hrivnak (Simmer's good friend and roommate) and Olaf Kolzig handled most of the goaltending chores for the Skipjacks in 1990–91. Simmer would join me in the booth when he was not in uniform. He had a great personality and did a terrific job on air. That was his last season as a player. He went on to do a combination of broadcast and front-office work for the Capitals. We roomed together in a house in Bowie, Maryland (along with Caps public relations guru Dan Kaufman) during the 1992–93 season. Capitals' management (general manager David Poile and director of player personnel Jack Button) paid for the fourth bedroom, and players acquired or recalled from the ECHL would stay with us for several days at a time. It was a bargain; the three of us paid only $300 rent per month. We took Polaroid photos of all who rotated through the fourth bedroom and posted them on the living room wall as a tribute. Simmer has since returned home to Ottawa and hosts a daily sports talk show on TSN Radio. I enjoy being a frequent guest.

My first broadcast with the Skipjacks (and my first game as a full-time, professional play-by-play announcer) was in Hershey on October 6, 1990. Hersheypark Arena was my favorite road building during my two seasons in the AHL. It had a great history. Wilt Chamberlain scored 100 points—an NBA record that still stands—in a game against the New York Knicks in Hershey on March 2, 1962. Plus, the building smelled like chocolate, and the hot dogs in the press room were outstanding. The tiny broadcast booth was about 10 rows off the ice, which was a great location to be able to describe the action. A fan just to the right kept a scorecard on a clipboard and would share the info (goals, assists, penalties) with the visiting broadcasters. I set up the equipment, watched warmups, and then began my first broadcast with Ubriaco. Things were going smoothly until I was handed a note by a gentleman in the press box below our booth during the first period: "Call your station. You are off the air." At that moment, I wasn't sure I would still have a job come the next game. While play continued, I scrambled to call the engineer at WLIF. It turns out one of us had accidentally knocked the phone wire out of the jack, which was located on the floor underneath our table in the cramped booth. I plugged it back in, and it was smooth sailing the rest of the way.

Less than three weeks later, the Bears headed south to Baltimore and the Skipjacks erupted for nine goals (yes—nine goals) in the first period in the span of 13 minutes, 48 seconds. Alfie Turcotte, who would lead the 'Jacks in scoring with 85 points that season, was involved in five of the nine. (His son Alex was a first-round pick by the Los Angeles Kings in 2019.) The nine goals scored by the Skipjacks—and the combined 12 goals in the period— both tied American League Hockey records and still remains the most goals I have ever seen in one period of a hockey game at any level. Every time the Skipjacks scored, the team fight song would blare out of the arena's public-address system. It's a tradition that began when the Baltimore Clippers played at the Civic Center (later re-named Baltimore Arena) in the 1960s. The Clippers were a New York Rangers farm team at one point; Hall of Famers Eddie Giacomin, Jean Ratelle, Doug Harvey, and Jacques Plante all spent some time with the club. I can still hear the song in my head: "Win you Baltimore Skipjacks! Win you Skipjacks from Baltimore! Fight you Baltimore Skipjacks! Faceoff, fight for a Baltimore score! Fight, fight, fight."

The Skipjacks had a small but rabid fanbase and a passionate booster club. A high school student once visited the broadcast booth to introduce himself; his family had season tickets. That student, Jason LaCanfora, went on to a terrific newspaper career with *The Washington Post* and *Detroit Free Press* before transitioning to the TV side with CBS Sports.

The Civic Center/Arena was home to the NBA's Baltimore Bullets (now the Washington Wizards) from 1963 to 1973 before their move to Landover, Maryland. At the south end of the arena, there was a stage in lieu of seats. Prior to the NHL's 1967 expansion, Philadelphia and Baltimore were reportedly competing for a franchise. According to legend, league president Clarence Campbell walked into the arena in Baltimore, took a quick look—and that's how the Flyers were born.

The Hershey Bears were our biggest rival. Due to the proximity between the cities (90 miles), the Skipjacks and Bears faced off 14 times per season (seven in each locale). The hour-and-a-half ride seemed like a trip around the corner considering where the other AHL teams were located during the 1990–91 season: Binghamton, Glens Falls, Rochester, Troy, and Utica, New York; New Haven, Connecticut; Springfield, Massachusetts; Portland,

Maine; and five teams in Canada (Newmarket, Ontario; Sydney and Halifax, Nova Scotia; Moncton and Fredericton, New Brunswick). We traveled by bus to all of the cities within the United States as well as Newmarket. For the one trip to the maritime provinces (Nova Scotia and New Brunswick), we flew to Canada and back to Baltimore at the beginning and end of the trip and via bus between the respective cities for each game. If I remember correctly, the AHL per diem at the time was $21 on gamedays and travel days away from home. The players, coaches, training staff, and broadcaster all received envelopes with cash at the beginning of road trips. If the team left from home after lunch time, it would be cut down to $12 per person on that day. Occasionally, to save money, the front office would strategically schedule the bus departure for 2:01 PM.

Our longest bus trip was from Baltimore to Portland, Maine. One weekend, the team played a home game in Baltimore on Friday night followed by a game in Portland the next evening. Management treated the players and coaches to a rare plane trip on Saturday morning. The bus, however, had to get to Portland from Baltimore for the return trip, and the equipment rode in the luggage hatch of the "iron lung" after the Friday home game—along with me, trainer Dan Redmond, equipment manager Rich Oberlin, and owner Tom Ebright. The four of us slept for most of the 500-mile, nine-hour excursion up the northeast corridor. We pulled into Cumberland County Civic Center around 8:00 AM, and the four of us emptied the hockey equipment bags and sticks from the bottom of the bus to the visiting locker room. Who was there to lend a helping hand? None other than Rick Bowness, the head coach of the Maine Mariners, who over the last three decades since has been behind the bench for more NHL games (as either a head or assistant coach) than anyone else in the history of the league.

During my first season with the Skipjacks, I enjoyed meeting the other team broadcasters, many of whom advanced to the NHL thanks in large part to expansion. Between 1991 and 2000, the NHL increased from 21 to 30 clubs. My peers from the American Hockey League who moved up to the next level include Rusanowsky (New Haven/San Jose), Joe Beninati (Maine/

Washington), Jim Jackson (Utica/Philadelphia), John Forslund (Springfield/ Hartford–Carolina–Seattle), Don Orsillo (Springfield/Boston Red Sox– San Diego Padres), Haynes (Capital District Islanders/Colorado), and Dan Kamal (Hershey/Atlanta). Steve Kolbe, who enjoyed a long career as radio voice of the Capitals, was one of our studio producers during my time with the 'Jacks. There was a camaraderie between all of us as we attempted to make it to the majors.

The bus rides may have been long, but they were a lot of fun. Players, who sat toward the back of the bus (mostly the veterans), usually played cards. There were a couple of television monitors, and we occasionally watched movies on VHS tapes. I would always bring reading material. Reggie Savage, a first-round draft pick of the Capitals, usually sat behind me and enjoyed borrowing my copies of *The Sporting News* and *Hockey News*. A few years later, I was on the call when Savage—while playing for the Capitals—became only the fourth player to score his first NHL goal on a penalty shot. His jersey from that game is still on display at the Hockey Hall of Fame.

We all had two seats to ourselves. The coaches (Laird and Trotz) sat in the front row—one on the left side of the bus and the other on the right. Redmond and Oberlin (the trainer and equipment manager) took the second row. I was in the third row on the left side. Defenseman Ken Lovsin usually sat across from me on the right side.

When we were scheduled to leave after a game, whether at home or on the road, the entire traveling party would place a dinner order prior to the game. There was usually a menu from a local Italian restaurant tacked to the locker room wall along with a blank sheet of paper. We would fill out our orders and place $10 in a nearby envelope. After the game the food would be waiting on our seat on the bus. So at the start of each bus ride, everybody would have either a chicken parmesan sandwich, pizza, or a pasta dish on their lap as we headed to the next destination. Our bus driver, nicknamed "Froggy," was quite a character. Due to the long hours we all spent together, it felt like he was a member of the team. Just like me, he became a target of occasional barbs and practical jokes from the players.

On October 3, 1990 (three days prior to our first game), the Capitals acquired Joel Quenneville from the Hartford Whalers. The veteran defenseman had played 12 seasons (and close to 800 games) in the NHL. The Caps had one of the deepest blue line corps in the league with Rod Langway, Kevin Hatcher, and Calle Johansson leading the way (and they traded for Al Iafrate during the season). Quenneville was at the back end of his career and wound up playing only nine games for the Capitals. However, he appeared in 59 games for the Skipjacks during the 1990–91 season. He was 32 years old at the time—four years older than Trotz and only four years younger than Laird. Quenneville acted as a third coach and fit right in with his teammates. He went on to win three Stanley Cups as head coach of the Chicago Blackhawks. As of this writing, Quenneville and Trotz are the second- and third-winningest head coaches in NHL history (behind only the legendary Scotty Bowman) and led their teams to a combined four Stanley Cup championships. Laird earned two Cup rings as a scout with the Los Angeles Kings. How lucky were all of us on those Skipjacks bus rides over three decades ago? Never in our wildest dreams did we expect three of our friends/teammates to achieve such great success behind the bench and in the front office.

Along with a few of my colleagues from the Skipjacks and Capitals organizations, we pledged to be in the building if Trotz ever had the opportunity to win a championship at any level. On May 29, 1994 (two days before Game One of the Rangers–Vancouver Canucks Stanley Cup Final), we traveled to Portland, Maine, for Game Six of the Calder Cup Final between Trotz's Portland Pirates and the Moncton Hawks (ironically coached by Laird). The Pirates won the game 4–1, and we joined the postgame locker room celebration. The party continued at various establishments around Portland, and at one point in the wee morning hours, Dave Starman accidentally dropped the Calder Cup on goalie Byron Dafoe's foot. Fortunately, Dafoe, who played in 415 NHL games, was no worse for the wear.

Nearly a quarter of a century later in 2018, I was on the call in Las Vegas for Westwood One Radio when Trotz won his next championship—the Stanley

Cup—in a five-game series victory against the expansion Golden Knights. After wrapping up my radio duties, I headed to the ice to congratulate Trotz and his family, and we took a photo together. I couldn't be more excited for him. My roommate had become a Stanley Cup-winning head coach.

In 2010 I had a FOX baseball assignment calling an interleague Chicago game (White Sox vs. Cubs) on Saturday, June 12, the day after the Blackhawks' Stanley Cup parade. When I arrived in the Windy City on Friday, confetti still littered the streets along the parade route. That night our crew (including producer Jeff Gowen, analyst Eric Karros, sideline reporter Chris Rose, and me) dined at Joe's Stone Crab. The restaurant was packed. Former Cubs pitcher Rick Sutcliffe happened to be sitting at the table next to ours. Midway through our meal, a roar erupted throughout Joe's. I looked toward the front entrance. There was Quenneville entering the restaurant with the Stanley Cup lifted high above his head. Along with his coaching staff, they circled around Joe's, giving patrons at every table a close-up look. Things settled down after a few minutes, and the Blackhawks coaches sat down to eat in a private room in the back of the restaurant. After we finished our main course, I walked back to congratulate Quenneville, my busmate in Baltimore two decades earlier. I mentioned who I was with, and assistant coach Mike Haviland asked if we wanted the Stanley Cup *on our table* during dessert. Who could turn down that offer? I will never forget the look on the face of Sutcliffe, a three-time All-Star and Cy Young Award winner. He acted like a little kid and asked us if he could take a photo with the Cup.

I enjoyed every second of my two seasons with the Skipjacks. Aside from the invaluable experience and reps while broadcasting the games on radio, I learned so much about how a professional organization operates. Although I wasn't a sales whiz, it taught me valuable lessons. I would not trade my two years in Baltimore for anything. There were fewer than 10 people on our office staff. I am still close with group sales executive Cliff Gault, my frequent lunch partner for two years, who has gone on to work with the Tampa Bay Lightning, Capitals, and New York Islanders. Community relations director Margaret Robinson and director of sales Sherrie Petti took me under their wing in Baltimore. They even brought me to a Tupperware party to give me something to do in a new city without many friends. Gault, Petti, Robinson, and I held a fun reunion with each other during the 2018 Stanley Cup Final in Washington. Kudos to any young broadcaster fortunate enough to start their career at the major league level, but in my opinion, they also missed out on a fantastic experience in the minors.

During my two seasons with the Skipjacks, Ubriaco, Simpson, and Starman were my most frequent color analysts. Occasionally, I would call games alone. Longtime major league baseball broadcaster Josh Lewin, who was handling play-by-play for the Triple A Rochester Red Wings at the time, was my analyst for a few games. Injured 'Jacks center Tim Taylor, who went on to win Stanley Cups as a player with the Detroit Red Wings and Lightning and in management with the St. Louis Blues, was my broadcast partner one night in Utica.

I once offered Jon Miller, the legendary baseball broadcaster who was with the Baltimore Orioles at the time and spent many years calling ESPN's *Sunday Night Baseball*, tickets so he and his family could attend a Skipjacks game. He was gracious enough to join me on radio between periods. His stories were so entertaining that the interview ran into the start of the next period. One of Miller's anecdotes was about his time during his college days spent broadcasting several California Golden Seals games in the early 1970s, when he and a few friends gained access to a TV truck and convinced owner Charles O. Finley (of Oakland A's fame) to hire them.

Prior to my second season with the Skipjacks, we switched radio stations from WLIF to WITH. During a meeting with WITH station manager Jim Ward, he asked if I would be interested in hosting a sports talk show in the late afternoon. He didn't have money in the budget to pay me, but I realized that it would be a good way to gain experience in a platform other than play-by-play and that the show would promote the Skipjacks. Ward told me that if I brought in someone to help with commercial sales, we could keep a percentage of the proceeds. I immediately thought of Jerry Coleman, whom I had first met in September 1990. I had heard about Coleman through a mutual friend, and his father owned a minority share of the Skipjacks. Coleman grew up in Baltimore and studied broadcasting at Ithaca College in upstate New York. We lived in the same apartment complex in Owings Mills and became friends. Coleman agreed to join me as the cohost of the show and as a salesperson. He is a hustler with a great sense of humor and was much more effective in the area of sales than I was. We modeled our show after a typical sports talk show on WFAN and, through some of my contacts, we were able to arrange top-notch guests from the world of sports and broadcasting.

The station was located on Light Street in downtown Baltimore. On game nights I would leave a bit early. Coleman would wrap up the show while I made the five-minute walk back to Baltimore Arena. When I was away on road trips, we brought in Nestor Aparicio, who was covering hockey and music for *The Baltimore Evening Sun*, as my fill-in. Aparicio was one of the beat writers covering the Skipjacks. During the summer of 1992 after I was hired by Home Team Sports and WTOP Radio—and moved closer to Washington, D.C.—it was the end of my Baltimore sports-talk run. Coleman and Aparicio continued to work together for a short time before branching off and continuing their careers. Three decades later, both of them continue to enjoy success on various media platforms in the Baltimore market.

Another avenue to help promote the Skipjacks was to broadcast several games on television. I set up a meeting during the 1990–91 season with John Zorbach, who ran the local cable access station for the city of Baltimore. He agreed to put together a production crew to make it happen, and we arranged for Home Team Sports to show the game on delayed tape. It turned out that the idea to collaborate on the TV package was one of the best decisions I ever made. The execs at both HTS and the Capitals watched some of the games and listened to my work. This helped lead to my hiring to call Caps games prior to the 1992–93 season.

For our initial telecast, we selected a home game against the Adirondack Red Wings; Starman was my color analyst. I needed to hire a radio crew to fill in for me that evening. Levy and Eric Spitz took time off from their duties at WFAN and drove down from New York. Levy did play-by-play, Spitz was his analyst, and John Schweibacher (a producer at WFAN who joined them for the ride) handled interviews between the periods. It was the first professional game Levy ever broadcasted. Not too long thereafter, he was doing NHL play-by-play on ESPN. Interestingly enough, the Adirondack head coach was Barry Melrose, who became Levy's longtime TV partner.

The next season (1991–92), we did a few more games on television. One of them happened to be against the Utica Devils—the New Jersey Devils affiliate—who were coached by Herb Brooks. Just 12 years earlier, Brooks had led the U.S. Olympic hockey team to their "Miracle on Ice" victory against the Soviet Union. I arranged to tape a pregame interview with the legendary coach on the stage behind one of the goals at the Baltimore Arena. It was the first professional television interview I had ever done, and my heart was pounding. Brooks was an intimidating figure, especially to a 23 year old who watched on television just more than a decade earlier as Brooks led his team—and country—to victory in one of the biggest sporting moments of the 20th century. Brooks sensed my nervousness but could not have been kinder and any more patient with me.

Many years later, during the pandemic in 2020, Todd Hlushko, a left wing with the Skipjacks who went on to play 79 NHL games with the Flyers, Calgary Flames, and Pittsburgh Penguins, posted the interview on Twitter. (He saved a VHS copy of the game, which he had played in.) When I watched the interview nearly three decades later, I couldn't believe how bold I was with one of the questions. I came right out and asked Brooks about a potential return to the NHL. Within his social media post, Hlushko either praised, made fun of, (or both) the amount of hair on my head: "Kenny had a great loaf back then."

That's exactly the type of humor I miss from the long bus rides with the Skipjacks. Even the radio broadcaster wasn't immune from the barbs. Early in my first season, I was not yet issued a team warm-up suit, which most of the players would wear on the bus. However, I did own a few Sergio Tacchini sweat suits, which were popular at the time. On one road trip, I made the unfortunate decision to wear one, which included a lot of pink on the front of the jacket. It wasn't long into the ride until I heard a voice from somewhere behind me: "Hey Albert, nice to see you wearing your mom's track suit." Needless to say, I never wore it again during any subsequent road trips.

During my two seasons with the Skipjacks, I filled in on seven more Islanders radio broadcasts. Whenever Isles TV play-by-play man Jiggs McDonald missed a game for a national assignment, Barry Landers shifted from radio to television, and I took Landers' spot. One such instance was during a road trip to Edmonton and Calgary in February 1992. The team had a few days off in between games and took a mini-vacation in Banff, Alberta. I used it as an opportunity to snow ski (for the first time in my life). I took a lesson in the morning, then practiced on the bunny hill. I felt brave enough to take the lift. My plan was to ski down the beginner's hill. Somehow, I wound up at the top of the Black Diamond mountain. There was nothing I could do but try and ski down on my own, which I somehow did while falling a few times along the way. During one of the mishaps, one of my skis went flying off my foot and into the vicinity of another skier. That was it for me. I have not hit the slopes since.

But that was not my most frightening incident.

I sat in the back of a police vehicle on March 16, 1992. *"Has your passport expired? Have you ever been arrested? Have you ever done anything illegal? Is anyone close to you in serious trouble?"* The two officers asked me these questions, as I was driven away from the tiny airport in Sydney, Nova Scotia. As a 24 year old in a foreign country, I was confused but very confident that the answer to all of their queries was a definite no. The interrogation continued for 15 minutes, and my heart pounded faster with each and every second. It wasn't exactly what I had in mind when our flight departed from Baltimore early that morning (with stops in Boston and Halifax before finally landing in Sydney).

As we pulled into the driveway of the team hotel, it was explained to me by the officers that the entire episode was set up by Trotz (with an assist from Capitals security chief Jim Wiseman), who had recently taken over as head coach of the Skipjacks. Trotz accidentally flubbed a few words during a pregame interview with me earlier that season. I made the mistake of playing the audio for some of the team's players, who all enjoyed a hearty laugh at his expense. Trotz was my roommate during all road trips. He assured me that he would retaliate. After months of elaborate planning, he sure did. The fake arrest was the ultimate practical joke.

Trotz, however, was a terrific roommate. I learned so much from him not only about hockey, but also about life. He even told me, a new contact lens wearer, that it was okay to wear contacts in the shower, assuring me they wouldn't fall out. It was Trotz who stayed up until 4:00 AM in our Binghamton, New York, hotel room during the playoffs in April 1991, working tirelessly with a screwdriver to fix his VCR because a VHS tape had gotten caught in the machine as he tried to edit power-play clips for the morning team meeting. Trotz used to assign me to fill out a form after every game (often during bus rides) that included approximately 20 columns across the page for each player's various statistics—early 1990s analytics—to be faxed to Capitals execs Poile and Button as soon as it was completed. We affectionately referred to the chart as the "Jack Button Sheet."

In February 1992 after Trotz was named Baltimore's head coach (replacing Laird), he was entitled to his own hotel room. However, he told me he didn't want to "change the karma," so we continued to room together for the remainder of the season. Our team did not make the playoffs, but 31 players who skated for the Skipjacks that season also played in the NHL at some point in their careers.

Trotz was always gracious with his time whenever I visited Nashville with the Rangers during his 15 seasons as Predators head coach, taking time out of his busy schedule on gamedays to have lunch. Jack's Bar-B-Que on Broadway was always a favorite spot. My broadcast partner Dave Maloney and Trotz's assistant coaches joined us on occasion. In 2015 I received a call out of the blue from Trotz during the NHL draft. I initially thought he dialed me by accident, but he wanted to pick my brain about an NHL veteran I had watched closely for the last few years whom the Capitals were considering signing as a free agent. I was shocked and flattered that he was asking me for a scouting report. But that's Trotz. He never leaves a stone unturned.

After the Skipjacks did not qualify for the playoffs in 1992, Spitz asked me to work as a reporter for WFAN covering Rangers postseason games. This entailed going into the locker room to record postgame sound bites, as well as taping recaps which were used on sports updates. The Rangers faced the Devils in the first round. I was sitting in the upper press box (nicknamed "the Halo") at Brendan Byrne Arena watching Game Four when I received a tap on the shoulder early in the second period. Devils radio play-by-play man Chris Moore had to leave because his wife Pam had gone into labor. I was asked to work the remainder of the game alongside analyst Sherry Ross. So, my first NHL postseason call was a relief appearance out of the bullpen! Hopefully I earned the save.

Just over a week later, I arrived in Pittsburgh to cover Games Three and Four of the Rangers–Penguins Patrick Division Final for WFAN. When I approached the front desk of the Westin Hotel to check in, I received a note from the gentleman behind the counter asking me to call Capitals executive Lew Strudler. To this day, I have no idea how Strudler knew where to find me. I hurried to my room and called him. Strudler told me that Jody Shapiro and Bill Brown wanted to talk to me about doing Capitals play-by-play for Home Team Sports. Strudler also mentioned that, as per WTOP program director Pat Anastasi: there would potentially be a full-time job in the afternoons there as well. It was the perfect combo. I would call Caps home games on HTS, while Rimer called the road games on an over-the-air station, and WTOP agreed to replace me on weekdays when the Caps had a game. A few weeks after accepting the dual role in Washington, I was honored and flattered to have been offered a potential radio opportunity by the Devils.

Former Capitals forward Craig Laughlin was an outstanding broadcast partner and is still going strong three decades later. He has done so much for the hockey community in our nation's capital. Pregame host/sideline reporter "Smokin'" Al Koken is one of the best in the business. We had a great production crew led by Bill Brown and Bill Bell. During one game "Mr. Hockey"

Gordie Howe, who was in town for a promotional function, joined Laughlin and me in the booth for a segment. It was always fun chatting with Ron Weber during my three seasons with the club. He was hired as the Caps' radio play-by-play voice for their inaugural season in 1974–75 and never missed a game—home or away—through his retirement in 1997.

The WTOP studio was located just off Wisconsin Avenue in Washington, D.C. I handled sports reports at 15 and 45 minutes past the hour during the noon to 8:00 PM shift. I would occasionally head out of the studio to cover press conferences and special events. On one memorable, sweltering hot weekend in our nation's capital, I was assigned to cover the Kemper Open in Potomac, Maryland. I had never been to a professional golf tournament. While working games in other sports, I would always dress nicely—usually a suit or sport jacket. So, for the first day of the Kemper, my attire included a long-sleeve shirt, slacks, and dress shoes. Unfortunately, I did not realize until I arrived that I would be walking the course and filing live reports from each hole…on a 90-plus degree day. Somehow, I got through it. With sweat pouring down my body and aching feet, I showed up the next day looking like the other reporters while wearing a golf shirt, khaki shorts, and sneakers.

The Capitals had a terrific team during my three seasons calling their games. Unfortunately, they lost to the Islanders in the first round of the 1992–93 playoffs. (The Isles won three games in overtime, including two in double OT.) During the 1994–1995 season, Laughlin and I worked a rare HTS road game in Boston. It was the only game I called at the old Boston Garden, though I was there for several other hockey and basketball games. My future broadcast partner, Keith Jones, scored the game-winning goal in a victory. The Caps upset the Penguins in an exciting first round before losing in five to the eventual Stanley Cup champion Rangers.

The 1994–95 season did not begin until January due to a lockout by the owners. During the abbreviated schedule, I called 17 Caps games (plus three more in the playoffs). Although I didn't know it at the time, the last Capitals game I called for HTS was Game Six of the first-round playoff series against the Penguins. Due to injuries the Caps wound up using three goaltenders (Jim Carey, Olaf Kolzig, Dafoe) in one game, which is very rare. The Penguins won that game 7–1 and eliminated the Caps on home ice in Game Seven.

Similar to my two seasons in Baltimore with the Skipjacks, I cherish the three years I spent at Home Team Sports. I gained invaluable experience, built relationships, and established my own identity in a market away from home. Not only was I given an opportunity to work NHL games full time, but I was asked to fill in on Washington Bullets and Baltimore Orioles games, as well as handle play-by-play for a variety of college sports (basketball, soccer, lacrosse, volleyball, and wrestling).

I called my first NBA game (Denver Nuggets at Washington Bullets) in March 1994 with analyst Phil Chenier. The next month, my father and I were both on the call for a Bullets–Knicks game in Landover for HTS and MSG, respectively. Our producers asked us to tape an interview with each other prior to the game. During one of my questions to him, I asked (with a straight face): "What was it like to call games when the players shot into peach baskets?" He stared back at me with a deadpan look on his face. I'm not sure how either of us didn't break out in laughter.

Just like during my high school years with Cox Cable, the time at HTS helped expand my versatility. My first event for HTS in September of 1992 was a men's soccer game in Charlottesville, Virginia, between the University of Virginia and Santa Clara. My color analyst was former UVA and U.S. National Team goalkeeper Tony Meola. From 1993 to 1995, I was given the opportunity to work a significant number of men's and women's college basketball games for HTS alongside analysts, including former Richmond Spiders head coach Dick Tarrant, ex-NBA star Kevin Grevey, and Glenn Consor, who has gone on to a long career as the Washington Wizards radio analyst. I worked the CAA men's basketball tournament in Richmond, Virginia, in 1994 and 1995. When Kent Culuko's game-winning three-point shot at the buzzer sent Lefty Driesell's James Madison Dukes to the NCAA Tournament in '94, I was so excited when my call was replayed on *SportsCenter*.

During the early-to-mid 1990s, I also did play-by-play of a World Basketball League game for SportsChannel America alongside former North Carolina State star Terry Gannon, as well as several "Hoop It Up" basketball tournaments in New York and Baltimore with color analysts, including NBA stars Mark Jackson and Rolando Blackman, longtime referee Earl Strom, and Dave Sims. I wanted to gain as much experience as possible and never turned down an assignment.

# WE ARE FAMILY

Family has always been a huge part of my life, and that starts with my parents. I am often asked what it was like growing up with a famous father. I never knew any different; it was normal to me and my siblings. Going to New York Knicks and New York Rangers games was a regular occurrence. When I was five years old, he started handling the sports reports on the 6:00 and 11:00 PM news on WNBC Channel 4 in New York. My mother and I would routinely watch on a 12-inch monitor in our kitchen while eating dinner. As opposed to friends, whose fathers had 9-to-5 jobs and were usually home at night, that wasn't the case with us. But I wouldn't trade it in for anything. (History would repeat itself when I kept a similar work schedule while my kids were growing up.) It was so exciting during my childhood to be able to attend so many sporting events as well as take trips either along with my father or with the entire family.

The most important attribute I learned by observing him throughout my life has been hard work and preparation. Whether we were at home or in a hotel the night before a game, he was always busy working on his charts, reading articles, watching other games, etc. That sounds just like what my life has become over the last three decades. I couldn't have asked for a better teacher.

I always took note of the great relationships my father had with all of his colleagues—whether it was a network executive or the stage manager in the booth. When I travel to arenas and stadiums around the country, I constantly run into myriad people who worked with him through the years and mention how kind he was to them. That includes other broadcasters, production folks, makeup artists, camerapersons, etc.

One of his best traits was his relationship with his color analysts. He always had great rapport with his partners and used his sense of humor to draw the best out of them. He also bestowed nicknames upon many of his broadcast partners, which elevated their persona to the viewers and listeners around the country. Some of my favorites were: Sal "Red Light" Messina, John "Johnny Hoops" Andariese, Ferdie "The Fight Doctor" Pacheco, and Mike "Czar of the Telestrator" Fratello.

His sense of humor remained even during dire times. After he was involved in an accident on the New Jersey Turnpike in April 2002 while sleeping in the back seat of a limousine following a late-night flight, my wife, Barbara, and I visited him in the hospital the next day. After he was diagnosed with a concussion, a doctor entered the room to quiz him on a variety of subjects. One of the questions was: "What season is it?"

The physician expected the answer to be spring. Instead—despite a traumatic brain injury less than 12 hours earlier—my father responded, "Baseball." At that point we knew he was fine.

That's the kind of quick wit my father always has had. He's always been funny and sarcastic. The sarcasm was passed down from generation to generation. When my daughter, Amanda, was young, she learned of his catch phrase, "Yes!" At the age of three, she would playfully repeat the word "No" to Grandpa Marv just to try and get under his skin.

He coauthored a book in 1993 alongside longtime *Sports Illustrated* writer Rick Reilly titled *I'd Love to But I Have a Game: 27 Years Without a Life*. I would have loved to use the title for this book, but it was already taken.

Whenever my Uncles Al and Steve came to our house, the barbs were always flying, and the competitive juices were flowing—whether we were all playing basketball in the driveway, tennis, or Ping-Pong in the basement. My mother went to the lengths of having a cement stoop installed, so my father and his brothers were able to recreate their youth and play stoop ball in our backyard. That's an inner-city game where one literally throws a ball against a stoop on the pavement in front of a building.

Following his retirement after the 2021 NBA postseason, I am frequently asked how my father spends his time. First of all, I never expected my father to retire, so that was quite the shock. He still does most of the same things that he did during his six decades as one of the nation's top sportscasters: a lot of reading (that's where I got it from) and he still watches every TV show, sporting event, and movie imaginable. His knowledge and recall of a wide variety of subjects has always been outstanding.

\* \* \*

I was an only child until I was almost five-and-a-half years old. Then, 10 months later, I was the oldest of four siblings. We usually did everything together. My mother would always set up four consecutive checkups at the doctor's office, four haircuts, or four dentist appointments in a row. I'm still a little bitter that I wasn't allowed to see a PG movie (*Grease* was the first), use a knife during meals, or get my own cup of soda at Burger King until the same day as my three younger siblings despite the fact that I was five and six years older than they were. My brother Brian and sister Denise (the twins) developed a similar interest in sports as I had. Brian would occasionally join me as my color analyst for games I announced off the television in my bedroom. He also formed his own fictitious radio station—WBDA (for Brian David Albert)—similar to my WKGA.

Denise followed my lead and became a Vancouver Canucks fan at a very young age. In fact, among the first words she spoke were "Don Lever" and "Curt Ridley." (Both were Canucks players during the 1970s.) I would show her their photos in the scrapbooks I kept; it was my version of reading to my little sister. Our sister, Jackie, had more of a passion for animals and cooking than sports. We always joked that when she would come to games with us at Madison Square Garden, her favorite team was "M&Ms." While pretending that she had little interest in sports, Jackie would often surprise us with the sports knowledge that she had absorbed. We also frequently played what we referred to as "the piano game." My siblings would sit on the bottom step of a staircase next to the piano in our family room. I would play a tune. Whoever yelled out the correct title would move up one step. The person who made it to the top step first would be declared the winner, and the prize was a ride on my shoulders. (I played the piano game with my kids as well.) We also played a lot of basketball and hockey in our driveway.

During my junior year at NYU in April 1989, we took a memorable family trip to Washington, D.C., to accompany my father to the White House, as he taped an interview for NBC's baseball pregame show with president George H.W. Bush (regarding his baseball career at Yale University). My mother, siblings, and I took a tour but did not envision that we would have an opportunity to meet the president. We were all ecstatic when a White House staffer said to us, "The President would like you to see the Oval Office." I thought I was dreaming. We were ushered in, met President Bush, and then *he* suggested that we take a group photo. The president reached down to slide a glass table out of the way so that he could pose with the six of us. My brother, Brian, was a high school freshman at the time. His social studies teacher knew about our trip and decided—on a lark—to mail an official school absentee slip to the White House with a note referencing that one of her students claimed he was with the president on April 8. Amazingly, a few weeks later, an envelope arrived at the school's office from the White House with the signed form. It said: "Dear Mrs. Rothman—Yes, Brian was with me. Please excuse his absence. President George Bush."

Missing school that day did not affect Brian academically. He attended Columbia University and Miami Law School, then spent several years as a news reporter in West Virginia, Florida, and New Jersey before starting his own businesses—TheLaw.TV, Newstation.com, and Videobolt.com. Jackie attended the Culinary Institute of America and became a terrific pastry chef at several restaurants in Manhattan. Denise has enjoyed a long career in the media, working in various production roles at *Good Morning America*, *Inside Edition*, and David Blaine Productions before founding media companies called The Moms and My Cancer Family. As an added bonus thanks to her relationship with Blaine, the magician/illusionist has often attended her kids' birthday parties and performed for all of us. Ironically, Brian and I both have two girls; Jackie and Denise both have two boys. Brian and his wife, Jen, live in Florida with daughters, Laya and Mia. Denise lives in Manhattan with sons Jaron and Jaylan. Jackie and her husband Mikhail live on Long Island with sons Jonathan and Logan. My parents divorced after 25 years of marriage. Both were re-married in the 1990s; my mother married Gary Oberlander, and my father married Heather Faulkiner. We have had the fortune of spending so many big family celebrations together.

Thirty years after my parents first met in 1964, fate went to work once again. A series of sporting and broadcasting-related events led to the initial meeting between my wife, Barbara, and me. I was a hired as a last-minute replacement by the NHL Radio Network to do play-by-play for the 1994 Stanley Cup Final. After the Canucks won Game Five (on June 9) to stave off elimination, I went to meet Jerry Coleman, my friend/colleague from Baltimore who coincidentally was in New York for a couple of days doing voiceover work. He had dinner that night with a few of his friends from Ithaca College, including Barbara Wolf. We met for the first time when I went to her apartment to meet Coleman after the game. Three days later, I took Barbara to Game Three of the NBA Finals between the New York Knicks and Houston Rockets, though she still claims it was not an official date. She became my wife just more than two years after we first met. We even had appropriately named Barbie and Ken dolls next to our wedding cake on August 10, 1996. In true Albert family fashion, my father worked a practice telecast that afternoon with his new NBC partner Sam Wyche at the Meadowlands during a New York Giants–Baltimore Ravens preseason game and then made the 20-mile trek to Livingston, New Jersey, in time to take photos prior to the wedding ceremony. Through the years both of our schedules have impacted the planning of many family events. We squeezed our wedding date in between my father's return from the Atlanta Olympics and the start of the NFL regular season.

We traveled to Hawaii for our honeymoon. Coincidentally, Al Michaels and his wife, Linda, were staying at the same hotel as us in Maui; I lost my sunglasses in a wave when conversing with him in the ocean. I did not warn Barbara (nor did I know at the time) that we would spend our first anniversary in Sacramento, California, where I was assigned to broadcast a WNBA game between the New York Liberty and Sacramento Monarchs. The life of a sportscaster's wife! Earlier that summer, we traveled to Rome, Florence, and Venice, Italy.

What a great year 1994 was. As a 26 year old, I was hired to work my first Stanley Cup Final, the New York Rangers won the Cup, I was hired by FOX, and, most importantly, I met my wife. Barbara and I have two wonderful daughters, Amanda and Sydney, who were born in different centuries.

Barbara and I lived in a Manhattan apartment (on 54th Street between 1st Avenue and Sutton Place) for four years before moving to Closter, New Jersey—10 miles north of the George Washington Bridge—on Monday, September 27, 1999. Just more than a week later, Amanda was born. I was in Chicago for a Bears–New Orleans Saints telecast on Sunday, October 3, and Barbara and I were nervous during the entire weekend that she would go into labor while I was away. Fortunately, everything worked out, and Amanda was born at 4:00 AM on Tuesday, October 5—just hours after Al Leiter and the New York Mets clinched a spot in the postseason with a victory in a one-game playoff against the Cincinnati Reds. Dr. Jonathan Lanzkowsky, who delivered Amanda at Mount Sinai Hospital in New York City, was a huge Mets fan and watched most of the game with me—much to Barbara's chagrin.

Fifteen hours after becoming a father, I worked the Rangers home opener against the Ottawa Senators. Most of our visitors had come to the hospital in the morning and afternoon; Barbara was going to rest at night, so I figured why not and headed six miles south to MSG. My in-laws had photos developed of Amanda earlier in the day. This was before texting and camera phones, so I proudly showed off the pictures to all of my friends and colleagues at the game. MSG's public relations guru Barry Watkins was kind enough to arrange for Amanda's birth announcement to be displayed on the scoreboard during one of the intermissions, and Sam Rosen and John Davidson mentioned her birth (along with photos) on the MSG Network telecast.

A few days later, I pulled out of our driveway to pick up Barbara and Amanda for the trip home from the hospital. After a few blocks, two women walking on the sidewalk alerted me to the fact that a passenger-side tire looked flat. I guess I must have been in new father mode because I didn't even realize that the car was wobbly. I switched cars, and fortunately my sister-in-law Ellen helped me secure the baby car seat in the other vehicle. Upon returning home with Amanda a few hours later, Barbara and I looked each other and said, "What do we do now?"

Just more than a month later—at the age of five weeks—Amanda made her first trip to a Rangers game at the Garden wearing a tiny white snow suit and strapped to Barbara in a BABYBJORN carrier. Despite the high decibel level in the arena, she slept for a good portion of the game but did wake up in time for a photo on the ice before we went home. Amanda was just shy of three months old when she attended her first NFL game—on the first weekend of the 21st century. The biggest story in the news during the prior weeks and months was that worldwide infrastructure would be brought down by the Y2K bug with the transition to the year 2000. The NHL and NBA did not schedule games on Friday, December 31, 1999, to avoid teams having to travel and potentially experience flight glitches. Fortunately, few major errors took place. We celebrated New Year's Eve at home, and then I drove to Philadelphia the next morning to prepare for the Philadelphia Eagles–St. Louis Rams telecast. Barbara and Amanda headed to Veterans Stadium on the day of the game and watched from the broadcast booth with Amanda bundled up to protect her from the frigid weather. Amanda was too young to realize it at the time, but she witnessed "The Greatest Show on Turf." Those 1999 Rams would win the Super Bowl later that same month.

The week she turned one, Amanda started walking. I had her on ice skates two days later. Like most parents of young children, we always peppered Amanda with questions and were so excited and proud when she comprehended and answered. I will admit that I may have taken things a bit too far when I taught her to throw both arms straight up in the air and exclaim "touchdown" over and over again. Barbara used to ridicule me, saying that I treated Amanda like a trained seal. Needless to say, Sydney had a mind of her own and never took part in such antics.

Amanda attended her first-ever day of school at the Jewish Community Center in Tenafly, New Jersey, on September 11, 2001. Barbara and I were in the building's café during Amanda's orientation when we first heard about a plane flying into the World Trade Center. We were less than 20 miles from Ground Zero. During our drive home (while heading north on the Palisades Parkway), we heard fighter jets flying above. We spent the next 12 hours glued to our television, watching in horror. The world changed drastically that day. Shortly thereafter, Barbara decided that the two of us would no longer fly together. Many other couples with young children have that same mind-set. I placated her wishes, even though statistically there is a greater percentage of an accident while we drive together. Through the years, we have traveled to locales in the United States, Bermuda, London, and even Italy on separate flights. We usually try to arrange it so we land within an hour or two of each other. Whoever is on the earlier flight checks the luggage, retrieves it, and checks in at the hotel. We have it down to a science. When traveling along with both kids, we all fly together.

Amanda was so fortunate to have five great-grandparents (three on my side and Barbara's grandmothers, Fanny and Eleanor) when she was born. I still had all four of my grandparents when I graduated from college in 1990. In February of 1991, a few days after my 23rd birthday, my grandmother Alida (my father's mother) passed away. I returned to New York for her funeral and missed a few Baltimore Skipjacks broadcasts. It was an honor to tell my grandfather, Max, that Amanda was named for his wife. Max lived another nine years before he died in April 2000 at the age of 84. Max split his time between Cliffside Park, New Jersey, and Coconut Creek, Florida; we visited with him frequently, especially after we moved to New Jersey. With three sons and a grandson in the business, we often joke that Max should be referred to as "The Father of Sportscasting."

For the first 15 years of my professional career, I took great pleasure in visiting my mother's parents—Julie and Stew Caress—whenever I had a work assignment in South Florida. Either I would visit them in Delray Beach or they would come to my hotel for a meal. In January of 2005, Stew met me at

Dolphins Stadium as I was there to host a taped college football skills competition show. Aaron Rodgers was one of the participants a few months before he was drafted by the Green Bay Packers. I chatted with Rodgers about his beloved San Jose Sharks (he told me he attended many of their games during his high school years). Marisa Miller was our sideline reporter; it was the first and only time I had my television makeup applied in a chair next to a *Sports Illustrated* Swimsuit Issue cover model!

Stew was a huge sports fan; I have great memories of attending baseball and football games with him as a youngster. Stew passed away in December 2007. Earlier that year in January, we celebrated Sydney's fourth birthday (and Stew's 87th) together at Walt Disney World. My grandmother Julie remained in Delray Beach until moving to the Cleveland area in 2015 at the age of 93. She may hold the record for the oldest person in history to move from Florida to Ohio. Ironically, since her move, I have been assigned to many more games in Cleveland (Cavaliers, Browns, Guardians) than South Florida, so my frequent visits with her continued, including one in January 2022, two months after her 99th birthday. Unfortunately, she passed away in September 2022, less than two months shy of 100. She lived a great life and was adored by her five grandchildren and 10 great-grandchildren.

It is only fitting that I equate both of my daughters' births with a sporting event. Sydney was born on January 27, 2003, the day after the Tampa Bay Buccaneers defeated the Oakland Raiders to win Super Bowl XXXVII. I missed a Rangers game (in Atlanta) to make sure I was home when she was born. Syd's birth was acknowledged on the Madison Square Garden scoreboard as well as at the next home game.

Similar to my childhood, both girls have grown up around the world of sports and broadcasting. Due to my schedule, they did not always experience the typical vacation destinations. Instead, spring break trips have been to cities such as Buffalo, Pittsburgh, and Montreal during the hockey playoffs. As Barbara likes to say, "It's not the norm, but it's our norm."

Both girls may have been inadvertently brainwashed by the world of sports as well. When three-year-old Amanda (who was just learning to read) accompanied us to a cemetery for an unveiling, she called out the names from a section of headstones. "Shapiro, Cohen, zhill-bear," she confidently proclaimed, pronouncing the final surname not as it was spelled (Gilbert) but with the French pronunciation of the former New York Rangers star. (The late Rod Gilbert loved this story.)

When Sydney was in nursery school, her entire class received an assignment during letter G week to draw a gorgeous garden. All of Sydney's classmates sketched trees, grass, flowers, etc. The teachers were concerned that she misunderstood the assignment, as she had drawn a building—with circles on the ice and stick figures, lines, and boxes to signify fans in the seats. When the teachers asked her to explain, it made perfect sense. "It's a Rangers game at Madison Square Garden," she innocently told them. Definitely my children.

Like most people who work in the world of sports, I was not always home on birthdays, holidays, and New Year's Eve. But that's the world I chose to be a part of and wouldn't change a thing, which made it extra special when my family travels with me or meets me on the road. I'm proud to say I was in attendance for the birth of both of my kids, two high school graduations, and one college graduation (so far). When Amanda was three, I was in Atlanta on a Wednesday and had to be back there on that Friday. I flew home on Thursday so I could go trick-or-treating with her on Halloween and then went back. Before Amanda turned four, I made sure to take her to a Knicks–Washington Wizards game at Madison Square Garden so she could see Michael Jordan play in person. Both girls may have been inadvertently brainwashed by the world of sports as well.

The girls made occasional cameo appearances during football telecasts thanks to director Michael Frank. In 2005 Amanda recorded a line for the game open (along with Ryan Macheska, the son of our producer). From the roof of Giants Stadium, they proclaimed together: "Giants–Vikings...next on FOX."

Two years later, Frank taped Amanda (eight years old) and Sydney (a few months before turning five) prior to the game in the broadcast booth holding copies of team rosters. They both took direction well and memorized the following lines:

Amanda: "Syd, it's time to stop studying."
Sydney: "But Daddy needs his nuggets."
Amanda: "But it's time!"
Both: "Happy Thanksgiving everyone."
Amanda: "Is my yellow crayon official?" (She played off my oft-repeated line, emphasizing how the superimposed first-down line is unofficial.)

When I'm not there for special events, Barbara pulls the weight of two parents. When we celebrated our 25th anniversary in 2021, I joked that due to my travel schedule, I had probably been present for only 14 of the 25. But there are perks, too. Amanda has celebrated many birthdays at the Garden, usually around opening night of the NHL season. Sydney has enjoyed birthdays at MSG as well and even traveled to Los Angeles for NHL All-Star Weekend around her birthday in 2017. I always tried to attend back-to-school nights. I have a stellar record at attending college move-ins; it works out since my schedule is pretty light in August. Parents' Weekends at Syracuse and Wisconsin didn't exactly work because those are during football weekends in September or October. I snuck in a bunch of visits to Syracuse (a four-hour drive from home), as well as side trips to Madison, Wisconsin, when on work assignment in Milwaukee or Chicago.

In 2009 they accompanied me to Washington, D.C., during a Rangers–Washington Capitals playoff series. We spent an off day at various attractions, including the White House. At one point, we lost sight of six-year-old Sydney. It should be impossible to lose a child *inside* the White House. But she was tired and wandered approximately 20 feet away from us and subsequently sprawled out on a couch behind a barrier, which was supposed to keep tourists away from sitting there. Only Syd! Fortunately, we were not escorted from the White House grounds. Three years later, the family joined me in

Indianapolis after I was hired to work the Super Bowl XLVI international telecast (along with Joe Theismann). When we met in the stands during the New York Giants' postgame celebration, the first thing Barbara told me was that in the final moments of the game as Tom Brady led the New England Patriots down the field for a potential game-winning score, nine-year-old Sydney turned to her and said, "Ma, I gotta pee." It was loud enough for the entire section to hear. Being that Barbara is a die-hard Giants fan, she told Sydney, "You're going to have to hold it in."

At a Rangers holiday party in December (for players, coaches, staff, and broadcasters), a young Sydney was invited to sit on the lap of Santa Claus and receive a present. She came running back to our table and said to me and Dave Maloney, "Why does Santa keeping saying 'bless you?' I didn't sneeze!" In 2016 a few weeks before Sydney's Bat Mitzvah, she made sure to tell me, "When you make your speech, please don't use your fake announcer voice." I turned that request into my opening line.

Barbara and the girls attended the 2010 Winter Olympics in Vancouver and the 2016 Summer Games in Rio. While I was busy working two games almost every day in Vancouver, they attended a few hockey games, as well as curling and ski events. Six years later in Rio, my schedule allowed me to attend events with them in the late afternoon hours, including gymnastics, fencing, water polo, swimming, diving, and beach volleyball. We spent my one off day on a memorable sightseeing tour, including a cable car ride up Sugarloaf Mountain and a trip to the top of "Christ the Redeemer." We saw many of the historic sights in Washington, D.C., and Amanda and I even swam with dolphins in Hawaii. We felt these were terrific opportunities for the girls to be able to learn when not in a classroom. They were life-changing experiences they will always remember.

While I missed a lot of their weekend events due to my schedule, I always felt like I was around during weekdays more than most fathers who worked traditional jobs. When I'm home, I'm home. I don't go to an office. My office is basically a broadcast booth located around the country. I drove Amanda and Sydney to and from school as often as possible. I accompanied both of them to sports classes at the JCC in Tenafly, New Jersey. It was usually me—and 10 moms. Those who didn't know me probably wondered how I could possibly be so available on Monday afternoons.

I enjoyed helping coach both girls in various sporting activities around town. Due to my schedule, I could never serve as the head coach, but I would be at their practices and games as often as possible. They both played T-ball, softball, and soccer during their childhood. Sydney attended a basketball clinic along with the daughter of comedian/actor Chris Rock, who was always very cordial. We ran into each other occasionally at Knicks games that I was broadcasting when he sat courtside.

Amanda loves ice skating and took several ice hockey clinics (she was the only girl most of the time). I drove her to the rink in Hackensack, New Jersey, whenever my schedule allowed. I enjoyed helping with her equipment and skates and then watching her learn the various skills. At Northern Valley Regional High School in Demarest, New Jersey, Amanda played on the field hockey and lacrosse teams. Sydney played lacrosse and tennis. During her junior year, the tennis team won the state championship, and all of the team members received championship rings. Both girls spent many summers at Lake Bryn Mawr Camp in Honesdale, Pennsylvania. They learned to be independent and build lifelong friendships—similar to my time at Kutsher's Sports Academy.

The girls enjoyed attending sporting events during their entire childhood, especially Rangers games. Amanda loved Mark Messier and burst into tears at his jersey retirement ceremony. Henrik Lundqvist quickly became a favorite of both girls after joining the Blueshirts in 2005. A digital imprint of Lundqvist and Syd was once the top of her birthday cake. Amanda and Sydney enjoyed helping out occasionally in the MSG media room by preparing cups of soda for the press.

I turned into a superhero in the girls' minds when I arranged a meet-and-greet with Miley Cyrus prior to a concert we attended at Nassau Coliseum. A few years later, Amanda and Sydney (and their friends) were jealous when they saw a photo of me with Taylor Swift, who was sitting two seats to my left in the front row at MSG while I broadcasted a Knicks game. Taylor actually took my cell phone and snapped the selfie herself. I guess she had a certain angle she liked best, and it wasn't the first time she had done it.

I couldn't attend too many sporting events with my children because I was usually working, but we always tried to fit in either a New York Mets or Yankees game every season, as well as U.S. Open tennis. Barbara became a master at schlepping the girls around to various stadiums. I'm not sure how she did it all. Occasionally, they would come to games just to see me for a few minutes before I left on a road trip.

Amanda and I enjoyed several "Albert doubleheaders"—the Open and a Mets game in the same day since the venues are located across the parking lot from each other. Amanda and I were in attendance when the Yankees defeated the Philadelphia Phillies to win the 2009 World Series. I flew home from Vancouver that day, and Barbara drove Amanda to a parking lot close to the George Washington Bridge. We made the exchange, and Amanda I were off to the Bronx. In 2016 Amanda and I attended the NHL All-Star Game in Nashville.

In hindsight, I am shocked that my parents allowed me (and my sister Denise) to run around Madison Square Garden wearing Canucks jerseys—let alone wear them to Rangers holiday parties. I am glad my girls were true blue Rangers fans, and we never had to deal with a similar issue. I doubt I would have let them wear an opposing team jersey at MSG. They did wear their Blueshirt gear to arenas on the road occasionally, and fans in some cities were friendlier to them than others.

Speaking of team apparel, I have accumulated a closet full of T-shirts from various teams, leagues, and special events that I either worked or attended through the years. Barbara once secretly sent a boxful of these shirts to a company who stitched all of the logos together as part of a 7' x 7' quilt. She thought I wouldn't speak to her for weeks after I learned that my T-shits were cut up. Quite the opposite; it was one of the best gifts she's ever given to me.

Amanda began her journalism career in second grade when she worked on the staff of the morning television program (*Hillside News Network*) at her elementary school for one week, and then on a regular basis in fourth grade. The students rotated positions weekly (anchor, producer, graphics, etc). Their five-minute show was beamed into every classroom in place of morning announcements. Sydney followed in her footsteps as an *HNN* anchor four years later. I couldn't believe a grade school had such an amazing program. At the age of eight, Amanda sang the national anthem prior to a women's basketball game at Columbia University (thanks to an invitation from associate athletic director Barry Neuberger). I was as nervous as I've ever been in my life while videotaping her from courtside, but she did great.

Amanda became editor in chief of the high school newspaper, and then it was on to Syracuse University. She had a terrific experience at the Newhouse School of Public Communications, studying broadcast and digital journalism. I am often asked if I attended Syracuse. Most people assume so because of the high volume of play-by-play broadcasters, including my father, who did. Now at least I can say I'm an honorary alum after I paid tuition for four years. I was a guest speaker in a few classes on the campus when visiting Amanda as well. Amanda and I enjoyed attending a Syracuse basketball game during our first campus tour and a Syracuse Mets minor league baseball game during one of my subsequent visits. She secured an internship with the athletic department and edited highlight videos at Orange football, basketball, and lacrosse games during her junior and senior years, which were distributed on the school's social media accounts.

After two-and-a-half months studying abroad in Australia as a junior, her stay was cut short in March 2020 due to the pandemic but not before she went to the Australian Open in Melbourne. Amanda would never miss the opportunity to attend a sporting event. She was a digital production assistant for NBC in Stamford, Connecticut, during the ensuing Summer Olympics and a producer/editor for the 2022 Winter Games. She was part of a team that won an Emmy for its work during the 2020 Tokyo Olympics. In addition to her Olympic work, Amanda has worked as a producer/editor at ABC, MSG Networks, SNY, and the NHL since graduating from Syracuse. In October of 2022, she started a full-time job at the NHL office as an NFT blockchain editor. I laugh and beam with pride that Amanda won a national Emmy at age 22, and Sydney won a championship ring at 17 while I've only waited 55 years for both. Like Amanda, Sydney was an editor for her high school newspaper and is studying journalism at the University of Wisconsin. She began her sophomore year in the fall of 2022. I love visiting her there. It is a beautiful campus, and I have enjoyed spending time at sporting venues such as Camp Randall Stadium and Kohl Center.

Barbara comes from a wonderful family. Her parents, Maxine and Herb Wolf, moved around a bit during Barbara's childhood and finally settled in Parsippany, New Jersey, (the home of the Tiffany headquarters, where the Super Bowl trophy is produced each year) when she was 10. Her older sister, Ellen, and husband, Eric, live less than 10 minutes from us in northern New Jersey, where they raised their daughters Danielle and Samantha. I first met Barbara's family at Danielle's third birthday party in 1994, and she was a flower girl at our wedding 20 months later. Barbara's brother, Rich, and his wife, Danielle, live in Westchester, New York, with daughter, Jojo, and son, Ben. Rich works in television sales. The entire family suffered a huge loss when Maxine passed away in May 2021; she is missed by all of us each and every day.

I could not have asked for a better partner over the last 27 years. Barbara has understood—and put up with—my crazy schedule better than anyone else I could imagine. She was a single parent for long stretches of time during football seasons, Olympics, and the hockey playoffs. We have a plaque in our family room with the inscription: "We interrupt this marriage to bring you football season."

During most major weather events—snowstorms, hurricanes, blizzards (or losses of power)—I always seem to be on the road. I was on the air calling an Eagles game in Philadelphia when Amanda underwent an emergency appendectomy, and Barbara did not inform me until the game ended in order to not break my concentration.

Barbara is the first to say she could not have done it without the assistance of our amazing family and friends who always stepped up to the plate. Special shoutouts to the Klaiman, Holzer, Sunshine, Sertner, Freeman, and Sherman families. And then there was Josephina Perez (nicknamed "Fina" by a young Amanda before she learned to pronounce her full name), who came into our lives when Amanda was six months old. She quickly became part of our extended family. Amanda and Sydney will always think of Fina as a second mother, considering she was around for their entire childhoods (and still is). She never lived with us full time but had her own room and was always on hand when needed. When Barbara was able to meet me on the road, especially when the girls were young, it was because Fina (and our family and friends) stepped up, helped out, and provided consistency and normalcy.

Barbara was a huge fan of both the Giants and Knicks when we first met in 1994 and quickly learned to love hockey as well. She can still name most of the roster from the 1986 and 1990 Super Bowl champion Giants. She watches as many of my games as possible, especially on football Sundays. Right from the start, Barbara has understood the nuances of broadcasting and provided excellent critiques. During our early years together, she took notes on a yellow legal pad, including her comments on the broadcast (not only on the announcing, but also technical aspects as well) and questions she might have about a rule or key play. We have an inside joke that whenever I say "extracurricular activity" during a broadcast, it's a test to see if she's watching or listening. I receive a text within 30 seconds if she is.

I was so proud to have my family by my side when I was inducted into the Closter (New Jersey) Hall of Fame in September 2018 and the New Jersey Jewish Sports Hall of Fame at the JCC in Tenafly, New Jersey, in May 2022. I was honored to share the night with CBS Sports' Tracy Wolfson, one of the top sideline reporters in the business. Eli Manning was the guest speaker and entertained the audience with terrific stories from his childhood and NFL career.

I have always taken pride in giving back to the community and enjoy supporting many charitable endeavors. I have shared my personal story about my premature birth at several March of Dimes fund-raisers through the years. I've helped emcee countless charitable events through the years to benefit, among many others, the Boomer Esiason Foundation, Garden of Dreams Foundation, the Viscardi Center, Hockey in Harlem, the Joe Namath Foundation, the Marty Lyons Foundation, the Cal Ramsey Awards, Champions in Courage, the Christopher and Dana Reeve Foundation, the Alan T. Brown Foundation, the Teddy Atlas Foundation, and the Mike Nichols Foundation. Although the sport of golf has never been my strong suit, I have enjoyed taking part in charity tournaments through the years. I'll never turn down a free golf shirt.

During the COVID pandemic, thanks to my friend David Steinberg connecting me with Fanatics CEO Michael Rubin, I donated a package to the "All-In Challenge," which offered the opportunity to sit in our broadcast booth at a game in all four sports. The winning bidder, Jeramy Utara, donated more than $25,000.

# THANKS, RUPERT!

On December 17, 1993, I was eating a pregame meal in the media room at the Capital Centre in Landover, Maryland, with our Home Team Sports production crew prior to a Washington Capitals telecast. Suddenly, producer Bill Brown was distracted by a local news report on the small television hanging in the corner of the room. Rupert Murdoch and his fledgling FOX network were awarded the rights to the NFC television package after submitting a stunning bid, ending a 38-year run between NFL and CBS. FOX did not even have a sports department at the time.

Brown had been a broadcast associate at CBS a decade earlier while working with legendary producer Bob Stenner, director Sandy Grossman, and the Hall of Fame broadcast tandem of Pat Summerall and John Madden. He knew many of the CBS production staffers who just learned they would lose their football duties within weeks. Never in my wildest dreams did I imagine this news would impact my life. After all, the NFL play-by-play men on CBS, NBC, and ABC were all giants in the industry, many of whom had been calling games since before I was born.

Within weeks FOX announced the hiring of the top two broadcast teams from CBS: Summerall and Madden, as well as Dick Stockton and Matt Millen. This established immediate credibility for the network. Skeptics previously joked that Bart and Homer Simpson would call the games. I heard rumors from both Brown and my agent, Alan Sanders, that FOX Sports was planning to hold auditions for additional play-by-play broadcasters and color analysts. A few months earlier, Brown had introduced me to Ed Goren, a longtime CBS producer who was one of the first executives hired by FOX Sports, in the press box at the MLB All-Star Game at Camden Yards. CBS carried the game, and I was there filing reports for WTOP Radio. I later learned that

George Krieger, another executive hired by Murdoch along with David Hill and Goren, had watched a lacrosse match that I had called for HTS. Krieger had a relationship with HTS exec Jody Shapiro and had Shapiro send a VHS tape of the match so he could watch with his son. I could count the number of lacrosse matches I worked in my life on one hand, but because Krieger's son was a lacrosse player, I was on my way to an audition with FOX.

I was asked to fly to Los Angeles in March 1994 to broadcast a game from the previous season involving the Green Bay Packers (and an opponent I can't recall) off a monitor with James Lofton, the former Buffalo Bills and Packers wide receiver who would be elected to the Pro Football Hall of Fame nine years later. We were sent team press releases and statistics, and I prepared my charts during the week prior to the audition. Lofton and I had dinner together at a Chinese restaurant across the street from our hotel the night before.

The following morning, we arrived at the FOX lot and were introduced to Hill, Goren, Krieger, and Stenner. Off we went…calling the first half of the game. I don't remember much about it—the entire day was a whirlwind—aside from the fact that I felt pretty comfortable. I had no idea how many other play-by-play folks would be auditioning and had pretty low expectations of actually getting hired to work NFL games on network television at age 26. Things like that just didn't happen. After wrapping up, we went back to the hotel. I headed to the pool and met Joe Buck and Tim Green for the first time. They had just finished their auditions as well (and wound up working together for the first two NFL on FOX seasons).

Over the next two months, Sanders kept in contact with the FOX execs and eventually told me there was a good chance I was going to be hired for one of the four open play-by-play slots. I received an invitation to head back to Los Angeles for a public relations tour and photo shoot with some of the other new hires in June. At that point it was official! Hill, Goren, and Krieger decided to take a chance on four young play-by-play announcers—three of us with limited football experience—all with fathers in the business. We were in the right place at the right time and received the biggest breaks of our lives. Aside from me and 25-year-old Buck, FOX hired 30-year-old Thom Brennaman (the son of Hall of Fame Cincinnati Reds broadcaster Marty Brennaman) and 33-year-old Kevin Harlan, the radio voice of the Kansas City Chiefs, whose dad, Bob, was the president of the Packers. The six FOX NFL crews during the inaugural 1994 season were: Summerall/Madden, Stockton/Millen, Harlan/Jerry Glanville, Buck/Green, Brennaman/Anthony Muñoz, and Albert/Ron Pitts along with the studio crew of James Brown, Terry Bradshaw, Howie Long, and Jimmy Johnson. Twenty-nine years later, following Buck's move to ESPN for the 2022 season, I am the only NFL game announcer from the original lineup who remains at FOX.

During the PR tour, I attended a dinner in Beverly Hills, California, along with most of the other FOX announcers. Buck, Brennaman, Harlan, and I sat at the left end of the table in silence (and awe), listening to the stories told by the legends at the other end who were now our peers. Game Seven of the NBA Finals between the New York Knicks and Houston Rockets played on a television just behind us. At one point, the waiter asked for appetizer orders. All of a sudden, in his unmistakable voice of God tone, Summerall stated with authority, "I'll have the 'Kick Ass Chili.'" Yes, that was an actual item on the menu.

The next month, during the initial NFL on FOX seminar in Anaheim, California, the excitement was indescribable. Many in attendance—executives, production folks, and broadcasters—had come from CBS, most of whom were unsure just a few months earlier if they would ever work NFL games again. FOX started its sports division from scratch, and its first preseason telecast was less than a month away. Madden was a larger-than-life presence anywhere he went. During every seminar throughout his years at FOX, whether in a ballroom, restaurant, or hotel lobby, we were all attracted to him like fly paper—eager to pick his brain and eavesdrop on each and every story he told. Madden wondered aloud why the network sports division branded itself as "FOX Sports" when it would only televise one sport (at least initially). He jokingly suggested it should just be "FOX Sport."

During the seminar we viewed commercials that would run throughout the summer introducing fans around the country to the new FOX Sports mantra: "Same Game, New Attitude!" We split up into breakout groups—producers in one room, directors, play-by-play broadcasters, color analysts, etc. in other rooms. I'll never forget sitting in the room with Summerall, Stockton, Harlan, Buck, and Brennaman. The four of us, who were the young hires, tried to soak in everything we could from Summerall and Stockton. We all filed away that advice for future use.

My color analyst, Ron Pitts, was a rookie broadcaster as well. The son of former Packers great Elijah Pitts, he played defensive back at UCLA, followed by a six-year career with the Packers and Buffalo Bills. We worked a practice game together in Chicago during the preseason, and our first regular assignment was on September 4, 1994, a game between the Los Angeles Rams and Arizona Cardinals in Anaheim. It was Buddy Ryan's first game as Cards head coach.

The Friday before the game, along with Brown and director Peter Bleckner, Pitts and I attended Rams practice in El Segundo, California. We then headed inside their facility, which was located at an adjacent elementary school. When veteran head coach Chuck Knox (age 62 at the time) walked into the room to meet with us, he seemed shocked to see broadcasters who looked so young. It was pretty intimidating for this 26 year old to sit in a room and ask questions of Knox (who began his NFL coaching career five years before I was born) and 60-year-old Ryan the following day in a hotel ballroom. I still have such vivid memories of that first game (a 14–12 Rams victory). The two Rams touchdowns were scored by Todd Lyght (on a 74-yard fumble return) and second-year running back Jerome Bettis.

Our crew—Pitts, Brown, Bleckner, associate director Larry Lancaster, broadcast associate Clark Pierce, and I—worked 10 games that season (including six in the western United States) and two "Battle of the Bays" between then-division rivals Green Bay and Tampa Bay. I text all five of them every year on September 4 to wish them a happy anniversary since the first game was such a huge milestone in all of our careers.

Prior to the 1995 season, FOX decided to flip-flop some of the crews, and I was paired with Hall of Famer Muñoz, one of the nicest gentlemen I've ever met. When we traveled around to meet with various teams, coaches, and players, I was in awe of the level of respect they all had for him. Our first game together was in Green Bay (the first regular-season game played by the Rams following the franchise's move to St. Louis). Reggie White stopped practicing and walked over to the sideline to say hello and chat with Muñoz. Later that season, we worked two games played by the expansion Carolina Panthers at Clemson University (during the construction of their new stadium in Charlotte).

I have loved working with all of my FOX partners—both personally and professionally. After one season with Muñoz, I was paired with the brilliant Green, who had played eight seasons with the Atlanta Falcons while also attending and graduating from law school and becoming an accomplished author. We spent seven seasons together (1996–2002). Unfortunately, Tim announced that he was diagnosed with ALS (Lou Gehrig's Disease) in 2018 but maintains the most positive attitude while continuing to write books and is an inspiration to not only his family and friends, but also millions around the country. One of the most memorable stories from my years with Green involved a production meeting with Brett Favre. They were teammates in Atlanta during Favre's rookie season (in 1991) and were assigned to room together during Falcons road trips. When I asked Favre what memories he had of Green, he joked, "Tim was on his bed writing books; I was on my bed reading *Penthouse.*" Speaking of Green's writing. I was honored when he featured me as a character in his 2009 novel: *Football Champ.*

Green and I were in New Orleans for a game in 1997 during Mike Ditka's first season as Saints head coach. We were scheduled to meet with the Hall of Famer early on a Saturday morning at the team facility. Before the days of GPS, Waze, and Google Maps, we usually followed printed directions provided by one of our crew members. Producer Rich Russo was driving and accidentally missed the exit; we wound up on the Lake Pontchartrain Causeway, which runs 24 miles each way! Needless to say, we arrived late. To his credit, Ditka was waiting for us, sitting by himself in a dark meeting room. Without missing a beat, he proclaimed, "John Madden is never late!"

Fortunately, Russo's driving skills did not have an effect on his career path. He is one of the most highly respected directors in the business and has worked multiple Super Bowls for FOX.

Another memorable moment while working with Green took place in 1999 in Atlanta. Our producer, P.T. Navarro, learned that James Brown—the "Godfather of Soul"—would be performing a postgame concert at the Georgia Dome following the Falcons game. Navarro arranged for Brown, a former high school quarterback (as he told us), to join Green and me in the booth for a segment during the game. I was shocked by how short he was. Live on the air, I suggested to Brown that he send it back to our studio for a "Game Break" provided by the "other" James Brown, then the host of *FOX NFL Sunday*. He followed my instructions well. Without missing a beat, Brown excitedly said, "From one JB to another!"

Green was a food connoisseur and was familiar with the hot spots in most NFL cities. Whenever we worked a game in New Orleans, we took a trolley to have lunch at The Camellia Grill near the campus of Tulane University. When in Atlanta, he usually brought us to Wright's Gourmet in Dunwoody for a Rebel Reuben sandwich. The list goes on and on; my taste buds are tingling as I think about some of our meals together.

From 2003 to 2006, Brian Baldinger was my broadcast partner. One of the most energetic analysts I have ever worked with, Baldinger had a tremendous work ethic and encyclopedic knowledge of the NFL. In the basement of his home in south Jersey, Baldy had magnets with the names of every player in the league, which covered the wall as if he were a team general manager. After a 12-year career as an offensive lineman (including six seasons playing for head coach Tom Landry with the Dallas Cowboys), Baldinger has gone on to an outstanding broadcasting career. His Baldy's Breakdowns on social media are a must-see for those who love the hidden intricacies of the sport. Thanks to Baldy's friendship with a member of Bruce Springsteen's crew, a group of us stood at the foot of the stage during a concert in Cleveland the night before we worked a Browns game. One of the perks of having friends in high places!

For five seasons from 2002 to 2006, I filled in on the B crew for three or four weeks every October along with Daryl "Moose" Johnston and Tony Siragusa when Buck was on postseason baseball duty. Stockton, who usually worked with Moose and Goose, would slide up to work on the A crew with Troy Aikman. Moose and Goose were both recent Super Bowl champions and they would always call the second-best FOX game on a given Sunday. It also gave me the opportunity to work with Stenner and Grossman, two giants in the industry.

On May 17, 2007, I received one of the greatest phone calls of my professional career. It was from FOX senior producer Bill Brown, who had hired me at HTS 15 years earlier. The FOX execs decided to pair me with Moose and Goose permanently, along with producers Pete Macheska and Barry Landis and director Michael Frank. I'll never forget just getting home from a field trip with my daughter Amanda's second grade class to the Closter Nature Center when I received the call from Brown. Not only would we call the No. 2 game on the FOX schedule every week, but also a divisional playoff game as well. Stockton had worked with Moose and Goose for the previous five seasons; he is a Hall of Fame broadcaster who not only called the NFL for over four decades, but also nine NBA Finals and the memorable 1975 World Series. I will always remember the voicemail I received from Stockton shortly after my promotion into his slot. He told me how much I deserved the opportunity and added other very kind words. Not many other broadcasters would have left a similar message for a younger announcer who replaced them. Stockton is a class act. His voicemail taught me a valuable lesson about taking the high road—even during periods of disappointment.

For the next eight seasons (2007 through 2014), I called NFL games on a full-time basis with Johnston and Siragusa. We were known around the country as "Kenny, Moose, and Goose." I'm not sure I ever had as much fun as we did during these years. We called big games every week, and there was never a dull moment with Goose around. During production meetings with players and coaches, I could always sense the respect level they had for both of my partners. Moose won three Super Bowl rings as a member of the Cowboys dynasty, and Goose was an integral member of the Baltimore Ravens dominating defense during their 2000 championship season. I've never seen players and coaches let their guard down during production meetings as often as they did whenever Goose was in the room. Favre would consistently sit with us for 45 minutes to an hour (as opposed to the usual 15 to 20 minutes we spent with other players) while swapping stories and enlightening us about his most recent hunting and fishing escapades. When we worked games in Philadelphia, Goose usually brought trays of Italian food cooked by his mom (nicknamed "Mother Goose") for Eagles coach Andy Reid, who always enjoyed a taste test during our meetings. We even held one meeting with Cowboys head coach Jason Garrett via speaker phone while Captain Siragusa gave us a ride on his boat in Fort Lauderdale, Florida.

Goose was usually restless during down time and often encouraged group activities. He was always ready for adventure. I was splashed by Shamu on camera while sitting with Goose inches away from the tank at Sea World in San Diego; sat in the passenger seat of a race car at a NASCAR track in Charlotte, North Carolina, while being driven three laps around the course at 140 mph; fired a gun at targets at a Dallas shooting range; took a swamp boat tour in Louisiana, petting baby alligators along the way; got soaked during a whirlpool jet boat tour in Niagara Falls; and visited Navy SEALs at their base in Coronado, California. These are experiences I never contemplated prior to working with Goose and will probably never partake in again, but they remain lifelong memories. One of the most amazing feats I've ever witnessed was when Goose entered the driver side of the race car feet-first through the open window—squeezing his head through before putting on his helmet—and whizzing around the track at high speeds with no trepidation.

Goose may have fooled people because of his engaging personality and jokester mentality, but he was always one of the smartest people in the room—whether talking football or about other topics. He was a gentle giant, always the life of the party, and lived life to its fullest each and every day. Goose tragically passed away in June 2022. Eleven days prior to his death, he texted me from his seat in the second row of Amalie Arena in Tampa. He was with his son, Anthony, attending Game Six of the Eastern Conference Final between the New York Rangers and Tampa Bay Lightning. I was all the way up in the press box, so I couldn't get down to see Goose, but I located him from afar, zoomed in, and took a photo. It was one of the biggest honors of my life to deliver the eulogy at his funeral in Kenilworth, New Jersey, in front of thousands of friends, family members, and former teammates. I counted at least five Pro Football Hall of Famers in attendance: Ray Lewis, Shannon Sharpe, Rod Woodson, Dan Marino, and Bruce Smith. If you were in Goose's inner circle, he would do anything for you. Prior to his passing, Goose was working on a charitable endeavor called "Goose Flights" to help transport children via Make-A-Wish New Jersey to make their wishes come true and also taking NFL alumni to medical appointments. Although he is no longer with us, Goose is still helping others thanks to his family and friends continuing his legacy.

One challenge in working with Goose was that he was down near the field with an open microphone. He could chime in at any time. Amazingly, the three of us hardly ever "stepped on each other." (That's TV talk for speaking at the same time.) Goose was usually positioned in the end zone with a monitor setup, which looked like he could be running NASA. He also roamed up and down the sidelines, and I was frequently amazed at the little things he could spot by looking at the foot or hand placement of an offensive or defensive lineman prior to the snap. This came from years of watching film and studying during his playing career, as he attempted to gain the slightest edge on each and every play.

I spent a total of 10 full seasons with Moose. (Laura Okmin joined us as our sideline reporter in 2015 and 2016.) During that time we called five NFL postseason games, a Pro Bowl in Hawaii, as well as several college football bowl games. Moose is a consummate professional (and one of the top analysts on network television). He was the ultimate team player, having spent 11 seasons with the Cowboys. (Ten of them were spent blocking for the NFL's all-time leading rusher, Emmitt Smith, who acknowledged Johnston during his Hall of Fame induction speech.)

When Johnston contacted various networks about an analyst job following his playing career, he was initially told that "running backs don't make good analysts because they only know their position." His response: "I was a fullback. I had to know what the other 10 players on my team were doing at all times, as well as the defense." He was right. Through the end of the 2022 NFL season, according to a database compiled by Tony Miller (unnecessarysportsresearch.com), Johnston has worked 399 games as a color analyst, the seventh most in network television history—behind only John Madden, Dan Dierdorf, Aikman, Phil Simms, Cris Collinsworth, and Paul Maguire.

Speaking of running backs—of all the players and coaches I have shaken hands with through the years, Adrian Peterson definitely had the hardest and firmest grip. When he walked into a production meeting, we all braced for impact. Longtime NHL player and coach Jim Schoenfeld ranks a close second on my list.

From 2017 through 2019, I was partnered with Rondé Barber. He is the only player in NFL history with at least 25 sacks and 45 interceptions, holds the record for most consecutive starts by a defensive back, scored 14 career touchdowns, and was elected to five Pro Bowls. Perhaps the most iconic play of Barber's career was his 92-yard interception return for a touchdown, which clinched the Tampa Bay Buccaneers' victory in the NFC Championship Game in the final football game played at "The Vet" in Philadelphia (in January 2003). Two weeks later the Bucs defeated the Oakland Raiders 48–21 in Super Bowl XXXVII. Barber is a great person, extremely hard worker, and a close friend. I could not have been more excited when it was announced in February 2023 that Barber would be inducted into the Pro Football Hall of Fame. In fact, I politicked for it both on television and social media for several years. He also has a great voice. He occasionally entertained our crew (and my family) with his terrific rendition of the *Hamilton* soundtrack. During our time together, he watched countless hours of game film and then put together a comprehensive, 15-page scouting report for each of our games, including notes on every player from both teams. He shared this with the production crew, and it was an invaluable part of my research.

Rondé's brother Tiki—a former New York Giants star—joined us for a few telecasts; they were excellent together. One of the highlights of our three years together came in September 2019, when Rondé was inducted into the Buccaneers Ring of Honor during halftime of our game between the Bucs and Giants, and Tiki joined us in the booth that afternoon. I joked that I was the third Barber triplet. It also marked Daniel Jones' first start as quarterback for Big Blue in an exciting game won by the Giants thanks to a last-second missed field goal by Tampa Bay. Jones led his club all the way back from an 18-point deficit and accounted for four touchdowns (two in the air, two on the ground). During our production meeting with Jones the day before the game, we were amazed how much he sounded like Eli Manning, who became his backup. They had so many similar mannerisms as well.

Later that season NASCAR star (and fellow FOX broadcaster) Jeff Gordon asked to sit in with us during production meetings with the Seattle Seahawks in Charlotte due to his relationship with producer Barry Landis. He was interested to witness how football broadcasters and players interacted with each other. It was fascinating to listen to the conversations between Gordon, quarterback Russell Wilson, and head coach Pete Carroll, who invited Gordon to speak to the entire team.

When we broadcasted Eagles home games, some of the fans sitting directly below our broadcast booth enjoyed giving both Johnston and Barber a hard time. Johnston's Cowboys—bitter rivals of the Eagles—won three Super Bowls in the early 1990s, and fans never forgave Barber for his touchdown return in 2003. Both handled it good-naturedly. In fact, Moose once responded by flashing one of his Super Bowl rings; that shut up his tormentors pretty quickly.

Another Super Bowl champion, Jonathan Vilma, joined me in the booth for the 2020 season. We certainly had an interesting start to our time together due to the COVID pandemic. We did a practice game together in August 2020 via Zoom from different countries. I was in Canada. We spent our entire first season socially distanced from one another during games and only shared a few meals together due to health and safety protocols. Things were somewhat back to normal in 2021. Despite his vicious mentality on the field, Vilma is soft-spoken with a kind personality off the field. He was the leader of the Saints defense during their championship run in 2009–10. I could listen to his stories about practice competitions with Drew Brees and Sean Payton and his back-and-forth battle calling signals against Peyton Manning in Super Bowl XLIV all day.

Through the years, I called several games on FOX with Aikman, John Lynch (the Hall of Fame safety who later became the general manager of the San Francisco 49ers), and Charles Davis (now the No. 2 analyst at CBS). They were all terrific partners and men.

Sideline reporters have been a major asset to our football crews through the years. They attend team production meetings and also speak with additional players and coaches on their own during the week to gather information for the telecasts. During broadcasts they provide injury updates, relay information from halftime chats with coaches, and add interesting anecdotes and stories. I've been fortunate to work with some of the best in the industry, including Chris Myers, Jay Glazer, Pam Oliver, Okmin, Kristina Pink, Lindsay Czarniak, Sara Walsh, and Shannon Spake.

Aside from calling NFL games on FOX since 1994, I worked several college football bowl games for the network as well. On January 3, 2007, I was involved in one of the most memorable broadcasts of my career, calling the Sugar Bowl alongside Bradshaw and Long, two of the stars of *FOX NFL Sunday*. I learned about the assignment a few months earlier and could not have been more ecstatic. I was trusted by Hill and Goren to anchor a marquee event on FOX along with Hall of Fame partners. Bradshaw had not worked a live game in more than a decade. For Long it was the first time. Prior to the season, James Brown departed for CBS, and Buck hosted *FOX NFL Sunday* in his place in 2006. The pregame crew spent most weekends on the road working from remote locations, the site of the game called by Buck and Aikman.

To prepare for the college broadcasts, I traveled from my NFL game site (along with producer Pete Macheska) on a couple of December weekends for rehearsals in empty stadiums along with Bradshaw and Long in Charlotte and East Rutherford, New Jersey. We called prior games off monitors in the broadcast booths to get Bradshaw and Long acclimated to both the rhythm of a game broadcast and the nuances of working in a booth, including the location of the cough button, which shuts off a microphone when needed. That technology came in handy while broadcasting a Rangers–Los Angeles Kings game at the Fabulous Forum in Los Angeles in the late 1990s, when I started to hiccup during live action.

We visited the campuses of Notre Dame and LSU to visit with players and head coaches Charlie Weis and Les Miles. I learned firsthand about Bradshaw's quick wit. During a production meeting the night before the Sugar Bowl, we all discussed our postgame travel plans. I mentioned that I was going to fly home early in the morning for a Rangers broadcast later that night. Bradshaw immediately blurted out (while imitating my voice and inflection), "Kick save by Giacomin!" I guess Bradshaw followed hockey during the 1970s and was familiar with Rangers goaltender Eddie Giacomin.

The bowl game ended up being an exhilarating and memorable telecast for so many reasons. I felt so good about it that I have never gone back and watched one second of it as I usually do. Later that week, Bradshaw was kind enough to mention Long and me during an appearance on *The Tonight Show* when he was asked by Jay Leno about the broadcast.

I called the 2008 Orange Bowl (Kansas–Virginia Tech), 2009 Sugar Bowl (Utah–Alabama), and 2011 Cotton Bowl (LSU–Texas A&M) with Johnston. Longtime University of Wisconsin athletic director and football coach Barry Alvarez was our third analyst in the booth for the Orange Bowl. The legendary Summerall was part of our crew for the Cotton Bowl. I had to "toss" it down to Summerall on the field at halftime so he could introduce a historical piece…quite the thrill.

During my 29 seasons calling NFL matchups on FOX, so many singular moments stand out from games I've worked:

- The first 8–5 final score in NFL history when the Atlanta Falcons defeated the Los Angeles Rams in 1994.
- Bill Cowher shoved a photo printout into the shirt pocket of referee Gordon McCarter as they exited the field at halftime during a game in 1995, showing that the Pittsburgh Steelers had the legal number of players on the field during a Minnesota Vikings field-goal attempt after his club was penalized for having 12 men on the field.
- Terrell Owens stomped on the Dallas Cowboys star at the 50-yard line after scoring a touchdown for the San Francisco 49ers in 2000.
- Ty Detmer threw seven interceptions, one shy of the NFL record, in the first game I called after 9/11.
- Michael Vick gained an NFL-record 173 rushing yards by a quarterback, including an electrifying, game-winning 46-yard touchdown scamper in overtime in 2002.
- In the New York Giants–Tennessee Titans game in Nashville in 2006, defensive lineman Mathias Kiwanuka released quarterback Vince Young from his grasp, thinking Young no longer had the ball and didn't want to get flagged for a penalty. The play helped lead to a Titans come-from-behind victory.
- In a St. Louis Rams game in 2007, Brett Favre broke Dan Marino's career passing yards record.
- After a tie game between the Philadelphia Eagles and Cincinnati Bengals in Cincinnati in 2008, Eagles quarterback Donovan McNabb admitted that he did not know NFL games could end in ties.
- The New England Patriots thrashed the Arizona Cardinals 47-7 in a snowstorm in Foxboro, Massachusetts. We were told in production meetings the day before that several of the Cardinals players had *never* seen snow in their entire lives. Just over one month later, Arizona won the NFC Championship Game and faced Pittsburgh in Super Bowl XLIII.

- No. 10 Eli Manning completed his first 10 pass attempts on October 10, 2010 (10/10/10) in Houston.
- Head coaches Jim Harbaugh and Jim Schwartz nearly came to blows during their postgame handshake in 2011.
- Tim Tebow led an incredible comeback in a Denver Broncos overtime win against the Chicago Bears in 2011.
- A 99-yard touchdown pass from Eli Manning to Victor Cruz against the New York Jets in December 2011 tied a record during the Giants' march to a Super Bowl title. As a native New Yorker, I have been fortunate to broadcast the last three Giants–Jets matchups that have been televised on FOX in 2003, 2011, and 2019.
- Robert Griffin III's remarkable NFL debut for the Washington Redskins in September 2012 included an 88-yard touchdown pass to Pierre Garcon in the first quarter of a 40–32 victory.
- Eli Manning and Drew Brees combined for an NFL record-tying 13 touchdown passes in a 52–49 New Orleans Saints victory against the Giants in 2015.
- Another tie game involving the Bengals occurred in Wembley Stadium in London against Washington in 2016.
- The first-ever punter-to-kicker touchdown pass (from Matt Haack to Jason Sanders) occurred during Miami Dolphins win against the Eagles in 2019.
- During a Green Bay–Cincinnati game in 2021, the kickers combined to miss five field goals in the fourth quarter and overtime. But both teams would advance to their respective conference championship games.

I called five divisional playoff games with Moose and Goose between the 2007 and 2011 seasons. In January of 2008, the Seattle Seahawks–Packers game included Favre's last postseason victory as a Packers player. Lambeau Field looked like a snow globe. It was one of the best atmospheres I've ever broadcasted a game from. During TV timeouts, the stadium crew kept busy shoveling snow off the yard lines.

In January of 2009, Arizona took a 27–7 halftime lead in Carolina en route to the NFC Championship Game. In January of 2010, the Saints defense knocked out Kurt Warner in the last game of his Hall of Fame career, and Reggie Bush scored two touchdowns on a 46-yard run and 83-yard punt return. In the January 2011 Seahawks–Bears game, Jay Cutler's 58-yard touchdown pass to Greg Olsen on the game's opening drive set the tone for a 35–24 Bears victory.

The most wild affair, though, was probably Saints–49ers in January of 2012. The teams combined for four touchdowns during the last four minutes of the fourth quarter. Vernon Davis scored the winning touchdown on a pass from Alex Smith with nine seconds remaining. In a nod to Vin Scully, who called the iconic Joe Montana to Dwight Clark game-winning score, aka "The Catch" in the 1981 NFC Championship Game in the same stadium, I repeated Scully's line, "It's a madhouse at Candlestick." Hopefully, a few people picked up on it. Our broadcast of this game (anchored by Landis and Frank) received a national Emmy nomination.

I called the Pro Bowl in February 2008 at Aloha Stadium in Honolulu (along with Moose, Goose, and Baldinger). Not a bad gig! I was assigned to two 3D telecasts produced by FOX: the 2009 BCS Championship Game between Florida and Oklahoma, featuring starting quarterbacks Tim Tebow and Sam Bradford, and the 2010 MLB All-Star Game. In the latter game, Will Ferrell joined us to present the starting lineups in a humorous fashion as only he could. I also called a Rangers–New York Islanders experimental 3D telecast at Madison Square Garden, so I completed a rare 3D hat trick (hockey, baseball, football). Good thing I didn't have to wear the 3D glasses during the game aside from brief on-camera segments.

Through the years FOX trusted me to work several other sports—baseball, hockey (between 1995 and 1999), college football bowl games, college basketball (legendary analyst Bill Raftery and I called Chris Mullin's first game as St. John's head coach in 2015), BIG3 hoops, PBC boxing, and even horse racing! In 1999 and 2000, I was the host of the NTRA on FOX series from iconic tracks such as Churchill Downs, Belmont Park, Pimlico, Santa Anita, and Hollywood Park.

The first 50 minutes of the horse racing broadcasts were scripted with features, interviews, and the post parade, and we always rehearsed the day before. Then…chaos would ensue. The two-minute race, which would be called by the track announcer, was followed by interviews with the winning owner, trainer, jockey, etc. It was always a scramble to make sure I had all my information and questions ready at the moment the race ended. I'll never forget the exhilarating feeling and roar of the huge crowds as the horses headed down the stretch toward the finish line within a few hundred feet of our broadcast podium. My broadcast partners, Jay Privman, Caton Bredar, and Ron Ellis, along with producer Pete Macheska and director Michael Frank were a valuable resource as I immersed myself in learning a new sport that I was not too familiar with. Longtime writer/FOX researcher John Czarnecki and horse racing guru Michael Ciminella (the father of actress Ashley Judd) were also huge assets. I'm not ashamed to admit that I purchased a copy of *Horse Racing for Dummies* after receiving my first assignment of that sport.

# 5

# THE WORLD'S MOST FAMOUS ARENA

Madison Square Garden has been my second home for almost my entire lifetime. My father was the radio voice of the New York Knicks and New York Rangers before I was born. In fact, he was on his way home from a Rangers game in Montreal when I was born (three months premature) on February 2, 1968. I often joke that I pushed to "come out early" so I would be born *prior* to the first event at the current MSG (on 33rd Street between 7th and 8th Avenues). That event on February 11, 1968, was a salute to the U.S.O. hosted by Bob Hope and Bing Crosby. The Rangers played their final game at the old Garden (8th Avenue between 49th and 50th Streets) earlier that same day. I was nine days old.

My mother started taking me to basketball and hockey games at the Garden at an early age and taught me how to keep score. I can still sense the smell and taste of Harry M. Stevens hot dogs and popcorn from the MSG refreshment stands back in the 1970s. During my childhood we would attend the Ringling Bros. and Barnum & Bailey circus annually, Harlem Globetrotters games (I was probably the only person in the building charting individual stats during the heyday of Meadowlark Lemon and Curly Neal), professional wrestling events (my sister Denise and I watched the WWF every Saturday morning and became huge fans), college basketball doubleheaders, and concerts (Madonna was the first, I recall, in 1985).

When I was old enough to take the Long Island Rail Road without adult supervision, I brought friends along to Rangers and Knicks games. Sometimes, we would spend one period in the radio booth sitting behind my father and Sal Messina. It was the best seat in the building at center ice right above where the Rangers exited the ice and between the team benches. Actually, the home radio booth remained in that location through the 2005–06 season, which was my 10th calling Rangers radio when Garden management decided to sell seats there for a premium price.

During my high school and college years, I moved up to the front row when I was "hired" as the radio statistician for my father (or his backups when he was on assignment) and Messina. Mike Emrick, John Kelly, and Howie Rose—all tremendous hockey broadcasters—filled in on Rangers radiocasts while I was handling stats. I felt like I was taking a master class, no matter who was in the play-by-play chair. I also kept the numbers on the television side for my father and John Andariese at Knicks home games from 1986–87 through 1989–90 (my four years at NYU). During college I may have had a busier schedule than during my broadcast career. I handled stats at most Knicks and Rangers home games, traveled on select NFL weekends to keep stats for my father as well as other NBC announcers (including Charlie Jones and Don Criqui), broadcasted NYU men's and women's basketball on WNYU Radio, worked select Islanders radio pregame and postgame shows during my junior and senior years and did four games of play-by-play as a college senior, played hockey on the NYU club team all four years, worked as an associate producer of *Mets Extra* at most home games between April and October, and—somehow—found a way to attend class. Oh, I also contributed articles to NYU's student newspaper, the Rangers' game program, and *Islander News*.

I inherited my work ethic from both of my parents. My father's schedule during my childhood was similar to what mine would become decades later. It must be in the DNA. During our first year living in Sands Point (when I attended first grade) through my high school graduation, he broadcasted Knicks and Rangers home games (and select road games), New York Giants on radio for several years before calling NFL games nationally on NBC, and college basketball and boxing on NBC. On top of all that, he was the 6:00 and 11:00 PM sports anchor on WNBC-TV in New York. I tagged along as often as he would allow. (We once took a family photo at the Channel 4 studios with professional wrestler Andre the Giant.) I also helped pull wire copy and wrote my own scripts. I always enjoyed using the Xerox machine.

During weekdays he would often do the sports report around 6:20 PM, hop in the car for the short ride to the Garden for a Knicks or Rangers radio broadcast, and then head back to Rockefeller Center after the game for the late news show. I'm not sure how he pulled off that feat for so many years. Despite the hectic back and forth, his calls were flawless; he never missed a beat.

During my father's high school years, he hustled his way to various roles: an internship with the Brooklyn Dodgers, a job as a Knicks ballboy, and as a statistician for legendary broadcaster Marty Glickman on local high school football telecasts. He was allowed to ride the Dodgers team bus back to Brooklyn from several home games they played in Jersey City and had personal conversations with Jackie Robinson. He even held the hand of Helen Keller as they walked across the stage during an assembly at Lincoln High School. He arranged credentials to sporting events and set up interviews for his high school newspaper, *The Lincoln Log*. My father once left a message for Stan Musial at the St. Louis Cardinals' hotel when they were in town to play the Dodgers. He thought the chances were slim that "Stan the Man" would call a high school student back. Sure enough, upon returning home from school one day, my grandmother told him that a Stan Musial had called. She wasn't a big sports fan and had no idea who Musial was. Musial was confused as well; he saw the name and thought it was someone from his stockbroker's office.

Not only did my mother raise four kids (with my father working or away most of the time), but she never missed volunteering on a committee at any of our schools. She opened a knitting/yarn store while I was in high school, then attended Hofstra Law School between the ages of 48 and 50. She practiced law for over two decades, including a ton of pro-bono work. We were all very proud of her. While she continued to practice law, the pride of being a grandmother superseded everything. She never missed an opportunity to change a diaper, play on the carpet with one of her eight grandchildren, attend their sporting events, and—when they were old enough—take them on trips.

In March 1965, before turning 21 (and months before their wedding), my mother made an appearance on national television as a contestant on

*What's My Line*, a long-running game show in the 1950s and 1960s during which celebrity panelists questioned contestants in order to determine their occupation. She worked at the U.S. Passport Office in Manhattan, and the panelists (including Buddy Hackett) tried to guess her profession by asking questions in a search for clues. Lucille Ball was the mystery guest on the same episode. I had heard about her appearance on the show throughout my entire childhood but did not know that a videotape existed. Amazingly, in the early 2000s, Mets and Knicks public relations guru Dennis D'Agostino told me he had been watching Game Show Network late one evening and noticed a woman named Benita Caress on *What's My Line*. He recalled that Caress was her maiden name. I was able to obtain a copy of the program and I surprised my mother with it more than 35 years later.

During my senior year at NYU, I was asked to host a Rangers radio pregame show for the first time. I remember how fast my heart was pounding (and my hands were shaking) while eating lunch in the food court at the Weinstein dorm in anticipation of my first-ever pro broadcast from the World's Most Famous Arena. During my five seasons living and working in Maryland (1990–91 through 1994–95), I didn't spend much time at MSG aside from broadcasting several Capitals games there or when I was home visiting family. However, there were four games—and one *very* special night—for me in the World's Most Famous Arena in June 1994.

I was working at WTOP Radio in D.C. one afternoon in May 1994 when I received a phone call from Alan Sanders. Little did I know that this call would change my life—in a number of ways. Sanders asked me: "If the Rangers advance to the Stanley Cup Final, would you be interested in calling the series for NHL Radio?"

I nearly fell off my chair. At the time, the Rangers and New Jersey Devils were in the early stages of the Eastern Conference Final, and the Vancouver Canucks were battling the Toronto Maple Leafs in the Western Conference Final. First of all, to have the opportunity to call the Stanley Cup Final on national radio—at the age of 26—would be the thrill of a lifetime no matter which teams were involved. On top of that, there was a chance it would be the Canucks (my favorite team as a kid) against the Rangers (my other favorite team, whose games my father had been calling for 30 years). Rose had called the 1993 Stanley Cup Final on NHL Radio with Mike Keenan, who had already been hired at that time to coach the Rangers in 1993–94. If the Rangers beat the Devils and advanced, Rose would be unavailable due to his role as the backup Rangers radio play-by-play announcer. He would most likely wind up with most of the games since my father (technically No. 1 on the depth chart, though Rose worked many more regular-season games) would be busy with the NBA Finals on NBC. Although I was rooting for a Rangers–Canucks final anyway, now it was personal.

Vancouver eliminated Toronto in five games, so the first piece of the puzzle was confirmed. Now I needed the Rangers to win their series; otherwise, Rose would be available to call a Devils–Canucks final. With the Devils ahead three games to two on May 25, Game Six took place at Brendan Byrne Arena. The day before, Rangers captain Mark Messier guaranteed a victory and then backed up his words. I was watching the ESPN telecast in my Rockville, Maryland, apartment, as New Jersey took a 2–0 lead in the first period. Goaltender Mike Richter made several incredible saves throughout the first 40 minutes, and Alexei Kovalev put the Rangers on the board late in the second period; then, Messier scored three goals in the third, including a shorthanded, empty netter, to set up Game Seven two nights later.

I needed another Blueshirts victory to guarantee my dream final—as well as the opportunity to call the series. Once again, I watched in my Maryland apartment. The Rangers took a 1–0 lead deep into the third period. Things were looking good; then, the unthinkable happened. The Devils' Valeri Zelepukin tied the game with 7.7 seconds on the clock. I'm told by people who were in the building that during the intermissions prior to the first and second overtime periods the fans were in stunned silence and looked like zombies while walking around the MSG concourses. The arena exploded (and I held my own personal celebration) when Stephane Matteau beat Martin Brodeur on a wrap-around early in the second overtime to send the Rangers to their first Stanley Cup Final appearance since 1979.

I worked the series alongside Sherry Ross, a longtime *New York Daily News* writer/columnist, Devils radio color commentator, and a pioneer in the world of hockey media. It was an incredible two weeks of hockey: beautiful weather in Manhattan and hockey and basketball on the back page of the tabloids almost every day, as the Knicks were deep into the NBA playoffs as well. I was able to purchase six tickets at face value ($40) for all four games at MSG thanks to Rangers PR guru Kevin McDonald (now the assistant general manager of the Colorado Avalanche), which my friends were happy to take off my hands. Greg Adams scored in overtime to win Game One for the Canucks. The Rangers won the next three games to set up a potential clincher on home ice on June 9. The Canucks had other plans, however, and won Game Five, a result which led to a life-altering meeting for me. I met my wife, Barbara, for the first time that night after the game. It was back to Vancouver for all of us and another Canucks victory in Game Six. I'll never forget the feeling of being in Madison Square Garden when the Rangers won their first Stanley Cup in 54 years on June 14, 1994, as well as my call on NHL Radio as the final buzzer sounded: "*Say good-bye to the ghosts of 1940! The New York Rangers have won the Stanley Cup.*" Thanks to Rose's prior commitment and the decision by NHL Radio's Gregg Baldinger to hire me as his replacement, I was in the building and at the mic when Messier and the Rangers gave generations of fans a moment that—to quote the team's TV voice Sam Rosen—"will last a lifetime." The championship was immortalized by a sign held by a fan in the stands that read "Now I Can Die In Peace!"

On June 5, an off day between Games Three and Four in Vancouver, I watched on television as Patrick Ewing and the Knicks defeated the Indiana Pacers in Game Seven of the Eastern Conference Finals to advance to an NBA Finals matchup with the Houston Rockets. It was the icing on the cake—both MSG teams were in the championship round simultaneously! With the Rockets leading the Knicks two games to one, New York hosted Game Four on Wednesday, June 15, less than 24 hours after the Rangers won the Cup. Messier and a few of his teammates brought the Stanley Cup to center court at halftime to a thunderous ovation. Two days later on June 17,

I attended the Rangers' championship parade down the Canyon of Heroes in lower Manhattan on a scorching hot day. My father was invited to be part of the festivities and was allotted a car for the entire parade route, and my brother Brian, sister Denise, and I tagged along. It was surreal to be in the parade in a slow-moving vehicle surrounded by more than one million screaming New Yorkers while constantly drowning in confetti. We then attended a post-parade celebration inside city hall and took a family photo along with mayor David Dinkins.

A few hours after the parade, I was back in the Garden to attend Game Five of the NBA Finals. During the second quarter, I glanced at Garden Vision and noticed what I assumed was one of the movie clips that are often played during timeouts. Most people did not yet have cell phones, and texting did not exist. NBC briefly switched away from the game to a news update, and at that moment, the live feed of the game on the video board above center court was replaced by what was happening on the freeway in California. It quickly disappeared after a few seconds. At halftime fans gathered around TV monitors at the concession stands and learned that the O.J. Simpson car chase was taking place 3,000 miles away.

The next hockey season did not begin on time due to a lockout. I was still working in Washington, D.C., and getting ready to call my third season of Capitals games when the work stoppage ended in January 1995. On January 20 I traveled to New York so I could be in the Garden for the Rangers' banner raising prior to their season opener against the Buffalo Sabres. The Stanley Cup was brought out to center ice for the ceremony, and the entire team surrounded it for one more celebration. Barbara attended the game with me; she acknowledges that this time it was in fact a date.

During the summer of 1995, I passed up potential TV opportunities at SportsChannel in New York with the New York Islanders and New Jersey Nets because I was really enjoying my work experience at Home Team Sports in Washington and still had a few years remaining on my contract. Later that summer, I was offered the Rangers radio job by MSG Network executives Joe Cohen (who has become a close friend and mentor) and Mike

McCarthy. Rose, who had been sharing the radio duties with my father, was offered the Islanders and Mets television roles by SportsChannel. I agonized for days with a constant pit in my stomach over two great situations. I wrote down the positives from both jobs on each side of a yellow legal pad—staying in Washington, where I was calling Capitals home games on television, as well as filling in on Washington Bullets (now Wizards) and Baltimore Orioles games or heading back to New York to call Rangers games on radio for MSG. It was the toughest decision of my life. I loved my job and felt such loyalty. I was so thankful to Jody Shapiro and Bill Brown for hiring me three years earlier and really enjoyed living and working in the D.C. area. I thought it would be my home for a long time and had established my own broadcasting style and identity during my time there. My fiancée Barbara (now wife) had already shipped her furniture from New York to my apartment in Maryland, but I grew up in Madison Square Garden, broadcasting Rangers games was my dream job, and I didn't know if the opportunity would ever come up again. Despite having strong feelings for my bosses and colleagues in D.C., I knew that in the long run it would be the correct decision.

Home Team Sports granted permission to allow me out of my contract but requested compensation from MSG. Sports fans may be familiar with the 2006 trade of broadcasting legend Al Michaels from ABC to NBC in exchange for increased usage of Olympic highlights; the rights to two golf tournaments; and Oswald the Lucky Rabbit, a cartoon character developed by Walt Disney in the 1920s. Eleven years earlier, I was traded by HTS for the rights to television control room access (without paying the usual fees) at Madison Square Garden during the next several seasons whenever HTS traveled to New York to broadcast Capitals and Bullets games against the Rangers and Knicks. It wasn't exactly Wayne Gretzky to the Los Angeles Kings, but it was still a memorable deal—at least in my mind. There is still something so magical about calling games at "The World's Most Famous Arena." I have worked Rangers broadcasts since 1995 and a quarter of the Knicks games on television for over a decade alongside Walt "Clyde" Frazier from our courtside broadcast location—just two seats away from celebrities such as Howard Stern, Ben Stiller, Chris Rock, Hugh Jackman, Spike Lee, and Taylor Swift. It never gets old.

My first game as radio voice of the Rangers was in Hartford on October 7, 1995—a 37-save shutout by Sean Burke in a 2–0 Hartford Whalers win. When I arrived at the Hartford Civic Center, there was a chocolate platter waiting for me from my former bosses at HTS—a very kind gesture. My first home game was four nights later, a 6–4 Rangers victory against the Winnipeg Jets. I recall interviewing Winnipeg's Kris King (a former Ranger who is now a senior vice president at the NHL) for our pregame show.

My father still worked some of the games (approximately 15 per year) during my first two seasons with the Rangers. I handled the pregame and postgame shows for those games. When both of us were away on assignment (I missed most of the weekend games during football season), we used a variety of fill-in voices, including Spencer Ross, Gary Cohen, Joe Beninati, Barry Landers, Bob Wischusen, and my uncle Steve. For the last decade and a half, Don LaGreca (cohost of *The Michael Kay Show* on ESPN Radio in New York) has worked the games that I have missed for national football, national hockey, and Knicks telecasts.

I really enjoyed working with Messina for my first seven seasons with the Rangers. I first met him when I was five or six years old when he began his radio career. He was a native of Astoria, Queens, and was a goaltender for the Long Island Ducks of the Eastern League. During the 1963–64 season, he was the Rangers' practice goalie and their designated backup goalie for all home and road games. In those days only one goalie on each team dressed for the games; the backup was in the crowd dressed in street clothes. Messina even roomed with Hall of Famer Jacques Plante during road trips. Unfortunately, he never got into an NHL game—not even for one second. Messina became an off-ice official at MSG and in the early 1970s he started handling color commentary on the radio while working a day job selling airline parts for a company on Long Island. He always had an enthusiastic and engaging personality, as well as a tremendous knowledge of the sport of hockey.

I sat to Messina's left as the statistician for seven seasons and then wound up on his right as his partner for another seven. My father and *New York Post* hockey writer Hugh Delano nicknamed Messina "Red Light" early in his broadcasting career, and it stuck. Messina was known for the occasional malapropism and was often the subject of practical jokes—all in good fun. He once referred to NHL forward Nelson Emerson as (former New York Jets running back) Emerson Boozer during a broadcast with Rose, and the two laughed uncontrollably on the air for the next 30 seconds while play continued. During a broadcast with me in Philadelphia, Messina was reading a promo for a soccer telecast on MSG and said "the Miami Hamms" instead of "Mia Hamm and the Washington Freedom." I looked over at our statistician (and longtime PR whiz) Scott Cooper. We could not control our laughter and still joke about it to this day. Messina seemed to have friends everywhere. We were working a game together in Florida in the late 1990s when—during the national anthem—all of a sudden, New York Yankees great Whitey Ford appeared out of the blue in our radio booth. Ford and Messina were members at the same golf club on Long Island. Ford knew Messina would be calling the game and stopped by to say hello. I was so thrilled for Messina when he was honored as the deserving winner of the Foster Hewitt Award in 2005 (for excellence in hockey broadcasting) during Hockey Hall of Fame ceremonies. I visit his plaque at the Hall of Fame whenever I travel to Toronto.

The Rangers were involved in some very exciting playoff series during my first two seasons. In 1996 they came back after losing the first two games at home to defeat the Montreal Canadiens four games to two before bowing out to the Pittsburgh Penguins in the second round. The next year Gretzky and Messier played together as teammates with the Rangers for one season (they had won four Stanley Cups together in Edmonton). The Blueshirts eliminated the Florida Panthers in five games in round one. During one of the home games at MSG, I sat in the stands after handling pregame chores, as my father and Messina called the game. During the second period, I received a tap on the shoulder. Messina had lost his voice. I was the color analyst for one of the only times in my life—the only pro game my dad and I ever worked together as play-by-play and color analyst. (He had joined me in the booth for an NYU basketball broadcast). My father was still working approximately 20 Rangers radio games per season and was on the call for this one alongside Messina, who was having issues with his voice and was not going to be able to continue. I slid into his seat and did color commentary for the remainder of the game, which I had only done in college on the occasional basketball game. It was strange not only working a broadcast with my father, but also working as the analyst. It was a fun night, and the Rangers won the game on an overtime goal from Esa Tikkanen.

The Blueshirts beat the Devils in five games in the second round, and the clinching game was in the afternoon on Mother's Day—May 11, 1997—at the Meadowlands. Adam Graves scored the series-clinching goal in overtime on a wraparound against Brodeur. It was almost a carbon copy of the Matteau goal against Brodeur three years earlier. The next day, on WFAN (our flagship station at the time), Steve Somers played Rose's call of the Matteau goal and my call of the Graves goal back to back. A Rangers team decimated by injuries then fell short in the conference final against the Philadelphia Flyers. Unfortunately, the Rangers would miss the playoffs the next seven seasons (from 1997–98 through 2003–04). We still had a lot of fun on the broadcasts during more seasons with Messina and then the next two (2002–03 and 2003–04) with former Ranger Brian Mullen.

On April 18, 1999, Gretzky played his last NHL game—a matinee against the Penguins at MSG. Unfortunately, I didn't call the game; Spencer Ross filled in on radio because I was assigned to a Flyers–Boston Bruins telecast on FOX. Barbara attended the game with her dad (and made sure to purchase a few commemorative programs for me). She was pregnant with Amanda at the time, but there was no way she would miss being in the building to witness history. I met her in New York City following my drive home from Philadelphia, and we attended Gretzky's retirement party at Windows on the World on the 107th floor of the World Trade Center. The entire Rangers and Penguins teams were on hand, as well as many other luminaries from the sport of hockey. Barbara and I took a photo with Gretzky. I always joke with Amanda that she was at both the game and party, too.

I often think about the road trips during Gretzky's three seasons with the Rangers. It was like traveling with The Beatles. There were always hundreds of fans waiting for Gretzky's autograph outside every hotel and arena—and sometimes at the private airport terminals. He would accommodate each and every one of them. Not a fan of flying, Gretzky often wandered up to the broadcaster section of the plane to take his mind off the turbulence. He sat with the four team announcers—me, Messina, Rosen, and John Davidson, who was one of the most respected people in the entire sport. Gretzky was so knowledgeable about football, baseball, and basketball as well. I said at the time that he could host a sports talk show.

Messier was one of the greatest leaders in sports history. I recall a road trip with the Rangers to western Canada during the 1995–96 season. The club played in Vancouver on December 28, then had an off day before a game in Edmonton on December 30. The team was scheduled to fly in the afternoon on the day between games, landing in time for the several Rangers, who formerly played for the Oilers, to meet up with family and friends. After we boarded the charter, the pilot announced that there was a mechanical issue. It would be at least four or five hours before they would either be able to gather new parts or have access to a different plane. Team management got together for a discussion, and the Edmonton group was told arrangements would be made for a commercial flight so they could arrive in time for dinner. Messier stood at the front of the plane and announced for all to hear, "We go as a team." He made it clear that no individual or group of individuals were more important than the others. Messier—and the entire group—waited for the new plane to arrive and flew as a team while missing dinner and quality time with their loved ones.

Dave Maloney became my Rangers radio analyst in 2005–06, and we are still working together nearly two decades later. Maloney is an unbelievable partner, and I have worked more games with him than any other analyst—in any sport—during my career. He was named the youngest captain in franchise history in 1978 at age 22, and the club reached the Stanley Cup Final during his first season wearing the "C." Maloney and my father became friendly around that time, and Maloney even began his broadcast career during the early 1980s while injured when he joined Messina and my dad in the broadcast booth for several games. By virtue of their friendship, I met Maloney for the first time when I was around 12. He was about twice my age and came to our house to play tennis and have dinner. I marvel at the fact that Maloney has had three distinctly different very successful careers: 10 seasons as a defenseman in the NHL; two decades as a broker with Wall Street firms, including Bear Stearns; and several different stints—totaling a quarter of a century—as an NHL television and radio broadcaster. He is an avid reader. Maloney usually carries around a 500-plus page novel and completes *The New York Times* crossword puzzle on a daily basis (sometimes between periods in the broadcast booth). He is highly respected around the league. His brother Don (his teammate with the Rangers) has been a longtime executive with the Islanders, Rangers, Arizona Coyotes, and Calgary Flames. Maloney and I have called more than 100 playoff games together, including long runs to the conference final in 2012, 2015, and 2022, as well as the Stanley Cup Final in 2014. He has been known to get emotional on air at times when a call goes against the Rangers. Maloney will always bleed Ranger Blue.

Our first season together followed a lockout, which wiped out the entire 2004–05 NHL campaign. Fans and media did not have high expectations for the Rangers following seven straight non-playoff seasons. Maloney and I had worked together a few times during prior years when he filled in for Messina or Mullen, but our first game as full-time partners was in Philadelphia on October 5, 2005 (Amanda's sixth birthday). The Rangers won the game 5–3. Jason Strudwick scored the first goal of the season, and Jaromir Jagr added a pair of power play goals. It also marked Henrik Lundqvist's first regular-season game in a Rangers uniform, though he backed up starter Kevin Weekes that evening. It wasn't long before Lundqvist took over the starting role, and he and Jagr (who scored a franchise-record 54 goals) led the club—coached by Tom Renney—to its first playoff berth since the spring of 1997.

During the first postseason game—at the New Jersey Meadowlands—I accidentally spilled a bottle of water on Maloney's laptop computer. I was scared for my life! Fortunately, there was no damage…and I made it home in one piece. The first season for Maloney in the booth coincided with the start of a magical run for Lundqvist and the Rangers. They reached the postseason in 11 of the next 12 seasons. "King Henrik" started 129 straight playoff games and won six Game Sevens. Maloney and I called so many exhilarating postseason games and series wins. I'll never forget walking from the arena to our hotel in Georgetown with Maloney—past the White House—around 2:00 AM, following Marian Gaborik's triple-overtime goal against the Capitals in 2012. Four years earlier, Maloney and I received a tour of the White House press area (thanks to my former colleague at WTOP Radio, Rich Johnson). Not only did the two of us take photos at the Presidential podium, but we actually attended a press conference in the West Wing's Briefing Room hosted by White House press secretary Dana Perino.

Pete Stemkowski, a Rangers forward from 1970 through 1977, has filled in for Maloney on radio for many seasons when the former captain works select games between the benches on the television side. Stemmer still proudly wears his championship ring from the most recent Maple Leafs Stanley Cup championship in 1967. In that series he assisted on Jim Pappin's Cup-winning goal, which may have actually deflected off Stemmer's leg. Still going strong in his late 70s, Stemmer is a true character of the game who never misses the opportunity to tell a joke or reminisce with a great story from his playing days. Stemmer scored the biggest goal of his career on April 29, 1971, just more than a minute into the third overtime of Game Six of the semifinals for the Rangers against the Chicago Blackhawks. My father was broadcasting the game on WHN Radio, and my mother was in attendance. I had just turned three a few months earlier and was at home on Long Island with my babysitter, Michael Levinson. My father knew that Levinson, a big sports fan, would be listening to the game on the radio. As the thrilling contest continued late into the evening, he said on air, "Michael, we'll be home a little late tonight."

I heard that story throughout my childhood. As it turns out, Levinson works part time in TV production. For more than two decades, he has run the FOX Box and score bug for the No. 1 FOX baseball crew. Whenever viewers have glanced at the score and inning number in the upper left-hand corner of the screen (as well as the number of balls, strikes, outs, etc.) during World Series games on FOX since the late 1990s, it has been Levinson inputting the info. We have worked many regular season and playoff games together through the years with me in the booth and Levinson in the production truck. Who would've ever thought that more than 50 years after Stemkowski's historic goal, I would work with both Stemmer and my babysitter from that same night?

During my first 10 seasons calling Rangers games, I sat two seats to the right of where I kept statistics during my high school and college days. The booth was located just above the "Willis Reed Tunnel" on the 33rd Street side of the Garden, where the Rangers would head from their locker room onto the ice. It was the equivalent of the fifth row between the team benches, and there were no seats in front of us. Although it was probably a bit too close to the ice (it was tough to see the near corners), it felt like I was right in the middle of the action while calling the play, and the atmosphere was tremendous. At times, when the paying customers stood up to my left or right, they blocked my line of vision. Actress Susan Sarandon (a huge Rangers fan) shot me a dirty look once when I motioned for one of her young children to sit down so I could see, though hopefully she appreciated that I was striving for accuracy. During the next seven seasons (2006–07 through 2012–13), there were various renovations at MSG, and we worked out of four different broadcast locations. There were three on the 31st Street (penalty box) side of the building and one in an auxiliary press box in the Zamboni corner. Finally, for the 2013–14 season, we moved to the newly built Chase Bridge, and the sightlines for hockey broadcasters from the bridge are among the best in the entire league.

During my early years working for MSG, I enjoyed calling several high school and college basketball tournaments. I worked the Lapchick Tournament on the campus of St. John's University and several ECAC Holiday Festivals at the Garden—all with R.C. "Bucky" Waters, the former head coach at Duke and West Virginia who had been my father's college hoops broadcast partner on NBC for many years. We were at the mic when Jack Armstrong's Niagara Purple Eagles upset St. John's in December 1997.

In the summer of 1996, I called Knicks games in the NBA Summer League played over two nights at Nassau Coliseum. My color analyst was Patrick Ewing, who had just finished his 11th season with the club. We got together the morning of the first game at MSG's Manhattan studios to call part of a game off a monitor so Ewing could learn the intricacies of television. He seemed to have fun with it. At one point during a commercial break, he jokingly said to me, "You're my mentor." Then-Knicks assistant Jeff Van Gundy joined Ewing and me for a segment during one of the telecasts. Years later, I ran into Ewing on occasion during his various stints as an NBA assistant coach, and he would refer to me as his "partner." It was very kind of him to remember the brief time we spent together.

That same year, 15 MSG broadcasters (including me) took part in a promotional music video for the network. "We're All Over It" was played to the tune of "This Magic Moment." Jay Black of "Jay and the Americans" was the lead singer, and the rest of us either posed with instruments (while pretending to play) or were backup singers. Most of us wound up keeping our day jobs, but it was a lot of fun.

Mike Quick was my analyst for televised high school basketball games played at MSG. He has been the guru of high school athletics in the New York metropolitan area for decades. During the 1990s several athletes who went on to become stars in the NBA and NFL announced their college decision on Quick's weekly MSG show. He was a huge resource; he knows all of the high school coaches and has an encyclopedic knowledge of their teams. We called games involving several players who went on to careers in the NBA, including Elton Brand and Al Harrington. He was also my analyst (along with former New York Jets great Marty Lyons) for the annual Empire Challenge, which we called annually from the late 1990s through 2019 at Hofstra University.

That high school football All-Star Game (Long Island vs. New York City) was founded by Boomer Esiason to benefit cystic fibrosis and various other charities. It was one of my favorite events each year. Boomer's son, Gunnar, was diagnosed with cystic fibrosis as an infant in 1993, and Boomer's efforts have raised an incredible $160 million to fight the disease and help find a cure.

More than 20 youngsters who participated in the game went on to play in the NFL. Quick was a huge advocate for the high school players he covered. One prime example is Jay Bromley, a defensive lineman from Queens, New York, who grew up in a tough environment and did not have a scholarship offer from any Division I colleges. In the 2010 contest, he finished with two sacks and seven tackles and was named the game's MVP. Quick and Lyons marveled over his performance throughout the entire telecast. Quick even suggested on air that he hoped Syracuse head coach Doug Marrone was watching. Sure enough, Bromley received an offer from the Orange, and the rest is history. He was a third-round pick by the New York Giants in 2014 and played six years in the NFL.

Beginning with the WNBA's inception in 1997, I called several New York Liberty games at MSG during their first few seasons. The women's professional basketball games were a lot of fun. The crowds were large and enthusiastic and usually offered a family-type atmosphere. The Liberty had a terrific team led by Rebecca Lobo, Teresa Weatherspoon, Vickie Johnson, Becky Hammon, and Sue Wicks. My analyst for most of the games was Doris Burke, who has gone on to an outstanding career with ESPN/ABC as an NBA broadcaster. I am honored that I was a part of the WNBA on the ground floor of its history.

The 2022–23 season marked my 27th as a Rangers broadcaster, which amounts to more than 1,500 games. After spending my entire childhood attending Rangers games and doing play-by-play in my head—re-imaging goals as I went to sleep—it is hard to fathom that it has been that long. Since my first season, the club has had four general managers (Neil Smith, Glen Sather, Jeff Gorton, and Chris Drury) and 10 head coaches (Colin Campbell, John Muckler, Ron Low, Bryan Trottier, Sather, Tom Renney, John Tortorella, Alain Vigneault, David Quinn, and Gerard Gallant). I have enjoyed getting to know each and every one of them. During Renney's reign, assistant coach Mike Pelino occasionally asked me to help compile statistical and analytical information. I enjoyed going back to my roots working with numbers.

I have also spent 12 seasons as the Knicks backup TV play-by-play announcer, filling in for Mike Breen when he is away on a national assignment. Working alongside Frazier never gets old. He is the only person in history to be inducted into the Basketball Hall of Fame as both a player and broadcaster. The point guard on the Knicks championship teams in 1970 and 1973 has been a joy to work with. He may be best known to the younger generation of Knicks fans for his wardrobe and unique vocabulary during telecasts, but he is one of the most astute basketball minds you will find. Frazier is always so kind to the fans; I have never witnessed him turn down a photo or autograph request (similar to his contemporary as a New York superstar, Joe Namath, whom I called Jets preseason games with in 1997). During one game we worked together, Ewing was in town as an assistant coach, and Willis Reed sat in a courtside seat. Our director, Howie Singer, took live shots of both former Knicks centers. Without missing a beat, Frazier commented, "It's great to see the second and third greatest Knicks of all time at the Garden tonight!" That's just one example of how quick-witted he is during telecasts.

There are many perks that come with working at Madison Square Garden, including attending concerts and other special events. In August of 2014, I was asked to interview tennis great Roger Federer on the floor of MSG to help promote a tournament he was going to play in at the World's Most Famous Arena several months later. He is one of the classiest superstars I have ever met. Even Lundqvist was on hand to meet one of his idols for the first time. It was neat to witness a star athlete so excited to meet an icon from a different sport.

Madison Square Garden is such a special place, and so many people who work there are like family to me—from the public relations staffs to security guards to the ice crew and Zamboni drivers. I grew up there, and my kids have as well. They never miss the opportunity to attend a Rangers or Knicks game or a Billy Joel concert. They were heartbroken when the Rangers lost in Game Six of the Eastern Conference Final to New Jersey in 2012 and again with the defeat in Los Angeles in Game 5 of the Stanley Cup Final two years later. They were sobbing after the Game Seven loss in the 2015 Eastern Conference Final while waiting for me to wrap up my broadcast. They experienced so many memorable playoff victories during the Lundqvist era. Barbara didn't miss a home game during the 2014 postseason run, and one or both girls were usually right by her side. I will never forget the looks on Amanda and Syd's faces when I met them on the Garden concourse following Artemi Panarin's overtime winner against Pittsburgh in Game Seven of the first round in 2022. I hope they get to experience the euphoria of a Stanley Cup championship at the World's Most Famous Arena as I did on June 14, 1994.

# 6
# ON THE ICE

have loved hockey for as long as I can remember. My parents first put me on skates around the time I started walking. My earliest memory of attending a New York Rangers game at Madison Square Garden (though I'm sure I went to several prior) was an afternoon game against the Philadelphia Flyers on February 23, 1975—weeks after my seventh birthday. I distinctly remember Jerry Butler scoring on a breakaway to give the Blueshirts a 1–0 lead. Ironically, four players on the ice that day would later become my color analysts: Terry Crisp, Rod Gilbert, Ron Greschner, and Pete Stemkowski.

For years I cut out every NHL box score from various newspapers and taped them into a black marble notebook. I still have all of them to this day. If West Coast game summaries were missing from the papers delivered to our house, I would cross my fingers and hope they would be printed two days after the respective games were played.

Our neighborhood was not wired for cable television until I was a senior in high school, so aside from Rangers away games on WOR Channel 9 (as well as select New York Islanders and New Jersey Devils road games), the only NHL games I was able to watch were on the league's syndicated packages throughout the 1970s and early 1980s. The only Rangers home games I recall watching on television were Game Four of the 1979 Stanley Cup Final, which was broadcasted on over-the-air television in New York—I had attended Game Three in person—and a game on February 23, 1983, on the UHF Hartford station (Channel 30) with a very grainy feed. Through the static, I watched Mark Pavelich score five goals for the Rangers against the Hartford Whalers.

I listened to as many games as possible on the radio—whether it was the Rangers, Islanders, Devils...or even the Whalers. We had a radio in our kitchen, which picked up the signal from Hartford, and I would sit at the counter for hours tuning in to Whalers games—especially whenever they faced my beloved Vancouver Canucks. Whenever I see Hall of Fame broadcaster Chuck Kaiton, I kid him about listening to his broadcasts as a youngster. During the first few Devils seasons, I occasionally called in to their "Dial-A-Devil" radio segments and chatted with broadcasters Larry Hirsch and Fred Shero. During the mid-1980s, while keeping stats for the Rangers radio broadcasts, I convinced Hirsch to allow to me to phone in live updates on the Devils radiocasts when the teams played games at the same time.

I loved skating and playing hockey at local rinks and was a member of club teams in both high school and college. My initial goal was to call hockey on the radio. Not only did I achieve that milestone—first as a backup with the Islanders, then with the Baltimore Skipjacks and Rangers on a full-time basis—but I transitioned to the television side as well. That began with the Washington Capitals, followed by stints on several national networks. I received the call to work two NHL games on fledgling ESPN2 during the 1993–94 season alongside analysts Darren Pang and Brian Engblom.

In 1995, less than a year after I began working NFL games on FOX, the network acquired the rights to the NHL. For five seasons I called play-by-play with a variety of analysts, including Denis Potvin, Terry Crisp, Craig Simpson, and Peter McNab. One of the games I'm still asked about (thanks to YouTube) took place at Nassau Coliseum on April 4, 1998. The goaltenders—Dan Cloutier of the Rangers and Tommy Salo of the Islanders—took part in fisticuffs (advantage Cloutier, who then challenged the entire Isles bench). Crisp was my color analyst 23 years after he played in the first NHL game that I recall attending. The 240 penalty minutes probably reminded him of his days as a member of the Broad Street Bullies. During another FOX telecast involving the two New York teams on Long Island, Potvin, the captain of four Islanders Stanley Cup teams, was my analyst. A shot appeared on our monitor of an anti-Rangers message written with Sharpies on the glass behind their penalty box. Without missing a beat, I remarked, "Denis, now I know why you asked to borrow magic markers."

Unfortunately, FOX lost the national NHL contract following the 1998–99 season to ABC/ESPN. Following the 2004–05 lockout, the rights shifted to OLN (Outdoor Life Network). I worked nine regular-season games for OLN during the 2005–06 season, including the deciding game of the Carolina Hurricanes–Devils series on Mother's Day. It was the final game I called with John Davidson. (We had worked several Rangers telecasts together before he became president of the St. Louis Blues prior to the next season.) The Canes went on to win the Stanley Cup just over a month later with Doc Emrick and Davidson at the mic.

OLN eventually was re-branded as Versus. Then prior to the 2011–12 season, Comcast— the owner of Versus—acquired a majority stake in NBC Universal. I had worked six games for Versus in 2010–11, then eight (after another name shift to the NHL on NBC) in 2011–12. I had already called Olympic hockey for NBC in 2002, 2006, and 2010 and had a relationship with the network's executive producer (and hockey fanatic) Sam Flood. He offered me a larger role with the NHL on NBC. In 2014 Flood asked me to work the Western Conference Final between the Chicago Blackhawks and Los Angeles Kings alongside Joe Micheletti and Engblom. The epic series was won by the Kings on an Alec Martinez overtime goal in Game Seven. Days later I filled in for Emrick (who was away at a family funeral) on NBC's telecast of Game One of the Stanley Cup Final between the Kings and Rangers with Eddie Olczyk and Pierre McGuire. That was my first time calling the Stanley Cup Final on television. Beginning with the 2014 playoffs, I became the No. 2 guy on NBC's depth chart behind Emrick and continued in that role for seven more seasons, calling one of the conference final series each spring.

It is extra special to call games during the playoffs involving teams whose fanbases haven't experienced deep runs. In 2016 I worked the Western Conference Final between the San Jose Sharks and St. Louis Blues. The Sharks won in six games to advance to their first Stanley Cup Final in franchise history. San Jose was beaten in six by the Pittsburgh Penguins, and I called the series on Westwood One Radio. The next spring I worked the Western Conference Final between the Nashville Predators and Anaheim Ducks on NBC/NBCSN.

The atmosphere in Music City was second to none both inside the arena and outside on Broadway. Thousands of fans would congregate in the heart of downtown Nashville—just blocks from the arena—to enjoy pregame concerts and then the games on giant video screens. The Penguins extinguished the Predators in six and were awarded the Cup in front of the Nashville fans. (I called the series on Westwood One along with Joe Micheletti.)

In 2018 the Vegas Golden Knights went on an unprecedented run during their inaugural season, becoming the first expansion team to reach the Stanley Cup Final in their first year since the 1967–68 Blues. I called the Western Conference Final between Vegas and the Winnipeg Jets on NBC and then the Washington–Vegas Final on Westwood One. The atmosphere in Las Vegas matched Nashville from the previous year…and then some. The save made by Capitals goaltender Braden Holtby on Alex Tuch in Game Two was a series-changer, and Alex Ovechkin and the Caps won their first championship with a Game Five victory in Sin City. Ovechkin might still be celebrating! Barbara and Sydney were there too; it was the second consecutive year Barbara attended the clinching game of a Stanley Cup Final. She was in Nashville the year before when the Penguins won the title.

The next spring, it was a lot of fun to call the last 19 games played by the Blues during their march to the first championship in franchise history. That included Game Two through Seven in the second round against the Dallas Stars (notably the double-overtime winner in Game Seven by St. Louis native Pat Maroon), all six games of the Western Conference Final against San Jose, and the entire seven-game final against the Boston Bruins on Westwood One.

From 2016 through 2020, I called the NHL All-Star Skills Competition for NBC. These are always fun, loose shows with events ranging from Fastest Skater to Hardest Shot to Accuracy Shooting. In 2017 at the Staples Center in Los Angeles, I had to apologize on national television after Snoop Dogg (aka DJ Snoopadelic) played unedited, uncensored music at ice level which could be heard by everyone both in the arena and by the television viewers. "We apologize for some inappropriate language you may have heard during the performance of DJ Snoopadelic."

The incident (and my apology) made it onto *The Howard Stern Show*, and Stern mocked my "announcer voice." A badge of honor! I was also at the mic in San Jose in 2019 when Kendall Coyne-Schofield made history by becoming the first woman to compete in the NHL Skills Competition (in the fastest skater event). A few months later, she was my broadcast partner on NBC for two games during the Blues–Stars series.

Brian Boucher became a frequent partner of mine during these years. He was a terrific addition to the NBC roster, following his retirement in 2013, and is now one of the top NHL analysts for ESPN. On the final day of the 2009–10 regular season, I was on the radio call for a rare winner-take-all game between the Rangers and Flyers in Philadelphia. The winning team would advance to the playoffs, and the losing team would be eliminated. With "Bouch" in goal, the Flyers won in a shootout and advanced all the way to the Stanley Cup Final. It was the only time the Rangers missed qualifying for the postseason between the 2005–06 and 2016–17 seasons. With my hockey season over and the girls on spring break, Barbara booked a trip to the Fontainebleau in South Beach before I even made it home from Philly. I have told Bouch the story, and he revels in the fact that he "sent the Alberts on vacation!"

During the summer of 2020 in the height of the COVID pandemic, the NHL returned to action following a four-and-a-half month pause. In the first three days of August, I called two qualifying round and/or round-robin games each day. On August 1 I called the Rangers–Hurricanes on radio from ESPN Radio's studio in Manhattan and then Calgary Flames–Jets off a monitor from Stamford, Connecticut at 10:30 PM. I would have bet my life savings if somebody had told me six months earlier that I would be calling a Rangers–Canes and Jets–Flames doubleheader in August! The next day, I called two games from Stamford: Arizona Coyotes–Nashville and St. Louis–Colorado Avalanche followed by Rangers–Carolina and Blackhawks–Edmonton Oilers on August 3. After the Rangers were eliminated in a three-game sweep by the Canes on August 4 and my radio duties were over, I hurriedly packed for Edmonton. I flew the next day and worked 34 playoff games in the bubble.

That often meant two games each day or three games the same day in a couple of instances.

Emrick announced his retirement in October 2020, a few months before the delayed start of the 2020–21 campaign. Late in the regular season, I received one of the most memorable phone calls of my life, and it came from Flood. He told me that I would be calling the 2021 Stanley Cup Final for NBC. It was the culmination of a lifelong dream. I had already called the Stanley Cup Final eight times on radio (seven nationally and in 2014 for the MSG Radio Network). But there would be something even more special about handling the call to a national television audience.

It's ironic how things work in life sometimes. In my next phone conversation with Flood—just a few days later—he informed me that NBC would not be retaining the rights to broadcast the NHL, following the postseason. Talk about going from the highest of highs to the lowest of lows.

The wild emotional pendulum would swing upward again less than two weeks later, when I was hired as the lead hockey play-by-play announcer by Turner, who agreed to a deal to share the NHL TV rights with ESPN for the next seven seasons. I was ecstatic to become their lead play-by-play voice. I couldn't have been any more excited to join the network that has done such an outstanding job with the NBA, MLB, and college basketball through the years.

As the playoffs began, I worked games for NBC in several series during the first round, then Colorado–Vegas in the second round and Tampa Bay Lightning–Islanders in the semifinal. I missed one game in the first round and another in the third due to my daughters' respective college and high school graduations. Because teams played only divisional rivals in 2020–21 (to cut down on travel due to health and safety protocols), there was not an Eastern Conference or Western Conference Final—just two semifinal series. Vegas–Montreal Canadiens was the other matchup. There were several thrilling moments during the Lightning–Islanders series. A blocked shot by Ryan Pulock at the final buzzer of Game Four prevented overtime, and an overtime goal scored by the Isles' Anthony Beauvillier in Game Six turned out to be the final hockey game played at Nassau Coliseum. Tampa Bay, the defending champs, won Game Seven on home ice—thanks to a Yanni Gourde shorthanded goal and Andrei Vasilevskiy shutout. The Canadiens upset the Golden Knights to set up a Tampa Bay–Montreal final.

The day before the series began, I taped segments for the NHL Awards Show for the second straight year. Due to the pandemic, the league did not hold their usual celebration with the award finalists and an audience. In 2020 and 2021, the winners were announced during a TV special. I was sworn to secrecy regarding the winners after we recorded the program.

Once the Stanley Cup Final matchup was determined, certain protocols were put back into place. After the Canadiens upset the Golden Knights in the Western Conference Final, our crew was going to have to fly back and forth between the U.S. and Canada throughout the series between the Lightning and Canadiens. The NHL reached an agreement with the Canadian government. Those of us in the league's traveling party would be allowed to cross the border and work the games without quarantining as long as we did not leave our respective hotels throughout the series—aside from going to games and practices and to pick up food. We were not able to eat at restaurants, take walks outside in either city, or sit out at the pool. In Montreal we had to take an NHL-sanctioned bus from the hotel to the Bell Centre (and vice versa) instead of walking five minutes. Fortunately, we were permitted to spend time on an outdoor, rooftop deck along with other league personnel and media— good news considering there were two full off days between Games Three and Four. We were tested for COVID every day during the entire series. (I lost count, but at that point, I think I had taken more than 100 tests throughout the past year.) But if all that was the tradeoff in order to work my first Stanley Cup Final on the TV side, I would've signed up for that 100 times out of 100. I would have stayed in my hotel room for a month leading up to the series if that's what it took. Despite the challenges it was a huge thrill to call the Stanley Cup Final with Olczyk, Boucher, and McGuire.

The Lightning won the first three games of the series. During one of the off days prior to Game Four, I spent time on YouTube watching Stanley

Cup-winning calls from previous seasons by the likes of Emrick, Gary Thorne, Dick Irvin, and Bob Cole. I did not necessarily want to have a pre-conceived call in mind, but I felt it was important to listen to the variety of ways they described the moment as various teams won hockey's holy grail.

Pat Maroon of the Lightning, who had already won the 2019 and 2020 Stanley Cup with St. Louis and Tampa Bay, tied Game Four at two apiece with just more than six minutes remaining in regulation. Montreal's Shea Weber was called for a double minor—a four-minute penalty for high sticking—at the 18:59 mark of the third period. The tension inside Bell Centre increased tenfold. I am usually very calm during broadcasts, but all of a sudden, my heart was pounding. If the Lightning scored on that power play, the Stanley Cup would most likely be theirs once again. The Habs killed off the final 61 seconds in the third. During the intermission I thought to myself that there was no way the Lightning would go without scoring with nearly three minutes remaining on their man advantage. Somehow, Montreal killed off the penalty, and Josh Anderson extended the series with his second goal of the game 3:57 into overtime.

We all boarded a charter flight back to Tampa for Game Five, which would be played on July 7. This time, the Lightning pulled it off before their home fans thanks to a second period goal from Ross Colton and yet another Vasilevskiy shutout. "Lightning Strikes Twice. The Tampa Bay Lightning win their second straight Stanley Cup," I proclaimed to the U.S. television audience as the final seconds wound off the clock.

Then, I laid out (or shut up in layman's terms) and let producer Matt Marvin and director Charlie Dammeyer tell the story with the sights and sounds from Amalie Arena. Then, another layout as the teams lined up to shake hands after battling so hard with each other for over a week. That's one of the greatest traditions in all of sports. I later learned that Chris Cuthbert used a similar phrase on the Canadian network telecast. Great minds think alike; it wasn't planned by either of us.

My first interaction with Turner was a Zoom call with Olczyk, our agent Lou Oppenheim, and network president Jeff Zucker, a huge sports fan who worked as the colead NBC researcher (along with Flood) at the 1988 Summer Olympics. Olczyk and I were paired on the top crew along with our good friend (and another former NBC colleague) Keith Jones, whom I had first met during his brief stint with the Skipjacks in 1992. I called his first two professional goals (during the last game of the 1991–92 season) as well as some of his games with the Capitals while working for HTS. After a preseason telecast in Boston, we opened the season with a Capitals–Rangers game in Washington, and Wayne Gretzky joined us live from the studio during a portion of the second period. We called three outdoor games during the 2021–22 regular season: the Winter Classic in Minneapolis; the Stadium Series in Nashville; and the Heritage Classic in Hamilton, Ontario. Gretzky joined us as a guest analyst for the entire game in Hamilton—just 25 miles from his (and Jonesy's) hometown of Brantford. It was one of the surreal moments of my broadcast career to look to my right throughout the entire game and converse with the greatest hockey player of all time, whom I idolized as a youngster.

Although I love the atmosphere and pageantry at NHL outdoor games, they are more challenging to call than typical games. The broadcast booth is much farther away from the ice than inside arenas, making it more difficult to see the uniform numbers. Typically, I always look directly at the ice while calling NHL games; during outdoor games I glance at the monitor frequently during live action since the cameras are able to zoom in and give a much closer look at the numbers. During the first outdoor game I broadcasted—Rangers–Flyers on the radio at Citizens Bank Park in Philadelphia in January 2012—I attempted to use binoculars but quickly realized the play was moving too fast and I wouldn't be able to see things happening away from the puck or penalty signals from the officials.

I called several additional outdoor games on radio from high booths—from Yankee Stadium, Citi Field, Lincoln Financial Field, and Busch Stadium. My first outdoor game on the TV side was at the Air Force Academy in Colorado Springs between the Avalanche and Kings in 2019. Olczyk and I worked from an ice-level location right up against the glass in single-digit temperatures. It was incredible to be so close to the action; that's the closest I ever have been for a hockey broadcast. But it certainly presented challenges as well whenever the puck was deep in either offensive zone or in the near corners.

Kudos to the NHL hierarchy (commissioner Gary Bettman, Bill Daly, Colin Campbell, and Steve Mayer), along with ice wizard Dan Craig and his staff. The outdoor games have become marquee events and have averaged more than 50,000 in attendance. They've also provided magical moments for millions and millions of fans who have enjoyed watching the games on television.

During the 2021–22 playoffs on Turner, I bounced back and forth during the first round (similar to the NBC years), working games in four different series. I mixed in Rangers radio games as well, including the triple-overtime series opener against the Penguins at Madison Square Garden. Igor Shesterkin stopped 79 of 83 shots—the second most saves in NHL history—but was beaten by Evgeni Malkin in the sixth period. Later in the round, Olczyk, Jones, and I enjoyed a whirlwind 48 hours. On Friday, May 13, we were in Pittsburgh for Game Six—a 5–3 Rangers victory. With limited flight options the next morning from Pittsburgh to Toronto, we took a car service (a little under four hours) from Pittsburgh to a hotel at the Buffalo Airport after the game, arriving around 2:30 AM. The next day, we drove across the border straight to Scotiabank Arena for Game Seven of the Toronto Maple Leafs–Lightning series. The car took us down the loading dock ramp, and we departed from the same spot after the 2–1 Tampa Bay victory and headed back to the hotel in Buffalo. We were in Toronto for a grand total of six hours and never breathed the outside air. After only four hours of sleep, I flew home from Buffalo. Following a quick nap, it was into Manhattan for Game Seven of the Rangers and Penguins, a game decided in overtime on an Artemi Panarin wrist shot from the right wing circle.

We were assigned to the Florida Panthers–Tampa Bay series in round two. It turned out to be a surprising four-game sweep by the two-time defending champs over the Panthers, who finished with the league's best regular-season record. I also called Game One, Two, and Five of the Rangers–Hurricanes series in Raleigh, North Carolina, for MSG Radio. Then, it was on to the Western Conference Final and another four-game sweep by Colorado over Edmonton. Games One and Four were run and gun. The Avs took the opener 8–6 on home ice; Colorado took Game Four by a 6–5 score in overtime after trailing 4–2 in the third period.

The Turner pregame crew (Liam McHugh, Gretzky, Paul Bissonnette, Rick Tocchet, and Anson Carter) traveled to Denver and Edmonton to do their shows on site during the conference final. Listening to Gretzky tell numerous stories from his playing career during meals and plane trips together was amazing; his recall of events that took place decades ago is incredible. We attended a junior hockey playoff game on an off day in Edmonton between the hometown Oil Kings and Seattle Thunderbirds. During the short walk from the hotel to the arena, Gretzky suggested that we took a group shot in front of *his* statue. Then, he spoke to the Edmonton club in the locker room prior to the game and introduced a "special guest"—Bissonnette—who read the starting lineups. The players went wild, and the guys showed the video during the TNT pregame show the next night. Two decades after traveling with Gretzky during his tenure with the Rangers, I felt like I was back with The Beatles again.

# NATIONAL
# PASTIME

guess I was predestined to become a baseball fan since my parents met while they were both working at Shea Stadium. I accompanied them to New York Yankees spring training in Fort Lauderdale, Florida, in March 1969 at just 13 months old. Like most youngsters, I played Little League baseball. The fathers of the kids on the team would take turns pitching. I remember one game in Port Washington, New York, when my father was pitching to me, and I hit a line drive right back into his midsection.

So many of my early sports memories involved the Yankees. I became a fan of the team while in first grade (during the 1974 and 1975 seasons) because a neighbor who was three years older told me he was a Yankees fan as we waited for the school bus one day. It was that simple. Although I have a photo with my parents at the original Yankee Stadium that closed for renovations in 1973, I was too young to remember attending a game there. The first baseball game I absolutely recall attending was with them in 1974, when the Yankees played against the Texas Rangers at Shea Stadium, where the Bronx Bombers played for two seasons while their ballpark was under construction. We arrived late due to traffic, and Jeff Burroughs was at the plate when we entered Shea, the venue where my parents had met 10 years earlier.

The only item I can honestly say I have ever stolen was a Billy Martin baseball card from a department store in the shopping center a couple of miles from our house. I was with my grandmother and spotted the card on top of the pack through its plastic. It was the only card I needed to complete my Yankees set. I opened the package, removed that single card, and took it home. I'm not exactly sure why I didn't just ask my grandmother to buy me the pack of cards. I felt so guilty that a couple of days later I went back into the store and placed a few dollars on the counter near one of the cashiers (more than the cost of the entire pack).

The first Mets game I remember attending was with my grandfather (Stewart Caress), and Woody Fryman pitched for the Montreal Expos. My parents surprised me with a trip to the new Yankee Stadium early in the 1976 season. They didn't tell me where we were going, but as we were driving on the Cross Bronx Expressway and I saw a sign for the stadium, I had a feeling. I'll never forget walking from the concourse area through the vestibule. Seeing the Yankee Stadium field in person for the first time was magical for this eight-year-old.

On July 19, 1977, I attended my first All-Star Game (in any sport). My grandfather Stew and I sat in an auxiliary press section, approximately 25 rows behind Yankee Stadium's home plate. It was a stifling, 100-degree evening. My father was there doing pregame and postgame interviews for WNBC and stopped by to visit us a few times. Three months later I watched alone in my bedroom as Reggie Jackson hit three home runs in Game Six of the World Series against the Los Angeles Dodgers. Jackson was an idol to most Yankees fans during the late 1970s. I had the opportunity to accompany my dad to Jackson's apartment one day during the offseason. He was going to tape an interview with the slugger along with WNBC colleague Dick Schaap. Inside the apartment Jackson handed me a baseball and autographed it for me. I also took a photo with him, which is still one of my most prized possessions.

On June 17, 1978, my father took me to a Yankees–California Angels game on a Saturday night. Ron Guidry set a franchise record by striking out 18 batters. It still ranks among the top individual athletic performances I've witnessed in person, and this occurred at the ripe age of 10. It's the first time I saw fans standing and clapping for a strikeout with two strikes on the opposing batter in the Bronx. Interestingly enough, Ken Brett (the brother of Hall of Famer George) pitched five-and-two-thirds innings of relief for California. Ken and I became broadcast partners two decades later.

Even from a very young age, my parents had me dressed in New York Knicks attire—and studying broadcast charts.

I was always around my father, Marv, and always around the broadcast booth—sometimes at the same time.

I wear a Pete Maravich camp shirt while hanging around my father and Richie Guerin while they call a game at Madison Square Garden.

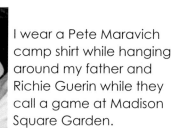

Our whole family visits George H.W. Bush at the White House.

Growing up I got a chance to meet so many sports stars, including Mr. October himself, Reggie Jackson.

I first met Wayne Gretzy when I was a teenager. Now we are *NHL on TNT* colleagues.

I helped found—and played on—the NYU hockey club and scored the first goal in its history.

My father and I pose at my wedding while holding microphones from our respective networks.

Washington Capitals general manager David Poile was in attendance when the Baltimore Skipjacks introduced me (and, of course, head coach Rob Laird) at a press conference in 1990.

I interview the Hatcher brothers (Kevin and Derian).

My broadcasting partner, Walt "Clyde" Frazier, is always the coolest and best-dressed man in the room.

You never know who you'll run into at Madison Square Garden. Taylor Swift was sitting two seats to my left at MSG while I broadcasted a Knicks game and took a selfie, which made my daughters jealous.

I enjoy calling the Winter Classic at Fenway Park with Eddie Olczyk and Keith Jones.

I hold my daughter, Amanda, while hanging out with Mark Messier after playing in the Christopher Reeve charity game at Madison Square Garden.

It was great fun announcing games with Moose and Goose (aka Daryl Johnston and Tony Siragusa).

I receive a unique opportunity to announce NFL games with identical twins—Tiki and Rondé Barber.

During the 2016 baseball season, I had the good fortune to spend a few minutes with the legendary Vin Scully prior to a game at Dodger Stadium during his 67th and final season in the Dodgers' booth.

I always enjoyed calling games with Tim McCarver, who was one of the best color analysts in the history of Major League Baseball.

Barbara and I celebrate at our wedding in 1996 with appropriately-named Barbie and Ken dolls next to the cake.

Amanda and Sydney hang out with me at our home away from home—Madison Square Garden.

Our family recreated The Beatles' famous walk across Abbey Road and used this photo for our 2014 holiday card.

My family celebrates my 50th birthday in a festive way that only they could.

On the afternoon of October 2, 1978, I was watching the telecast in my bedroom when Bucky Dent hit the iconic home run at Fenway Park, which pushed the Yankees into the postseason after trailing the Boston Red Sox by 14 games in the standings in July. I sprinted out of my room and into the backyard and gave my father and uncles a detailed report on what had just transpired. Later that month, I attended Game Four of the World Series with my grandparents Stew and Julie. We witnessed the moment when Jackson was infamously hit by a thrown ball but was not called for interference.

At some point during the late 1970s, my dad brought me onto the field at Yankee Stadium. He was there to handle pregame interviews for WNBC. He introduced me to one of the bat boys, who offered to give me a bat from the player of my choice. I asked for a Thurman Munson model. While at summer camp, I was devastated when I heard the news that Munson had died in a plane crash on August 2, 1979. I still have the bat. I also have an actual seat from the old Yankee Stadium; it was Yankees blue with a black No. 6 painted on the seatback. The chair was bolted to the floor in my childhood bedroom in Sands Point. Unfortunately, while I was away at camp during the early 1980s, a crew hired by my parents to paint my bedroom walls decided that the chair could use a new coat and took it upon themselves to paint it white! I was horrified when I noticed it upon returning home in late August. I wanted to sue the painters. I still have the chair to this day, but it doesn't mean as much to me as when it was in its original state.

During the early-to-mid 1980s, the Yankees started to decline, and the New York Mets were on the upswing thanks to the acquisitions of Keith Hernandez and Gary Carter and the development of prospects such as Darryl Strawberry and Doc Gooden. During ninth grade I attended Strawberry's first major league game on May 6, 1983, against the Cincinnati Reds. Shea Stadium was an easy, half-hour ride on the Long Island Rail Road, and around that time, my parents allowed me to take the train with friends to Mets and New York Jets games. (The Jets moved to the Meadowlands prior to the 1984 season.) Tom Seaver and Mario Soto were the starting pitchers.

There was a huge buzz surrounding Strawberry's debut; he went 0–4 and scored a run.

Over the next few seasons, my father would occasionally arrange for me to sit in an empty booth in the press box at Shea down the first-base line, and I would announce games into a tape recorder along with a friend. My dad had done the same thing at Ebbets Field in Brooklyn three decades earlier. I started to root for the Mets as well (yes, you could call me a frontrunner) and attended several of their postseason games in 1986 against the Houston Astros and Red Sox, including Game Seven of the World Series. I listened to part of the clinching game of the National League Championship Series against the Astros while riding a bus from the Port Authority Bus Terminal to Brendan Byrne Arena for a New Jersey Devils–Vancouver Canucks game. During my childhood I tried to attend every Canucks game in the New York metropolitan area—three per season. It turns out three of my future color analysts played in that game for the Devils: Peter McNab, Andy Brickley, and Ken Daneyko.

On October 25, 1986, I passed on a ticket to Game Six of the World Series at Shea Stadium because I felt obligated to honor my commitment to handle stats for the second game of a preseason doubleheader at MSG. It was Greg Gumbel's first game as the backup Knicks broadcaster, so I felt like I should be there to pass him notes and statistical nuggets throughout the game. Gumbel was filling in for my father, who was at Shea to handle interviews for NBC. I also worked the first game of the twinbill and made some extra cash, handling stats for longtime Detroit Pistons broadcaster George Blaha. My college roommate Rich Ackerman—along with his brother Michael—were the lucky beneficiaries of the World Series tickets, as they were on hand to witness the Bill Buckner play.

I was standing at the bar in the Madison Square Garden media room watching in shock (along with other members of the media, including future Devils TV voice Steve Cangialosi) as Mookie Wilson's slow roller trickled through Buckner's legs. Game Seven took place two nights later (following a Sunday rainout), and I attended with Ackerman. It was the first time I witnessed a World Series-clinching game in person. We were sitting on the mezzanine level down the third-base line. During the middle innings, Ackerman mentioned to me that Jerry Seinfeld was sitting directly behind us. I wasn't familiar with the name; Seinfeld was in the infancy of his stand-up career, but Ackerman had already seen him on television and was a fan. For some reason Ackerman (as a college freshman) had printed business cards. He asked Seinfeld for an autograph on the back of one of the cards. Two innings later, Ackerman turned to Seinfeld and asked if he would call him to let him know if he was going to be performing in New York in the near future. He then inadvertently handed Jerry the same business card he autographed and didn't realize it until we returned to our NYU dorm. For years I expected Seinfeld to include a story in his comedy set about "the guy who asked for my autograph—and then gave it back to me!"

Decades later, Ackerman relayed the story to Seinfeld when the comedian cohosted a show on WFAN with Steve Somers. (Ackerman was there handling the sports updates.) Seinfeld said he never even realized that Ackerman had given him back the card with the autograph because he attempted to buy a Mets championship T-shirt outside Shea Stadium after exiting Game Seven and realized he had been pickpocketed, and his wallet was missing. It was like a plot right out of an episode of *Seinfeld*.

During my years working on *Mets Extra*, I developed relationships with the team broadcasters. In fact, I asked Bob Murphy to record an answering machine message for our dorm room. For the next three years, anyone who called to leave a voicemail for Ackerman or me would be greeted by the unmistakable voice of the legendary Mets announcer in his Midwest accent: "Kenny and Rich aren't here right now…Please leave a message, and they'll get back to you as soon as possible."

I helped produce *Mets Extra* until a month after my college graduation when I moved to Baltimore in June 1990. During my first few summers in Maryland, I enjoyed attending Baltimore Orioles games (including their final game at Memorial Stadium on October 6, 1991), as well as minor league baseball games in small towns around Maryland and Pennsylvania.

It was exciting to watch the development of Oriole Park at Camden Yards. I attended the inaugural game (an exhibition against the Mets) and then the regular-season opener after Jerry Coleman, Nestor Aparicio, and I did our radio show prior to the game from a hotel rooftop behind the outfield stands. Rick Sutcliffe pitched a gem. His 2–0 shutout against the Cleveland Indians took only two hours, two minutes. My future color analyst, Bill Ripken, drove in one of the two Orioles runs. I covered the 1993 All-Star Game at Camden Yards for WTOP Radio and attended the games on September 5 and 6, 1995, when Cal Ripken Jr. tied and then broke Lou Gehrig's major league record for consecutive games played.

I was given my first opportunity to call MLB games during the 1994 and 1995 seasons on Home Team Sports, filling in for Mel Proctor. I worked alongside former Orioles outfielder John Lowenstein and also handled some pregame segments with Hall of Fame pitcher Jim Palmer.

After moving to New York in 1995, I was assigned by the MSG Network executives to substitute for Al Trautwig as the pregame and postgame show host for two Yankees series in Kansas City and Texas in late July/early August 1996 while Trautwig was on assignment at the Atlanta Olympics. I also did two innings of play-by-play on these games with Hall of Fame pitcher Jim Kaat. Then-Yankees radio broadcaster Michael Kay was my partner on the TV postgame shows. I was under strict instructions from Barbara to apply a heavy dose of sunscreen during the trip since our wedding would take place a week later and I would be taking a multitude of photos. Kay and I share a birthday, and for many years, we have had a contest to see who would text first as the clock struck midnight on February 2. During my brief stint, the Yankees acquired Cecil Fielder (on July 31). Prior to his first game with the club, I interviewed Fielder on the pregame show; I borrowed the first cap he was given by the Yankees equipment staff. I attempted to demonstrate by putting it on my head, but my head was so big that Fielder's hat did not fit!

In October of 1996, Barbara and I attended Game One of the American League Championship Series between the Yankees and Orioles. Our seats were in the upper deck down the first-base/right-field line. There was a long delay after Derek Jeter hit a ball just over the right-field fence in the bottom of the eighth inning. As Orioles outfielder Tony Tarasco settled under the ball, we couldn't see what was happening. From our seats that area of the field was a blind spot. In 1996 cell phones were primitive. There was no texting or internet available on cell phones; they were only used to make actual calls. So, we had no idea what happened until we got back to our apartment in New York City and watched the news. A 12-year-old fan named Jeffrey Maier reached out and caught the ball, and umpire Richie Garcia awarded Jeter a home run—much to the chagrin of the Orioles and their manager Davey Johnson. The Yankees won the game on a Bernie Williams walk-off homer in the 11th inning. They would go on to win the series in five games and capture the first of their four titles in a five-year stretch. Around a decade later, Barbara and I were eating dinner at a restaurant near our home in northern New Jersey. There were two couples sitting at the table next to us. Barbara said hello to one of the women, whom she knew. The woman then introduced us to the other couple and said, "These are Jeffrey Maier's parents."

I started calling Major League Baseball games on a regular basis during the 1997 season on a FOX cable package. Over the next five seasons (1997–2001), the games aired on FOX Sports Net, FX, and Fox Family—usually on Thursday and Saturday nights. My primary analyst was Jeff Torborg, one of the nicest men I've ever had the pleasure of meeting and working with. Torborg spent 10 seasons as a major league catcher (he was behind the plate for three no-hitters, including Sandy Koufax's perfect game in 1965 and the first of Nolan Ryan's seven no-hitters) before embarking on a long coaching and managerial career. He seemed to know everybody in the sport of baseball and was kind enough to introduce me to the likes of Tom Seaver, Don Sutton, and countless others. I learned so much about baseball from Torborg not only from the broadcasts, but also from countless meals and flights together as well. He usually traveled with his wife Suzie (a former Miss New Jersey); I always enjoyed my conversations with them. Torborg and I once grabbed a postgame dinner in St. Louis along with Seaver and his

Mets television partner Gary Thorne. It was certainly a memorable evening listening to "The Franchise" entertain us with stories from his Hall of Fame career.

On another occasion Torborg and I were working a Mets game at Shea Stadium. Upon exiting from the Diamond Club elevator, we walked past a display, which included busts of many of the great figures in club history. Without missing a beat, Torborg said to me, "I should be on that shelf. I was a bust as Mets manager!" It was one of the funniest, self-deprecating lines I've ever heard. As an added bonus, Torborg taught me all of the shortcuts out of the Yankee Stadium and Shea Stadium parking lots. He had played, coached, and managed at both ballparks for many years and perfected the art of the quick escape.

I worked on a semi-regular basis with Kevin Kennedy (the former Red Sox and Texas Rangers skipper), Steve "Psycho" Lyons, and longtime major league pitcher Ken Brett, as well as several games with other former stars. During a game in Cleveland with Keith Hernandez, a scorching foul ball headed back into our broadcast booth. Using cat-like quickness, Hernandez left his chair and slid under the desk. My reaction time was a bit slower, and fortunately the ball missed me. My next line on air: "Excellent job by the 11-time Gold Glove Award winner to get out of the way." That is a prime example of homework on a broadcast partner's career paying off at the opportune time.

On Thursday, August 14, 1997, I was in Baltimore to work an Orioles–Seattle Mariners game, and Randy Johnson was scheduled to pitch for Seattle. Due to an issue with the lights at Camden Yards, the game did not start on time. In fact, after a two-and-a-half-hour delay, it was postponed due to the power failure. I went to a late dinner in the Little Italy section of town with some of my colleagues. Palmer and Ripken happened to be sitting at the next table.

During the 1998 season, I called several St. Louis Cardinals and Chicago Cubs games during the Mark McGwire/Sammy Sosa home run chase. A check of my scorecards reveals that I called McGwire's 27th, 67th, and 68th longballs. Both McGwire and Sosa eclipsed Roger Maris' single-season record of 61 home runs.

I was working a St. Louis Rams game at the Trans World Dome in St. Louis on September 27, 1998. As quarterback Tony Banks was standing under center, a roar from the crowd broke the concentration of Banks and his teammates, and the Rams were flagged for a false start. It turns out McGwire hit his 70th home run at that exact moment across town at Busch Stadium. Thousands of fans at the football game were listening to the Cardinals game on transistor radios and reacted as McGwire went deep.

On April 15, 1999, Tim McCarver—the lead FOX Network baseball analyst—was assigned to work a FOX cable game for the first time: a Thursday night affair between the Yankees and Orioles with starting pitchers Roger Clemens and Mike Mussina. When I asked my bosses at MSG weeks before if I could miss the New York Rangers game in Ottawa that night to work the baseball telecast, I had no idea it would turn out to be Wayne Gretzky's last career game in Canada (the "Great One" announced his retirement earlier that week) and second to last game of his career. I was as nervous during the Yankees–Orioles telecast as any game I had ever worked up until that point. McCarver had already called 10 (of his record 24) World Series on television. I had the feeling throughout the game that I had to be on my toes even more so than usual in order to be ready for anything that McCarver would throw at me. I quickly learned that he was one of the best ever at "first guessing"—predicting what would take place before it happened. I went on to work around 25 more games with McCarver over the next decade and a half and enjoyed each and every second of them. It was my honor and pleasure to attend the ceremony in Cooperstown when he received the Ford C. Frick Award during Hall of Fame Weekend in 2012. After McCarver passed away in February of 2023, he was universally lauded as the greatest color analyst in the history of the sport. I couldn't agree more.

During the 2001 season, I worked six Mets radio broadcasts (in Philadelphia, Tampa, Baltimore, Chicago, and Atlanta) alongside Gary

Cohen and Ed Coleman when Murphy missed a chunk of games due to medical issues.

In 2005 I was asked to work several Washington Nationals telecasts during their inaugural season, following their move from Montreal. Once again, I was filling in for Proctor, the former Orioles/Washington Bullets play-by-play man who was hired by the Nats but had basketball commitments early in the season. My color analyst was ex-Mets pitcher Ron Darling, who has since enjoyed a fabulous TV career with the Mets and Turner. It was fun working games at RFK Stadium. I had attended and covered (for WTOP Radio) several Washington Redskins games there but had never done an actual broadcast from RFK.

My first experience calling postseason baseball came in October 2001, when FOX assigned me to the first two games of the Astros–Atlanta Braves National League Division Series in Houston alongside analyst Rod Allen. Proctor was scheduled to call the weekend games due to my football duties. I was actually in Atlanta already for Friday meetings with the Falcons and attended Game Three that evening as the Braves completed a sweep.

The FOX cable package ended following the 2001 season, and Ed Goren asked me to join *MLB on FOX* on one of the four Saturday crews, initially working with a rotating set of analysts often borrowed from the home team's broadcast.

More than 99 percent of the events I have worked throughout my career involved calling play-by-play. During both the 2003 and 2004 American League Championship series between the Yankees and Red Sox, I was asked by FOX to handle sideline reports and postgame interviews for Games One, Two, Six, and Seven at Yankee Stadium. Both years the games at Fenway Park fell primarily on weekends when I was away on football assignments. These games were all super-charged, emotional, and among the most thrilling sporting events I've ever attended. I literally had a front-row seat—down the first-base line in between the Yankees dugout and photo box.

On occasion last-minute broadcast assignments wreak havoc with personal events. Prior to receiving word about working the ALCS, we had scheduled (and sent out invitations for) our daughter Amanda's fourth birthday party at 3:00 PM on Wednesday, October 15, 2003. That was the same day as Game Six (if necessary) of the Yankees–Red Sox series. We did not change the date of the party because (a) the series could have ended in four or five games and (b) if it was the only game that night, it would start at 8:00 PM, and I could attend the party then head to the Bronx. The day before, the Chicago Cubs and Florida Marlins met in Game Six of the NLCS at Wrigley Field. Had the Cubs won, they would have advanced to the World Series for the first time since 1945. Thanks in part to Steve Bartman reaching out from the stands and hindering Cubs left fielder Moises Alou from catching the ball, the Marlins forced a Game Seven, which would be played in prime time, moving the Yankees–Red Sox matchup to a 4:00 PM start. Fortunately, the magician whom we had hired for the party (nicknamed "Magic Al") was a big sports fan and agreed to a date change without an additional fee. To Cubs fans, the name "Bartman" meant a huge missed opportunity. To me it meant a birthday party date change. Such is the life of a sportscaster.

I attended the pregame manager meetings with Joe Buck and McCarver prior to Game Seven of the 2003 ALCS. As we exited their respective offices, I mentioned to both Joe Torre and Terry Francona that I would be handling the postgame interviews (in the winning clubhouse) and that I will "see you after the game" just as a heads up. Prior to the ninth inning, with the game tied after the Yankees scored three runs in the bottom of the eighth inning, I left my position and headed to an area in the bowels of the stadium between both clubhouses so that I would be in position to enter the winning clubhouse. I watched the next three innings on a small, black-and-white monitor with a few NYPD officers while listening to Buck, McCarver, and guest analyst Bret Boone in my earpiece. When Aaron Boone (Bret's brother) sent the Yankees into the World Series with his 11th inning home run, I heard the roar of the crowd (and Buck's call in my ear) before I saw it on the monitor due to a brief delay. I immediately turned to my left and sprinted toward the Yankees clubhouse. I was almost run over by team personnel hustling the other way to head through the tunnel and to the field to join the celebration.

Curt Menefee handled the interview with Aaron Boone on the field, as I was getting set for the trophy presentation. I introduced Mrs. Jackie Autry to a national television audience, and she presented the William Harridge Trophy to members of the Yankees ownership group. As Torre stepped onto the podium amidst champagne flying everywhere, he proclaimed to me, "You told me you would see me after the game!"

How in the world he remembered that after one of the most intense games he has ever been involved in, I will never know. Nineteen years later a five-second clip from my interviews on the podium was included in episode four of *The Captain*, the ESPN documentary which chronicled Jeter's life and career.

Following the trophy presentation and clubhouse interviews with Torre, Mariano Rivera, and other Yankee stars, my night was over—or so I thought. It was well after midnight and time for the FOX affiliates around the country to join their late local news. As I removed my earpiece, I noticed New York City mayor Michael Bloomberg standing to my left at the side of the podium. His young aide scurried toward me and whispered, "Would you mind bringing the mayor on next?"

I politely explained that we had already signed off. He then whispered in an even lower tone, "Can you fake it?" I proceeded to interview Bloomberg for the next five minutes—a chat heard by only the two of us—but hopefully I saved the job of his assistant.

The next year in October 2004, it was the Yankees and Red Sox in the ALCS for the second consecutive season. Similar to the previous year, I worked Games One, Two, Six, and Seven at Yankee Stadium. The Yankees won the first three games. After the Sox took Games Four (a Dave Roberts stolen base in the ninth inning helped prevent a Yankees sweep) and Five, I returned for Game Six in the Bronx, following a football weekend. Curt Schilling started the game despite a torn tendon in his right ankle. This game is remembered for both Schilling's bloody sock as well as Alex Rodriguez slapping at pitcher Bronson Arroyo's arm (and knocking the ball loose) as they converged toward first base. A-Rod was called out for interference. The play unfolded right in front of me. I was probably the closest person to the incident aside from the first-base umpire. I interviewed Schilling live on national TV in the hallway outside the visiting clubhouse while the game was still going.

The following night the Red Sox took a 6–0 lead after two innings against Yankees starter Kevin Brown, and the result was never in doubt. I waited in the tunnel behind the Red Sox dugout at Yankee Stadium as Boston wrapped up an unprecedented comeback in Game Seven of the ALCS. It was the first time a Major League Baseball team came back from an 0–3 deficit to win a postseason series. I ran onto the field behind players and coaches as they celebrated, then conducted postgame interviews. After the scene shifted to the clubhouse, my first question on national television to team president Larry Lucchino: "How does it feel to defeat the 'Evil Empire'?" That was the term he had coined earlier to describe the Yankees.

A year later I was asked to handle sideline duties for Game Six of the NLCS in St. Louis after Albert Pujols extended the series with a three-run homer in Houston off closer Brad Lidge in the top of the ninth inning two nights earlier. The Astros defeated the St. Louis Cardinals 5–1 in what turned out to be the final game at the old Busch Stadium. Lyons handled the trophy presentation, while I interviewed Tony La Russa, the losing manager. These situations are always uncomfortable, but La Russa handled it with a lot of class.

During the 2006 regular season, I was assigned to work a Marlins game in South Florida alongside Lou Piniella, the longtime Yankees fixture who managed the Cincinnati Reds to the 1990 World Series title. "Sweet Lou" was in between managerial stints with the Tampa Bay Devil Rays and Chicago Cubs. It was a thrill working with Piniella, who was an integral member of the Yankees during my childhood. We learned shortly before the game that Piniella did not know how to keep score! Someone on our production crew came up with a great idea. We asked one of the managers for a blank, oversized lineup card—like the ones hanging on the dugout wall. Lou filled out the card as if he was managing the game. He made adjustments on the card when a pinch hitter or relief pitcher entered the game and marked which player made the last out of each inning. During an on-camera segment early in the game, Piniella held up the lineup card, and we shared a laugh about the fact that he never learned to keep score.

I was back in the Yankees clubhouse after they eliminated the Angels in Game Six of the 2009 ALCS. As I turned to my right to interview pitcher CC Sabathia, I sensed a figure standing inches to my left. Mayor Bloomberg was on the scene again. This time he walked onto the podium in anticipation of being interviewed. Producer Pete Macheska screamed into my earpiece, "Do not turn to your left. Don't ask the mayor a question!"

Election Day was just around the corner, and according to FCC regulations, had I spoken with Bloomberg, FOX would have had to grant his opponent equal time. The mayor stood there stoically—live on national television, though probably embarrassed—while I ignored him as if he was invisible. The next day, Bloomberg's staff threatened to revoke the network's parking privileges for all of their production vehicles on the streets around Yankee Stadium. The mayor's office quickly relented when reminded about the equal-time rules. All was forgiven.

Among the Yankees I interviewed before and after Bloomberg's "appearance" on the podium was manager Joe Girardi, whom I had worked FOX games with in 2007 in between his stints as skipper with the Marlins and Yankees. Girardi joined me again (along with A.J. Pierzynski) during the 2019 ALCS between the Astros and Rays.

Early in the 2010 regular season on April 17, McCarver and I were assigned to a late afternoon Mets–Cardinals game at the new Busch Stadium. Little did we know when Jaime Garcia threw the first pitch of the game to Jose Reyes that the game would not end for six hours, 53 minutes. It was scoreless for the first 18 innings. The Mets scored in the top of the 19th to take a 1–0 lead. When Yadier Molina singled in Pujols in the bottom half of the inning, I proclaimed, "The Cardinals have tied the game at one."

McCarver had the perfect response: "Of course they did!"

The Mets finally won the game 2–1 in 20 innings. I never left the booth for a trip to the men's room; perhaps that will be my claim to fame. There was a restroom nearby, and I could have gone; during baseball games the commercial breaks are usually between 90 seconds and two minutes. I never expected the game to take nearly seven hours. Once a game goes past 12 or 13 innings (or into the third overtime during the hockey playoffs), my philosophy is why not be a part of history. I root for these rare games to go as long as possible. Twelve years earlier (on July 30, 1998), I called a 17-inning game between the Mariners and Indians at the Kingdome in Seattle, which took five hours, 23 minutes. A fellow by the name of Rico Rossy entered the game in the eighth inning for the Mariners. He stepped up to the plate with the bases loaded in the 14th, 16th, and 17th innings…and did not drive in a single run!

In May of 2010, I was on the call for one of the most bizarre moments I've witnessed during my career when Kendrys Morales of the Angels broke his leg as he jumped onto home plate while celebrating his walk-off grand slam.

My jigsaw puzzle of a schedule occasionally requires me to ask off an assignment due to a conflict—usually around playoff time in one of the sports since the schedule is not set in advance. I was assigned to call a Mariners–Chicago White Sox game in Seattle on April 21, 2012. The NHL playoff schedule was released about two weeks earlier, and the New York Rangers were scheduled to play Game Five of their series with the Ottawa Senators on the same day. FOX kindly replaced me on the baseball telecast. As I was setting up in my Madison Square Garden booth, the baseball game happened to be on the TV monitor in front of me. I noticed on a graphic that after eight innings the Mariners did not have a hit. Wouldn't you know it? Philip Humber pitched a perfect game—only the 21st in the history of Major League Baseball, and I was scheduled to be there. Instead, Dave Sims had the honor of making the call. I have never witnessed a perfect game or no-hitter in person as either a fan or in a working capacity. I came close twice in the two years prior to the Humber perfecto: Boston's Daisuke Matsuzaka pitched seven-and-two-third innings of no-hit ball in a game I called on

May 22, 2010, in Philadelphia, and Anthony Swarzak of the Minnesota Twins went seven-and-one-third innings without allowing a hit in an emergency start on May 28, 2011, against the Angels. Years earlier, my friend Rich Bianchi offered me a ticket to the Yankees–Mariners game on May 14, 1996. I turned him down due to a prior commitment, and Gooden pitched a no-hitter! Bianchi and I met when we both lived in the D.C. area. We often had lunch together and loved the spinach and artichoke dip at Houston's Restaurant. He always joked that it was so good that we would write about it someday. Well, Bianchi, here's the mention in print.

I was assigned to call four playoff series between 2015 and 2019: Toronto Blue Jays–Rangers in 2015, Dodgers–Nationals in 2016, Milwaukee Brewers–Colorado Rockies in 2018, and Astros–Rays in 2019.

The decisive Game Five of the 2015 Toronto–Texas series is one of the events from my career that I'm asked about most frequently. It featured the Jose Bautista home run (and subsequent bat flip) during a wild, 53-minute bottom of the seventh inning. The atmosphere in Rogers Centre during the latter innings was as tense as I can recall in any game that I've ever been a part of.

One of my favorite aspects of calling baseball games has been visiting so many historic ballparks. The two oldest stadiums in all of sports—Fenway Park and Wrigley Field—are among my favorites. It always feels so magical walking into the same parks where legends of the sport have been playing since early in the 20$^{th}$ century. I enjoyed working games in the previous Yankee Stadium and Shea Stadium, where I attended many games as a kid. I called games at Tiger Stadium, Veterans Stadium, Milwaukee County Stadium, Three Rivers Stadium, Riverfront Stadium, Busch Stadium, Candlestick Park, Jack Murphy Stadium, the Metrodome, the Kingdome, the Astrodome, and many others before they were replaced by new venues.

Yankees–Red Sox matchups are always special, no matter the locale. Aside from working as a sideline reporter at the 2003 and 2004 American League Championship Series, I called several of their matchups through the years in both cities. In 2013 I worked a Saturday game during the final Yankees series in Boston after Rivera, the legendary closer, had announced his retirement. I was having dinner with Barbara and statistician Ben Bouma at Abe and Louie's Steakhouse. Then, all of a sudden, a standing ovation started at the front of the restaurant and continued throughout. Rivera had walked in with his family and was immediately noticed by all of the diners—Yankees and Red Sox fans alike.

Through the years, some of the biggest names in the history of the sport spent time with us in the broadcast booth. I was calling a game in Minneapolis in the early 2000s with Hall of Famer Paul Molitor when another Hall of Famer—Harmon Killebrew—came into our booth for a brief interview. Both Molitor and our statistician, Marty Aronoff, had idolized Killebrew during their childhoods and were so excited to be in his presence. On another occasion Mr. Cub, Ernie Banks, brought a handwritten note to our booth thanking us for mentioning him during that day's telecast. Icons Yogi Berra and Joe Garagiola—childhood friends who grew up in "The Hill" neighborhood in St. Louis—once joined our telecast for an inning during a game at Busch Stadium. Al Kaline in Detroit, Tommy Lasorda in Los Angeles, and Ralph Kiner and Paul O'Neill in New York all did the same. Bob Brenly proudly brought the World Series trophy into our booth during an Arizona Cardinals–New York Giants NFL game at Sun Devil Stadium one week after his Diamondbacks defeated the Yankees in Game Seven of the World Series. Not sure the viewers in New York enjoyed that. Phillies slugger Ryan Howard joined us for a segment during an Eagles game at Lincoln Financial Field in Philadelphia and then was driven via golf cart across the parking lot to Citizens Bank Park for a Phillies playoff game later that day.

And then there was the time in 2017 when I was working a Yankees–Red Sox game at Fenway, which went 16 innings. Alex Rodriguez was in the FOX studio in Los Angeles working as an analyst. During the latter innings, the producer alerted me to throw to LA for a "Game Break." The show's host, however, had exited the studio for a brief moment. "Now for a game break, to Los Angeles we go...*Alex Rodriguez*." It was probably the first (and maybe only) time in his career A-Rod had to narrate a highlights package solo. He handled it as smoothly as an easy ground ball to the left side of the infield.

During the 2016 baseball season, I had the good fortune to spend a few minutes with the legendary Vin Scully prior to a game at Dodger Stadium that I worked for FOX. It was Scully's 67th and final season in the Dodgers booth, and I made an appointment with a member of his crew to have a photo taken with the greatest baseball broadcaster in the history of the sport. This was common practice throughout the season. Visiting players, managers, coaches, broadcasters, and other media members were allotted a few moments with Scully upon request. Hours before the game, I entered the booth, and Scully gave me a warm greeting as if we were long lost friends. Although I had been in his presence on many occasions in various media rooms around the major leagues, we had never officially met.

I assume he watched some of my broadcasts the prior October when I called the National League Division Series between the Dodgers and Nationals; he did not travel to Washington for the away games. Scully's colleagues wanted the numerous photos he took on a daily basis to look professional, so cell phone cameras were not permitted. A gentleman in the booth took the photo with a professional camera and emailed it to me a short time later. I had watched a recent interview Scully had done along with long-time Los Angeles Kings broadcaster and Hall of Famer Bob Miller, during which they discussed Scully attending New York Rangers games while growing up in New York. I mentioned to him that I am the Rangers radio broadcaster and asked what he remembered about his Blueshirts fandom. Without missing a beat, in his iconic voice, he told me, "I used to get into Madison Square Garden with my school ID card...I watched Davey Kerr... and Bryan Hextall...and Lynn Patrick." He had no idea I would ask him about the Rangers and may not have thought of those names for decades upon decades. What a memory he had! It was a magical moment.

I had been approached earlier by Dodgers management about potential interest in a play-by-play position with the club upon Scully's retirement. It was one of the most flattering propositions I have ever received. I considered it for a few weeks but ultimately decided to stick with the status quo due to my various gigs with FOX, MSG, and NBC at the time as well as family considerations.

In March of 2023, I called two quarterfinal matchups at the World Baseball Classic in Miami with Hall of Famer John Smoltz. The first was televised on cable channel FS1, and the second one was on FOX. Both games were instant classics. Puerto Rico scored four runs in the top of the first inning before Mexico came all the way back to win 5–4 to advance to the semis. The next night, the United States defeated Venezuela 9–7 in dramatic fashion—on a Trea Turner grand slam in the top of the eighth inning. Team USA had led 3–0 and 5–2 before Venezuela took a 7–5 advantage in the bottom of the seventh. The atmosphere (and tension) in the ballpark reminded me of Game Five of the Blue Jays–Rangers ALDS in 2015.

# 8

# MOVE OVER,
# BO AND DEION

D ating back to my high school years calling games in myriad sports for Cox Cable of Great Neck, Long Island, I have always enjoyed the variety. So many terrific play-by-play broadcasters—including many Hall of Famers—only called one sport. Others have been lucky enough to work two or three different sports throughout their careers. I began my NHL broadcasting career (on a full-time basis) in October 1992. I called my first NFL game in September 1994. After working a select number of Major League Baseball games from 1994 through 1996, I started calling games on a regular basis in 1997. My first NBA broadcasts were on a fill-in basis with the Washington Bullets on Home Team Sports in 1994. I called college basketball on and off for two decades on various networks and, since the 2008–09 season (with the exception of 2011–12, 2012–13, and 2013–14), I have called approximately 20 New York Knicks games per season on MSG Networks.

I am proud to say that I have been the only play-by-play broadcaster to call all four major North American sports on a full-time basis in the 21$^{st}$ century. There are a handful of other broadcasters who have called play-by-play in the NHL, NFL, NBA, and MLB at some point during their careers, though not necessarily in the same calendar year. Two of them share my last name. My father, Marv, was the longtime voice of the Knicks and New York Rangers; the lead play-by-play announcer for the NBA on both NBC and Turner; called NFL games for four decades (New York Giants radio, national games on NBC and CBS, as well as *Monday Night Football* on Westwood One); and also called select baseball games as a fill-in for NBC in the late 1970s. His youngest brother Steve (my uncle) called NBA games for four different teams (New Jersey Nets, Golden State Warriors, New Orleans

Hornets, Phoenix Suns); NHL games for the New York Islanders and New Jersey Devils and filled in on Rangers radio broadcasts as well; New York Mets radio and TV; and New York Jets radio.

Two pioneers in sports play-by-play broadcasting, Marty Glickman and Bob Wolff, worked games in all four sports during their illustrious careers. Glickman was a track and football standout at James Madison High School in Brooklyn before heading to Syracuse University. He qualified as a sprinter for the U.S. team at the 1936 Summer Olympics in Berlin, Germany. He was scheduled to compete but was replaced (along with Sam Stoller, who like Glickman was Jewish) on the 4x100 relay team by Ralph Metcalfe and Jesse Owens. It was thought that Glickman and Stoller were replaced to avoid embarrassing Adolf Hitler, the chancellor of Germany. Glickman became the longtime voice of the Knicks and Giants (and later the Jets). He also did some hockey (Rangers) and baseball broadcasts. My father initially met Glickman while working as a Knicks ballboy in the late 1950s and kept statistics for Glickman at high school football games. Marv called his first Knicks game in Boston on January 27, 1963, when Glickman could not travel back from a track event in Europe due to a snowstorm. Richie Guerin, who would become Marv's broadcast partner two decades later, led the Knicks with 20 points. I only met Glickman on a few occasions but will never forget the sight of one of the greatest sportscasters in history attending my wedding in August 1996—just four days before his 79th birthday.

Wolff called two of the most iconic events in sports history—Don Larsen's perfect game during the 1956 World Series and the 1958 NFL Championship Game between the Giants and Baltimore Colts—and is a member of both the Baseball and Basketball Halls of Fame. Aside from his national work in both baseball and football, he was the longtime voice of the Knicks and Rangers. I had the pleasure of meeting Wolff on several occasions at Madison Square Garden. He was kind enough to ask me for an anecdote that he included in his 2011 memoir, *Bob Wolff's Complete Guide to Sportscasting*. That was quite an honor.

Like Wolff, Dick Stockton has called a number of memorable moments and events, including the Carlton Fisk home run during the 1975 World Series and nine NBA Finals on CBS. He was a mainstay on NFL telecasts on both CBS and FOX for more than four decades and also called a few NHL games on FOX during the mid-1990s. He attended Syracuse at the same time as my father. They remained friends, and I've been told that Stockton once played the piano at my parents' Manhattan apartment while I was listening from my nearby crib. We became colleagues at FOX from 1994 until his retirement in 2021.

Spencer Ross—another student of Glickman—may hold the record as the voice of the most New York sports teams. He worked on a full-time basis for the New York Yankees, Jets, Devils, and Nets while also serving as a part-time play-by-play broadcaster for the Rangers, Islanders, Knicks, and Giants. Sean McDonough, Ted Robinson, and Bob Wischusen—all terrific broadcasters—have called games in all four major league sports as well. My apologies to any other four-sport, play-by-play callers whom I inadvertently left out.

Here are a few interesting tidbits about legendary broadcasters that you may not know:

Monty Hall, the longtime host of *Let's Make a Deal,* was once the voice of the New York Rangers. Jack Buck was one of the original voices of the St. Louis Blues. Pro Football Hall of Famer Dan Dierdorf also called Blues games during the 1980s. Mike "Doc" Emrick called select NFL games for CBS during the early 1990s, including Brett Favre's first game with the Green Bay Packers (in which his first NFL pass completion was to himself), as well as a Pittsburgh Pirates game (his favorite team since childhood) with Bob Costas on MLB Network in 2016.

Uncle Al was a longtime NBA and NHL voice. Steve and Al both worked national boxing telecasts for many years—Al on USA Network, Steve on Showtime. Steve was inducted into the International Boxing Hall of Fame in 2018. Al was a goalie at Ohio University and was once invited to a Rangers training camp. He also called the Stanley Cup Final for several years in the

1980s on USA. Steve was the only Albert to call World Hockey Association games (in the early 1970s for the Cleveland Crusaders).

I am often asked by fans I run into at arenas, stadiums, airports, and restaurants about my "brothers" Marv, Steve, and Al. My uncles and dad get a kick out of that; it makes them feel younger. I guess some people don't realize that I am between 18 and 27 years their junior and part of the next generation. I have been called "Steve" countless times while walking through Madison Square Garden and various airports around the country. Sal Messina worked with all four of us and somehow he managed to keep all of our names straight!

During my three decades at FOX, I have been fortunate to work with some of the best in the business. My full-time football producer/director tandems have included: producers Bill Brown, Pete Macheska, Keith Pelley, Rich Russo, P.T. Navarro, Barry Landis, and Fran Morison and directors Peter Bleckner, Michael Frank, Bryan Lilley, Scott Katz, and Jeremy Green. I have also worked with producers Bob Stenner and Richie Zynotz and directors Sandy Grossman and Artie Kempner, who have all worked Super Bowls, as well as Ray Smaltz, Larry Lancaster, Eric Mandia, Chuck McDonald, and Bo Garrett. I have worked FOX baseball with Macheska, Michael Weisman, Jeff Gowen, Carol Langley, Eric Billigmeier, Lancaster, Aaron Stojkov, John Moore, Jim Lynch, and Matt Gangl on a regular basis, along with Bill Webb, one of the greatest directors in the history of sports television. John Filippelli, who has run the award-winning YES Network in New York for the last two decades, was one of my *NHL on FOX* producers as well. I enjoyed working with Tom McNeeley, David Gibson, and Derek Manning during NBC and FOX boxing shows. Many of the producers and directors that I've worked with have been known to imitate me via my headset during broadcasts—in the fake announcer voice that Sydney asked me not to use at her Bat Mitzvah.

The Knicks and Rangers production crews on MSG Networks deliver network-quality broadcasts. Howie "The Electronic Wizard" Singer has been an integral part of the Knicks team for 40 seasons, including the last two decades as director. He also works national NBA telecasts for TNT. I have known producer Spencer Julien since he was three years old. His family lived around the corner from us in Sands Point, New York, and he used to spend countless hours playing street hockey in our driveway. Chris Ebert and Larry Roth do a terrific job producing and directing Rangers hockey; their longtime truckmates Steve Napolitani, who became the Islanders TV producer in 2020, and Brian Gallagher are among the best in the business in their roles as well. The brother/sister tandem of Kevin and Paula McHale and directors Bobby Lewis and John Giannone have done outstanding behind-the-scenes work on Knicks and Rangers telecasts for many, many years. Similar to my experiences on weekends with my FOX football crews, I've spent so much time with the Rangers and Knicks crews on the road that they have become like family. Giannone was a terrific sportswriter with the *New York Post* and *Daily News* before transitioning to the broadcast side— first with CNN and then MSG. He is one of the best in the business. During certain times of the year, I probably have more meals with my close friends/ colleagues Dave Maloney and (Rangers MSG host/reporter) Giannone than with my actual family.

New York sports fans are very lucky to be able to enjoy the work of so many Hall of Fame caliber broadcasters. At Madison Square Garden, Sam Rosen has been the TV voice of the Rangers since 1984. Mike Breen began his career with the Knicks in the early 1990s on the radio side before making the move to television. He has called more NBA Finals nationally than any other broadcaster in NBA history. I am lucky to call them both col- leagues and friends. In September 2013, Breen and Yankees voice Michael Kay spearheaded a dinner in Manhattan with most of the radio and tele- vision play-by-play voices from all of the New York pro teams. It was one of the most enjoyable nights I can remember; the stories flowed for hours. Somehow, we were able to find a date where all could attend. It occurred on a Monday night, the day after the baseball regular season ended and before the start of the NHL and NBA seasons.

Kevin Brown, Joe Whelan, and Paul Hemming, who were hired by Turner for the inaugural 2021–22 NHL season, do a top-notch job. The NBC hockey production staff was an absolute pleasure to work with, and the roster included John McGuinness, Matt Marvin, Josh Freedenberg, Steve Greenberg, Jon Norton, Charlie Dammeyer, Jeff Simon, Billy Matthews, Carlos DeMolina, Lisa Seltzer, Kaare Numme, Tim Nelson, Kaitlin Urka, Jenny Glazer, Rene Hatlelid, Dan Reagan, and countless others.

The support staff—statisticians and spotters—in the booth are vital to a play-by-play broadcaster. Ben Bouma has stood over my left shoulder for NFL games since 1994, NHL telecasts on both NBC and TNT, Major League Baseball games, and six Winter Olympics. It is hard to describe everything that Bouma does during football games. Two hours before kickoff, we head to the field to gather last-minute information, chat with coaches we have relationships with (and usually take a pregame lap around the field). Aside from handling the usual spotter duties (pointing on my chart to personnel entering the game or the player who makes a tackle, recovers a fumble, or delivers a key block), Bouma is very helpful with both the rules and game management situations in all three sports. I feel it is extremely important during the final minutes of a football game to let the viewers know if the team with the ball and the lead can run out the clock. If not, at what point can their opponent potentially get the ball back? (Bouma and I have devised our own chart consisting of time remaining, the down, and timeouts.) We use hand signals that we have developed together during the last three decades. If a stranger entered the booth and watched us, he or she would think we were involved in a pantomime competition. Bouma and I met just after his graduation from Penn State when he worked in the ticket sales department for the Washington Capitals. He then spent several years as the assistant public relations director for the Pittsburgh Pirates. Over the last two decades, he added Mike Tirico, Emrick, Steve Levy, McDonough, Hannah Storm, and Andrea Kremer (among others) to the stable of broadcasters he has worked closely with.

During my years working in Washington, I was introduced to Marty Aronoff—perhaps the best and most well-known sports statistician of all time. During the 1970s and 1980s, Aronoff worked just about every big sporting event on network television with the likes of Warner Wolf and Stockton. We first worked together on college basketball games for Home Team Sports. Because of my background keeping stats, Aronoff joked that I was the only play-by-person whom he would allow to look at his charts to decipher information—as opposed to only relying on note cards he passed along. Aronoff became a good friend and worked as my statistician for FOX Saturday baseball games for close to two decades. We also worked select NFL and NBA games together, and Aronoff made a point to join me for a few Rangers radio broadcasts in Washington, D.C., so that we could say we worked all four sports together. Aronoff might have earned more frequent flyer miles than anyone in the history of sports television. I was once with him at a check-in counter at Lambert Airport in St. Louis. Aronoff knew I would get a kick out of him asking the airline employee how many miles were in his account. The answer was over three million, and that was just on a single airline!

I met Eric Mirlis—known to his friends as "Mirl"—during our time together at New York University. During my sophomore year (his freshman year), he posted a petition on the wall in the lobby of our dorm in an attempt to acquire cable television for the building. It didn't work, but we became friends, and Mirl joined our radio staff at WNYU. Upon graduating in 1991, Mirl was hired by the Islanders to work in their PR department, followed by various positions at the NBA, CBS Sports, and FOX Sports. From 1994 to 2006, Mirl was my primary statistician on NFL telecasts. We have also worked numerous NBA, NHL, and MLB games together, so like Aronoff, he has been on my side for all four sports.

Another close friend and fellow NYU grad and WNYU radio broadcaster, Barry Hochhauser, has also worked with me on all four sports but primarily football. During my early years with FOX, Hochhauser, Bouma, and Mirlis rotated between the two positions (statistician and spotter) each week. They weren't always available due to their other obligations, so having three people for two spots worked out. Hochhauser is a lawyer by trade and has had a front-row seat to just about every Knicks home game since the late 1980s as the team's official scorer. Dave Korus, who has the same role (official scorer) with the Boston Celtics, has been my football statistician since 2007. He spends hours upon hours preparing for each game and shows up every Sunday with volumes of information, including historical nuggets and player career highs and career longs. I have worked countless games in various sports with longtime Knicks/multiple sport statistician Dave Fried, Dennis D'Agostino (formerly a key member of the PR departments of both the Mets and Knicks), and John Labombarda (of the Elias Sports Bureau). They are all tremendous assets to any broadcast they work. Dave Brooks, a good friend who works in the world of finance (and the captain of the NYU basketball team in the mid-1980s), has filled in as a football spotter and hockey statistician on numerous occasions. I always enjoy working hockey games with Eric Hornick, Emmett McGuire, and Bob Fitzgerald. I also worked several football games with "Mr. Stats" Elliott Kalb. They are all invaluable. My brother Brian, sister Denise, and brother-in-law Rich (and even Barbara on a few occasions) followed in my footsteps and handled stats in the Rangers radio booth during my early years at MSG.

During the 2005 hockey lockout, I was hired by Westwood One Radio's Howie Deneroff to work as the sideline reporter for a few *Monday Night Football* games. My father called the games alongside Boomer Esiason. It caused a bit of a dilemma whenever I did a report and tossed it back up to the booth. I wasn't comfortable ending my thoughts with "Dad" or "Marv," so I generally went with "back upstairs" or "back to you guys." Similar to the Rangers broadcast in 1997, it was strange to work on the same broadcast as my father. I had listened to (or watched) thousands of his games through the years at home, in the car, or while handling statistics sitting inches away from him. During the few Westwood One NFL games we worked together, I was still listening to him—but on a headset while preparing my next report.

I was honored to receive the call from Deneroff to work the Stanley Cup Final, as well as several NHL outdoor clashes and All-Star Games on national radio from 2016 through 2020.

As of January 2023, according to Tony Miller and the website of unnecessarysportsresearch.com, I am fourth on the all-time list of play-by-play broadcasters who have worked the most U.S. network telecasts in the four major sports leagues—trailing only Marv Albert, Dick Stockton, and Kevin Harlan—with a total of 1,289 games. My 476 NFL broadcasts rank eighth all time, my 412 NHL games rank fifth, and my 401 MLB games rank 10th.

# 9

# ON THE
# ROAD AGAIN

have so many great memories of trips with my father—both alone and with my entire family—during my childhood. Just after turning nine, I accompanied him to Morgantown, West Virginia, for a college basketball game between the Mountaineers and Notre Dame. Perhaps it was a make-up trip after the chicken pox kept me from attending the NHL All-Star Game in Vancouver a month earlier. He introduced me to Fighting Irish head coach Digger Phelps, whom he knew from Phelps' time as head coach at Fordham University in New York. Phelps invited me to work as a ballboy during the game. I handed the players towels and water cups during timeouts. I wrote him a thank you note, and we became pen pals. I immediately became a huge Notre Dame basketball fan. The Fighting Irish had a great team led by Kelly Tripucka, Orlando Woolridge, and Bill Hanzlik. Over the next several seasons, Phelps invited me to assist when they played annually at Madison Square Garden against opponents such as Fordham and Manhattan. I worked several New York Knicks telecasts with Tripucka decades later and enjoyed letting him know that I had worked his bench as a youngster.

Another family road trip that stands out was a journey to Washington, D.C., where my dad was assigned to call a Georgetown basketball game in the early 1980s. Luckily, my beloved Vancouver Canucks were scheduled to play the Washington Capitals the night before, and we secured tickets to the game. The six of us—me, my parents, and my siblings (ages nine, eight, and eight at the time)—boarded an Amtrak train at Penn Station in Manhattan. Not too long after we departed, it started to snow...and snow...and snow. The trip down the northeast corridor took a lot longer than we expected. Both the Friday hockey game and Saturday college basketball game were postponed. We happened to be staying at the same hotel as the Canucks in the Maryland suburbs. The next morning, as I wandered through the lobby, I happened to run into Canucks coach Roger Neilson. I introduced myself as a huge Canucks fan from New York, and he was kind enough to chat with me for the next 15 minutes. We exchanged letters a couple of times per year. Once I started broadcasting NHL games professionally, I always enjoyed running into Neilson at various arenas around North America. He passed away in 2003 at age 69, but his legacy has carried on with so many of his former players and coaching colleagues still involved in various positions within the NHL.

I have had the good fortune to visit 41 states as well as seven Canadian provinces and cities on three other continents. I've enjoyed calling sporting events at both Wembley Stadium and O2 Arena in London; in Edinburgh, Scotland; Frankfurt and Dusseldorf, Germany; Turin, Italy; Sochi, Russia; Rio de Janeiro, Brazil; and Pyeongchang, South Korea. I've also worked in a behind-the-scenes role at Olympic Games in Seoul, South Korea and Barcelona, Spain. For those keeping score at home, the nine states I have yet to visit: Alaska, Idaho, Iowa, Montana, Nebraska, New Mexico, North Dakota, South Dakota, and Wyoming. I have called four different sports in the span of a week on a few occasions during the month of October. I recall a memorable 19-day stretch in late September/early October 2019 when I worked five different sports…boxing, NFL, MLB playoff games, NHL, and NBA.

Not all trips are as glamorous as others. While many of my road excursions include team charter flights, first-class seats, and five-star hotel suites, things don't always go as planned due to weather issues and airline cancellations. My travel follies have included a six-hour, overnight taxi ride from Buffalo to New Jersey; a seven-hour, overnight car ride from Atlanta to New Orleans; and a battle through a snowstorm in an SUV in the wee morning hours from Allentown, Pennsylvania, to New Jersey. Usually a two-hour trip, that ended up taking six hours (including 45 minutes stuck in a snowbank near Newark Airport).

In October of 2009, I was assigned to a Pittsburgh Steelers–Minnesota Vikings game in Pittsburgh on a Sunday afternoon. FOX also asked me to handle postgame interviews after the clinching game of the American League Championship Series between the New York Yankees and Los Angeles Angels of Anaheim. Game Six was scheduled for a Saturday night in the Bronx, and the Yankees led three games to two. I traveled to the Steel City for Friday practice and meetings at the Steelers facility. My plan was to head back to New York on Saturday morning. Heavy rain was in the forecast for Saturday night in the Bronx. I decided to fly to Philadelphia and then would evaluate whether to continue to New York or turn around and go back to Pittsburgh. When I arrived in Philly, the game was still on, so I continued north (via car). As I was about to cross the George Washington Bridge—around 6:00 PM—the game was postponed and re-scheduled for Sunday night. I stopped off at home for a half hour and then headed back to Pittsburgh (in a car service arranged by FOX). Six hours later (around 1:00 AM), I arrived at the hotel. Following the football game (a shootout between Ben Roethlisberger and Brett Favre), I flew back to New York and went straight to Yankee Stadium. So I went from New Jersey to Pittsburgh to Philadelphia to New Jersey to Pittsburgh to New York...in the span of less than 72 hours.

One of my craziest periods of back-and-forth travel took place during the NHL's Western Conference Final round in 2014. I was assigned (for the first time) to call it on NBC. Wouldn't you know it? The New York Rangers advanced to the third round for only the third time in my 18 seasons calling their games on radio. The Rangers were set to open the Eastern Conference Final in Montreal on the afternoon of Saturday, May 17. Game One of the West Final was scheduled for the afternoon of Sunday, May 18. There was only one problem: the second-round series between the Los Angeles Kings and Anaheim Ducks went to a Game Seven on Friday night, May 16. If the Kings won, the Western Conference Final would begin in Chicago; if the Ducks took Game Seven, the WCF would begin in Anaheim. There would be no way to get from Montreal to Anaheim in time under that scenario, so

Don LaGreca headed to Montreal to call the Rangers–Montreal Canadiens series opener on the radio. I watched the Kings–Ducks game at home. As it turned out, the Kings were victorious, and I was headed for Chicago the next day. I watched on TV as Carey Price was knocked out of the game in a collision with Chris Kreider, changing the complexion of the series. Over the next two weeks, I crisscrossed North America and worked the remaining 12 games in the round (the final five games in the Eastern Conference on radio and all seven in the Western Conference on television):

May 18—Chicago (West Game One)
May 19—Montreal (East Game Two)
May 21—Chicago (West Game Two)
May 22—New York (East Game Three)
May 24—Los Angeles (West Game Three)
May 25—New York (East Game Four)
May 26—Los Angeles (West Game Four)
May 27—Montreal (East Game Five)
May 28—Chicago (West Game Five)
May 29—New York (East Game Six)
May 30—Los Angeles (West Game Six)
June 1—Chicago (West Game Seven)

It was 12 games in 15 days, and there were never consecutive games in the same time zone. I had an early morning flight or redeye almost every day—sometimes both in the same day. There were four overtime games, one which went to a second overtime (including a seven-minute, 56-second stretch without a stoppage, meaning continuous play-by-play). It was exhilarating. I ran on adrenaline and never felt tired. My voice held up thanks to Halls cough drops (my favorite) and gargling a concoction of hot water, baking soda, and salt that was prescribed by a friend, Gwen Korovin, a professional voice specialist who has worked with many world-famous singers. Her dad,

Hesh, was a beloved head counselor during my summers at Kutsher's Sports Academy.

I made sure to take a photo on my cell phone of my hotel room number during this wild stretch. I can't tell you how often I've tried to get into the room number that I was assigned to in the previous city. When checking into a hotel, Barbara and I sometimes associate the room number with athlete's uniform numbers. For example, if we are given room 1056, she will say, "Clyde Frazier/Lawrence Taylor."

Following the Western Conference Final round, I called the Stanley Cup Final (Game One on NBC, Games Two through Five on radio). In all, I was behind the mic for each of the last 17 NHL games played in 2014, a streak which had probably never been accomplished before. The next spring, during the second round of the playoffs, I called 13 games in 14 days, including 11 straight, all seven games of the Rangers–Capitals series, five Tampa Bay Lightning–Canadiens matchups, and one Chicago Blackhawks–Minnesota Wild game. Then, during the Western Conference Final, I called three games in Anaheim for NBC and several games of the Rangers–Lightning series (on both TV and radio).

London is one of my favorite cities, and I have been fortunate to call three NFL games and two Knicks games there. My first trip to Great Britain was in 1997 to call NFL Europe games in Edinburgh, Scotland, and Dusseldorf, Germany, on consecutive weekends. NFL Europe was a terrific training ground for players, coaches, officials, and broadcasters. The most famous alum is Pro Football Hall of Famer Kurt Warner, who led the league in touchdowns and passing yards as a member of the Amsterdam Admirals in 1998. Less than two years later, he was a Super Bowl champion and NFL Most Valuable Player. I first met FOX rules guru Mike Pereira that week. He officiated one of the two games I worked. The FOX execs flew me to London on the Concorde, and the flight took less than four hours! Between games I was assigned to a flat (apartment) in downtown London just a few blocks from Buckingham Palace and spent most of the week sightseeing. I ate lunch—and bought a few T-shirts—at "The Albert," a pub built in 1862.

London is a great walking city. During my subsequent trips, I have taken numerous selfies outside the palace, as well as Parliament and Big Ben, and rode the London Eye. I've visited the Churchill war rooms, Stonehenge, and even the U.S. ambassador's residence in London for NFL cocktail parties. Along with Barbara, Amanda, and Sydney, we took a family photo while crossing the street Beatles-style on Abbey Road, which we used as our holiday card in 2014. It was such a perfect photo that we never sent out cards after that; there's no way we could top it.

I checked the state of Arkansas off my list during a road trip with the Knicks to Memphis, Tennessee, in January 2015. The town of West Memphis, Arkansas, is located 10 miles from downtown Memphis and across the Mississippi River via the Hernando de Soto Bridge. With assistance from the hotel concierge in Memphis, I grabbed a taxi, traveled across the state line, and enjoyed lunch at a casino/dog track in West Memphis before heading back to Memphis to prepare for that night's telecast.

I finally made it to Oklahoma in July 2017 during a trip to Tulsa to cover BIG3 basketball on FOX. I crossed Oregon off my list when I covered the U.S. Olympic Track and Field Trials in Eugene for NBC prior to the 2018 Olympic Games. My trip to—or actually through—states 40 and 41 (Alabama and Mississippi) was not planned. In November of 2018, I was scheduled to fly from Newark to New Orleans in the early afternoon for a Knicks–New Orleans Pelicans game the following evening. The Knicks were on a road trip, and I did not work the previous game, so I was scheduled to travel on a commercial flight. Weather reports indicated snow flurries in the late afternoon. However, the precipitation began much earlier—and harder—than expected, wreaking havoc with the entire flight schedule. After numerous cancellations and delays—and six hours in the airport—I was hoping to at least fly to any city within driving distance of New Orleans. I found a flight to Atlanta, which took off around 9:00 PM, landing just before midnight. During the entire flight, I was online searching for early morning flights from Atlanta to New Orleans. Every flight had been booked solid due to all of the cancellations earlier in the day. My only option, which would guarantee my arrival in New Orleans in time for the game the following night, would be a seven-hour ride in a car service, which Barbara was able to arrange while I was in the air. I slept through most of the drive through Alabama but woke up around 5:00 AM and got out of the car at a rest stop in Mississippi.

Although so much of life on the road is spent in airplanes, taxis, Ubers, and hotels, the ability to sightsee is an added bonus during downtime. I have taken a few tours of the White House and visited the Washington Monument, the Capitol, and Ford's Theater during trips to Washington, D.C., with my family. During trips to Dallas, I have taken a tour of the Texas School Book Depository and stood on the grassy knoll, including a visit on November 21, 2013, the day before the 50th anniversary of the assassination of President Kennedy. I have toured Graceland in Memphis; The Alamo in San Antonio, Texas; Mann's Chinese Theater in Los Angeles; Pearl Harbor in Honolulu; Bourbon Street in New Orleans; the Henry Ford Museum in Dearborn, Michigan; the Arch in St. Louis; the Liberty Bell and Betsy Ross Museum in Philadelphia; the Negro Leagues Museum in Kansas City, Missouri; the Pike Place Fish Market in Seattle; Rock & Roll Hall of Fame in Cleveland; and Country Music Hall of Fame and Museum in Nashville.

You never know who you might wind up next to or near on a commercial flight. Mario Lopez and I were once seatmates on a redeye flight from Los Angeles to New York; we both reclined our seats, fell asleep, and never said one word to each other. I have sat directly in front of Harry Connick Jr. and Hillary Clinton; directly behind Geraldo Rivera, James Carville, Chris Wallace, and Monica Seles; and a few rows away from Al Roker, Glenn Close, Matt Damon, Willie O'Ree, and Lenny Wilkens.

Traveling with a professional sports team is not reality. It's like traveling with the president of the United States. After a game the bus (there are usually two buses for hockey and basketball teams—one for the players, coaches, and trainers and the other for broadcasters and team personnel) drives directly onto the airport tarmac, leading to easy access up portable steps and onto the plane. Once on board there is enough food to feed a small army. Upon landing, it's back on the bus for a short ride to the hotel in the next city. However, there could be a glitch from time to time.

During a Rangers road trip, we landed in Nashville in the middle of the night. Those of us with luggage stored underneath the plane would walk around to the other side of the aircraft to wait for our bags. On this particular night, my luggage was stuck somewhere in the hatch, and it took the baggage handler an extra moment or two to retrieve it. By this time everyone else in our traveling media party had retrieved their luggage and was already on the minibus. By the time I had my luggage in hand, I looked up, and the vehicle started to pull away (following the team bus). Nobody realized that I was missing! Fortunately, my luggage had wheels on the bottom. I started running across the tarmac—for at least 100 yards—dragging my suitcase in one hand and briefcase in the other. Luckily for me, the security gate had not yet opened, and the bus was forced to slow down. I was finally close enough to bang on the back window. Once I was safely on board, my broadcast partner Dave Maloney vowed to never leave me behind again. We still joke about it to this day. Whenever we get on a bus after a flight, Maloney bellows, "My partner is here!"

A few years later, I was scheduled to fly with the Rangers for a Sunday afternoon game in Boston. The charter flight was set for Saturday afternoon from Westchester Airport. Upon arriving at the private terminal, we all received word that the team plane had suffered a bird strike during the short flight from its hangar in Pennsylvania. The pilots were fine, but the airplane would be out of service for a few weeks. I assumed the team travel coordinator, Jason Vogel, would arrange a couple of buses for what would be a three-to-four-hour ride (depending on traffic). However, because MSG always does things in a first-class manner (and had other aircraft at their disposal around the metropolitan area), within an hour two private planes (with seating for 10) and two helicopters (six seats apiece) arrived on the tarmac. When I saw that I was going to be on the helicopter with Henrik Lundqvist (as well as forward Artem Anisimov, defenseman Matt Gilroy, the team's internet writer Jim Cerny), I figured we would be safe.

I had never been on a helicopter. I have to admit I was a little nervous during the takeoff, which goes straight up, but the ride was smooth, and we landed after a little more than an hour on a beautiful, sunny day in Boston with not a cloud in the sky. That's just one example of how well Madison Square Garden CEO James Dolan treats his teams. The Rangers and Knicks always stay in five-star hotels, share a beautiful, state-of-the-art practice facility, and are provided with every resource they need in order to perform on the court and ice. This carries over to the team broadcasters as well. I have enjoyed each and every minute of the 28 years I have worked for MSG Networks. During any interactions I've had with Mr. Dolan (usually in the bowels of the Garden before or after a game), he has always been very kind and complimentary of my work.

In April of 2013, the Rangers played a Friday night game in Buffalo, and I was assigned to a FOX baseball game at Citi Field at 1:00 PM the following afternoon. The team was scheduled to charter back to Westchester, New York, after the game, and I assumed there wouldn't be any snow-related issues in Buffalo during the month of April. As we assembled on the media bus outside KeyBank Center following the game, I started to hear murmuring about a potential issue with the flight. It turned out there were heavy winds somewhere on the flight pattern between Buffalo and Westchester, and the pilots thought it would be prudent to wait until the next morning to fly home. I went into scramble mode. It was 11:00 PM, and I had to be in Queens around 10:00 AM for manager meetings prior to the New York Mets game. I went with the entire Rangers traveling party back to the team hotel. It was too late to rent a car; all of the agencies in Buffalo had closed. I attempted to arrange a car service. No luck. I was finally able to hail a taxicab. It wasn't exactly in great shape; the car was a bit rickety. But the driver could not have been nicer and was pretty amenable to the long distance once we agreed on the price. I slept on and off during the six-hour ride from Buffalo to northern New Jersey. We had to stop at an ATM close to my house so I could pay the driver, and Barbara had a hot coffee waiting for him when we pulled into my driveway around 6:00 AM.

Unfortunately, it was not my first trip home via car from Buffalo. In December 2007, I called a New York Giants–Buffalo Bills game with Daryl Johnston and Tony Siragusa. Most of the game was played in a hailstorm. Giants running back Ahmad Bradshaw scored on an 88-yard touchdown run, one of the signature plays of the season for Big Blue, whose season culminated with a Super Bowl XLII victory in Glendale, Arizona, less than two months later. The elements proved to be tough—even for Goose, who came up to our booth for the second half. It was the only time during our eight seasons together that he left the field. When the game ended, our crew headed to the airport in Buffalo—only to learn that every flight had been canceled. Instead of staying overnight in Buffalo, those of us who lived in the New York metropolitan area decided to pile into two cars and drive home. The storm had actually slowed down, and it was a pleasant, easy drive. We all stopped at McDonald's along the way. Goose's car arrived there first. He purchased the biggest order of burgers and fries I have ever seen for our group of eight and then had that spread all over the table when I walked in.

In late December 2010, I called a St. Louis Rams–San Francisco 49ers game in St. Louis. Beginning on Saturday night, we heard reports about a big snowstorm developing in the northeast. When the game ended at 3:00 PM on Sunday, our flights had still not been canceled…but they were by the time we arrived at the airport a half hour later. I went into scramble mode once again. I was scheduled to work a Rangers game at MSG the next evening and didn't want to be stuck in the Midwest for a few days. Somehow, I managed to switch to a flight from St. Louis to Detroit, then connect to Allentown, which under normal circumstances would be about a two-hour drive to my house. During the approach to Allentown, I could see the snow was coming down pretty hard. The pilot announced that our flight was the last that would land in the northeast as all of the other airports had already shut down. While I was in the air, Barbara—once again assisting on the ground—managed to switch the car service that was scheduled to pick me up at Newark Airport to Allentown and requested an SUV. I got into the vehicle around 11:00 PM. The first hour of the ride wasn't bad. Once we crossed into New Jersey, I could sense trouble. Now it was a full-fledged snowstorm. Around Newark Airport, we wound up stuck in a snow ditch for about 45 minutes. Somehow, we made it out…and pulled into my driveway around 4:00 AM. The rest of my crew was stuck in St. Louis until Tuesday evening. Blues president John Davidson set them up in a suite at a game on Sunday night while I was flying home. Our director, Mike Frank, did not believe that I actually made it back to New Jersey. I sent him a photo the next morning of myself standing in the snow in my driveway while holding up a newspaper and pointing to the date. By the way…it was a clear day with no precipitation by the afternoon, and I made it to MSG with no problem.

Two years later in 2012, Moose, Goose, and I were in Chicago for a Bears telecast. During our Saturday night production meeting, we started receiving notifications about flight cancellations on Sunday due to a pending storm (Hurricane Sandy). Fortunately, Goose had friends in high places and was able to arrange a private jet from Gary, Indiana, to Morristown, New Jersey, following the game on Sunday for six of us who lived in the northeast. If not, we would have been stuck in Chicago for a few days. Thanks to Goose's good friend and business partner, Dirk Vander Sterre, we all made it home on Sunday night.

Occasionally, the best-laid plans can affect non-work-related trips as well. In August of 2021, I was scheduled to fly with my family to move Sydney into her University of Wisconsin dorm the next day for her freshman year. Three days before our trip, Barbara and I began to hear reports about a potential hurricane heading our way. We looked into moving our flight up to the previous day instead. We finally decided to drive all the way from New Jersey to Madison, Wisconsin, which is more than 900 miles. I looked into renting an SUV, but availability was scarce for a one-way trip. There was no way I was going to drive home as well. It turned out it was the most cost-effective to drive our own vehicle and then ship it home from Madison (with a big assist to good friend and former sideline producer Nick Gagliano). Once the plan was in place, it alleviated Barbara and Sydney's fears about not arriving on time due to weather and/or flight issues. We somehow fit everything into the car, and the four of us headed out early Sunday morning on our family adventure. We drove west across Route 80 through New Jersey and Pennsylvania, hitting a few rest stops along the way. In the early evening, we stopped for a quick, surprise visit in the Cleveland suburbs with my then-98-year-old grandmother Julie.

We continued for a few more hours and finally checked into a hotel after midnight in South Bend, Indiana. We had driven 10 hours (not including our stops)—and were only four hours from Madison. After sleeping for six hours, we continued our journey—but not before taking family photos in front of the University of Notre Dame's golden dome, just a few miles from our hotel. We headed west, then north past Chicago's O'Hare Airport and arrived in Madison around 1:00 PM—around the same time we would have had we flown. Yes, I checked if our original flight had taken off. Of course it did, and it landed on time. But we will always remember the 14 hours we spent in the car. It was great family time and something we will probably never do again. Over the next few days, while setting up Sydney's room, we learned that a number of other families had done the same thing upon hearing the weather reports. Helpful hint: if you ever ship your car on a flatbed truck, make sure to remove the EZ Pass tag. I did not and wound up with $90 in charges from the journey from Wisconsin back to New Jersey. But that was a small price to pay for less family stress.

During New Year's weekend of 2021–22, I was scheduled to work my first Winter Classic on the television side (for TNT). The Wild hosted the St. Louis Blues at Target Field in Minneapolis on Saturday night of January 1. Most of the previous Winter Classic games were played in the afternoon, but with my luck, this one was scheduled for 7:00 PM local time. FOX did me a favor and assigned me to the closest NFL game the next afternoon—Las Vegas Raiders at Indianapolis Colts (a terrific Week 17 matchup between two teams still mathematically alive for a postseason spot). There was no way I could take a chance and fly from Minneapolis to Indiana on the morning of the football game with a noon kickoff. I had two choices: a 10-hour drive or charter a private plane. I chose the latter. I was nervous for weeks that there would be some type of glitch with my plan. If there were any weather or ice issues and the NHL pushed the game to Sunday, I would have had a huge dilemma—with commitments to two different networks. Although I often feel like I am in two places at once, this would be literally impossible. Fortunately, the game went off without any issues. I made it to the airport around 11:00 PM (with Ben Bouma), and we landed in Indianapolis about 90 minutes later. The pilots then told me that there had been an ice storm earlier in the day along the route and they weren't sure if the weather would take a turn for the better, which it did. Thankfully, they withheld that information until after we arrived in Indianapolis.

Despite the thousands and thousands of hours I have spent in airports and on planes, trains, and automobiles traveling from city to city with various challenges along the way, I have *never* missed a game (knocking on wood right now) due to a travel issue. There have been many nervous moments along the way, especially when traveling on the day of a game. I only missed one game due to illness when I lost my voice prior to a Rangers–Capitals radiocast in 1996. I am so thankful to my tremendous bosses at FOX, MSG, NBC, and TNT over the last three decades who have allowed me to juggle such a unique schedule. On several occasions I worked two games in the same day in different sports: a Knicks game followed by a Rangers game or a Giants or Jets game followed by a Rangers game at night. Former NFL referee Gene Steratore once joked that he would call extra penalties to extend the game so that I would arrive late to MSG. I replied that I would have the last laugh—control of the microphone during the football game. I once pulled off a miracle: broadcasting games that were played in Portland, Oregon, (Knicks–Portland Trail Blazers) and Beijing, China, (Olympic hockey) within hours of each other in February 2022. The secret? Both games were called off monitors (in New York and Connecticut).

In May/June 2022, I called the NHL's Western Conference Final for TNT. Commercial travel between Denver and Edmonton isn't exactly a piece of cake. As we prepared to broadcast Game Four in Edmonton, everyone on the Turner crew made arrangements to either head home (if the Colorado

Avalanche completed a sweep) or fly back to Denver (if the Edmonton Oilers extended the series). There was one hitch: the United States government still required a negative COVID-19 test to fly into the country. I was a bit nervous about the possibility of a false positive, in which case a 10-day quarantine in Canada would be required. Earlier in the season, many of us elected to travel via car to Buffalo following broadcasts in Ontario because a COVID test was no longer required when driving across the border. So in order to get home after the Avs swept the series (despite trailing 4–2 in the third period of Game Four), I took a red-eye from Edmonton to Toronto (along with Keith Jones and Liam McHugh). We then took a car from Pearson Airport to the airport in Buffalo and flew home from there. Had Edmonton won Game Four, the plan was to still fly to Toronto, followed by a three-hour car ride to Detroit, and then a flight to Denver. Wouldn't you know it? The U.S. altered their regulations less than a week later and a negative test to fly into the country was no longer required.

Sometimes I've traveled to be in a film. Through the years many sportscasters have had the opportunity to play themselves (not much of a stretch) in motion pictures. I received my first offer in the summer of 1997 from a New York-area producer named Steve Klein, and it was a local shoot. I was to play the role of a play-by-play man on his film *Game Day*, starring comedian/actor Richard Lewis (of *Curb Your Enthusiasm* fame). Lewis grew up in New Jersey and is a huge sports fan; he and my dad became friends during the 1980s when he sat courtside at several Knicks games. We spent an entire day shooting my scenes at a college gymnasium in upper Manhattan. Lewis played the role of a former college basketball coach who received a chance at redemption with a small, second-rate program. Taking part in a movie shoot for the first time was a lot of fun. A year later, I attended the screening in Manhattan. It was surreal to see and hear myself on the big screen. Unfortunately, *Game Day* went straight to video, but I always smile when a friend tells me they caught part of it on cable.

In September of 2000, I headed to Charlotte, North Carolina, to take part in another movie shoot. This was for *Juwanna Mann* (starring Vivica

A. Fox as well as several NBA players). Miguel A. Nuñez Jr. played the role of a pro basketball star who was kicked out of his league following an outrageous on-court stunt. He then dressed as a female named Juwanna Mann and joined a women's league. I was scheduled to fly from LaGuardia Airport to Charlotte around 4:00 PM on a weekday afternoon with shooting set to begin very early the next morning. I was told to bring three suits as well as several different shirt and tie combinations. I packed the entire wardrobe in my checked luggage. An older and wiser version of myself would have kept one suit and shirt with me in a carry-on bag on the plane just in case. When I arrived at the airport, the weather was perfect, and there were no flight delays.

About a half hour after I had checked my suitcase, the sky suddenly turned dark, and it began to downpour. The monitors listing all of the flights, including mine, started to flicker with delays and cancellations over the next few hours. Somehow, I was able to get the last seat on a flight that left around 10:00 PM. If not, I would have missed the 6:00 AM pick-up from the hotel to the Charlotte Coliseum for filming. Upon arrival at the Charlotte Airport around 11:30 PM, my heart sank. My luggage did not make it onto the new flight. I asked the taxi driver to stop at a 24-hour pharmacy so I could at least buy a toothbrush, toothpaste, and razor before heading to the hotel (another issue because I always use an electric razor).

After sleeping no more than four hours, I headed to the hotel lobby early the next morning wearing the same casual clothes I had traveled in. I explained what had happened when I arrived at the arena. I was directed to a trailer with my name on the front door—right next door to the trailer for my analyst in the film, Kevin Frazier, who was a sportscaster at the time and has gone on to a long career as cohost of *Entertainment Tonight*. Fortunately, I was able to borrow a suit jacket, shirt, and tie from him...and was good to go (while still wearing the underwear, pants, and socks from the previous day). We sat at the courtside press table during the entire shoot, so only the top half of my body could be seen. The filming of my scenes only took a few hours. I headed back to the airport around noon. I happened to check the baggage claim before going through security to fly back to New York. At that exact moment, my bag happened to be riding around the carousel. It had arrived in Charlotte on a flight that morning. I grabbed it, checked it at the counter, and brought it back home without it ever getting unzipped.

I also can be heard (but not seen) on a famous TV show. During the Thanksgiving week episode of *Friends* in November 2001 (featuring guest star Brad Pitt), my voice resonates in the background broadcasting a Green Bay Packers–Detroit Lions game. I worked both Packers–Lions matchups during the 2000 season, so the audio was pulled from one of those telecasts to reflect the game played that day. No, I have not received any residuals. That's too bad, considering the six regular cast members each reportedly receive $20 million per year—just from reruns.

I have worn a chauffeur hat on occasion. Well, not in the literal sense, but I have had some interesting folks in the passenger seat of my car, beginning with John "Hot Rod" Williams during the summer of 1986 with the Staten Island Stallions. I once drove Keith Hernandez from Yankee Stadium to the iconic Elaine's Restaurant in Manhattan and Joe Theismann from our hotel to Gillette Stadium in Foxboro, Massachusetts. I gave Rangers forward Nigel Dawes a lift from the Garden City Hotel to Nassau Coliseum and dropped off NCAA champion basketball coach Gary Williams at Providence Airport. But perhaps the most memorable ride was when I took Regis Philbin to and from our mutual friend Rich Ackerman's birthday dinner.

Ack befriended Philbin at their gym: the Reebok Club on the west side of Manhattan. Philbin was a huge sports fan and was familiar with Ack from hearing his sports updates on WFAN. In 2008, when Ack turned 40, I extended an invitation to Philbin (through a third party) to attend his celebratory dinner in Manhattan. Despite spending most of the evening at a charity event, Philbin was kind enough to show up for dessert and entertain seven of us—all strangers to him aside from Ack—with stories for close to an hour. Philbin even talked about the dinner on his show the following morning. Ten years later, as Ack turned 50, 15 of us treated him to dinner at his favorite restaurant, Peter Luger Steak House, in Brooklyn. To our delight, Philbin agreed to attend. He asked Ack how he would be getting to Brooklyn. He replied that I would be picking him up, and Philbin asked if he could tag along. So, I drove Philbin (and Ack) to Brooklyn and then back to Manhattan after dinner. He was 86 at the time but still as sharp as a tack; the stories he told us were incredible. During the dinner despite only knowing Ack (and to a much lesser extent me), Philbin was a gem...conversing and taking photos with everyone at the table and even wearing one of the "ACK 50" T-shirts that Barbara had ordered for everyone.

The only time I've ever experienced an earthquake was in Kansas City, Missouri, on the Saturday morning of a baseball broadcast in September 2016. While sleeping around 7:00 AM, I was awoken by what felt like my bed slightly shaking. I immediately checked the Internet; it turned out a 5.6 magnitude quake in the Pawnee, Oklahoma, area was felt as far away as Kansas City—more than 300 miles northeast.

In November of 2022, things finally felt back to normal (following the pandemic years) when I embarked on a 12-day trip to Washington, Detroit, Los Angeles, Edmonton, San Francisco, and New Orleans to call six games in three different sports (three NHL, two NFL, and one NBA) in all four time zones. I took flights from nine different airports during this stretch—the six cities named above plus connections in Vancouver, Houston, and Atlanta. A few weeks later, I enjoyed a dream weekend: a Friday night Rangers telecast at MSG, a Knicks/Rangers TV doubleheader at MSG on Saturday, then a Giants–Washington Commanders game at MetLife Stadium on Sunday. This was reminiscent of a December 2019 weekend: a national boxing telecast on FOX in Brooklyn on Saturday night followed by a New York Jets/Rangers twinbill on Sunday—three sports in just over 24 hours.

I definitely have travel pet peeves. I am always among the first to board a flight. I like guaranteeing space for my carry-on bag in the overhead compartment and would rather get settled in my seat and start reading instead of wasting time standing in line. I roll my eyes at rookie travelers in front of me on the TSA PreCheck line who still take off their shoes and belts and remove laptops from their bags. Another waste of time. And never grab the side or headrest of my seat—and use it as a springboard! It's mind-boggling to me that people are oblivious enough to actually do that.

I've been told that I sleep with my eyes partially open. This has unnerved numerous flight attendants, one of whom admonished me for not responding to her question. I woke up a moment later, and she apologized. On a charter flight with the Rangers, defenseman Darius Kasparaitis turned around from his seat (in front of mine) and was a bit spooked when he noticed me asleep with my eyes half opened. I woke up to the sight of Kaspar taking a photo of me on his cell phone.

# 10
## FIVE RINGS

had just turned 12 when the Winter Olympics got underway in Lake Placid in February 1980. I was an avid NHL fan but didn't know much about the collegiate hockey players who were representing the United States. I read about the 10–3 thrashing of Team USA by the Soviet Union in a pre-Olympic match at Madison Square Garden on February 9 and distinctly remember watching the Olympic opener with my dad in our house three days later—a 2–2 tie with Sweden on a last-minute goal scored by Bill Baker of the U.S. squad. In the early evening on Friday, February 22, my mother mentioned to me that she heard the final score on the radio: the United States defeated the Soviet Union in Lake Placid, New York, 4–3. I'm not sure I totally understood the magnitude of the victory. I watched the game—and Al Michaels' "Do You Believe in Miracles" call—on tape delay that night on ABC. After getting home from Hebrew school that Sunday, I was glued to the television in my bedroom in the early afternoon as the Americans won the gold medal with a come-from-behind, 4–2 win against Finland. Many folks—even rabid sports fans—think that Team USA won the gold medal when they defeated the Soviets. However, the Olympic hockey tournament for many years included a round-robin final round. If the United States had lost to Finland, it may not have won a medal of any kind. In fact, during the second period intermission, coach Herb Brooks told his team, "If you lose this game, you'll take it to your grave!"

In 1984 the United States sent an exciting, young team to Sarajevo to try and duplicate the Miracle of 1980. There was a lot of hype around the squad, especially the "Diaper Line," which included 18-year-olds Pat LaFontaine and David A. Jensen and 17-year-old Eddie Olczyk. I was an autograph collector at the time and decided to write a letter to one of the players on the team before they headed to Yugoslavia; I arbitrarily selected Olczyk. I'm not even sure where I sent the letter to; perhaps I found an address for the U.S. Olympic training center in Colorado. Lo and behold, a few weeks later I received an 8 x 10 team photo in the mail with this inscription in the bottom right-hand corner: "To Ken, Thank You For All Your Support! Ed Olczyk #12."

It became a prized possession and hung on the wall of my bedroom for many years. What are the odds that Olczyk and I would call hundreds of Olympic and NHL hockey games together, and that he would become my partner when I called the Stanley Cup Final on television for the first time in 2021? Another miracle perhaps.

I had the tremendous opportunity to work in behind-the-scenes roles for NBC at both the 1988 and 1992 Summer Olympics (in Seoul, South Korea, and Barcelona, Spain). In Seoul I was a researcher/runner at the boxing venue, which turned out to be a hotspot of controversy. (A runner is an intern/gopher who performs various tasks for the production crew.) I arrived in Seoul a few weeks before the start of the Olympics and was assigned a dorm-style room in the Press Village along with a roommate, Sean Kennedy, who was a runner at a different venue. Another of our fellow runners was Dan Abrams, who went on to a long career as a television host and legal commentator. Prior to the start of the Olympics, most of my daily duties took place at the production trailers outside the boxing arena. As the athletes started to arrive, I conducted interviews with some of the boxers and their coaches in order to compile biographical information for the announcers (my father, "The Fight Doctor" Ferdie Pacheco, and sideline reporter Wallace Matthews). There were several memorable incidents during the two-week tournament: a decision that went against American Roy Jones despite his total domination, the disqualification of U.S. boxer Anthony Hembrick after he showed up late to the arena due to a confusing fight schedule, and the throwing of chairs and the attack of an official in the ring followed by a sit-in for more than an hour by a South Korean bantamweight who had been docked two crucial points during his bout. I had a ring-side seat for all of the above. Aside from the craziness, I had the opportunity to watch some world-class boxers, including Jones; Ray Mercer; Riddick Bowe; and my future broadcast partner, Lennox Lewis.

I worked 14-to-16-hour days in Seoul but was thrilled to be at an Olympic Games for the first time. I soaked in the atmosphere around the Olympic Park as often as possible. I even happened to bump into (no pun intended) diver Greg Louganis the day after he struck his head on the springboard during the preliminary rounds in an infamous incident before he went on to win two gold medals. Fortunately, I had my camera with me, and we took a photo together. During some rare down time, I ventured into downtown Seoul and happened to see track and field star Carl Lewis at a sneaker shop and snapped a photo with him as well.

Due to the climate in Seoul, the 1988 Summer Olympics were held later than usual—from September 17 through October 2. The dates caused a bit of an issue with the beginning of my junior year at NYU, where classes started in early September. I devised a plan with the help of chancellor L. Jay Oliva, whom my fellow WNYU broadcasters and I had befriended at Violets basketball games because he hardly missed any home or road contests.

New York University students usually took 16 credits per semester (and needed a minimum of 12 to live in a dorm). Most classes awarded four credits, but others offered just two. Two professors—one in the journalism department (Mitchell Stephens) and a history professor (Jack Peckett) who also worked in the athletic department—allowed me to take their classes, though I would miss the first three weeks. I was required to take some work with me to Korea, though I'm not sure how much of it I actually completed, and upon my return give a class presentation summarizing my time at the Olympics. I also set up an independent study through the journalism department for another four credits and wrote a few papers about my experiences in Seoul. I made up the other four credits during later semesters. Thanks to Chancellor Oliva, it worked out perfectly!

During my years at NYU, Oliva became a close friend and supporter. Prior to my graduation from NYU, Oliva presented me with the Chancellor's Service Award for Leadership based on my work as an administrator with the

NYU hockey club. Following his retirement as the school's president, I was honored to be among a small number of speakers during an event in Oliva's honor at his beloved NYU Skirball Center in 2009, along with the new president, John Sexton, and a few others. Neil Diamond—a former NYU student—serenaded the audience with a rendition of "Sweet Caroline."

Four years later in the summer of 1992, my father asked me to handle the statistics in Barcelona during the basketball competition. Despite the fact that I had already been broadcasting professionally with the Baltimore Skipjacks for two seasons and had just been hired by Home Team Sports to broadcast Washington Capitals games, I couldn't pass up the opportunity. I joked that this would be my last hurrah as a statistician. What better way to complete my duties as a stats guy than keeping track of the numbers while watching the Dream Team from a court-side seat? It was the first time the United States sent a basketball team filled with professionals to the Olympics. As opposed to my long days in Seoul, the schedule in Barcelona was quite easy. I worked all of the games played by the U.S. men's team, the U.S. women's games that were carried by NBC, and a select number of other games. My father, Mike Fratello, Quinn Buckner, and researcher David Kahn, who went on to become the general manager of the Minnesota Timberwolves, and I all rode together to every game from our downtown hotel to the arena in Badalona while being driven by a local named Miguel, who became an honorary member of the crew. We had the pleasure of watching the greatest basketball team ever assembled, featuring Michael Jordan, Larry Bird, Magic Johnson, Charles Barkley, David Robinson, Patrick Ewing, Scottie Pippen, Clyde Drexler, Karl Malone, Chris Mullin, John Stockton, and Christian Laettner, as they won all eight of their games en route to a gold medal. They outscored their opponents by an average of 44 points per game in the process. During an off night in Barcelona, I attended my first (and only) bullfight—along with broadcaster Don Criqui and his son.

I watched the Olympic hockey tournaments in 1988, 1992, 1994, and 1998 with keen interest. In February of 1994, I was calling a women's college basketball game in Charlottesville, Virginia, the day of the gold medal game between Canada and Sweden. I set my VCR to tape the hockey game and made sure to avoid listening to the radio during my two-hour drive home so that I wouldn't accidentally hear the score. When I arrived home, I watched the game, which culminated with Peter Forsberg's iconic shootout-winning goal. The moment quickly became the image on a postage stamp in his home country of Sweden.

NHL players participated in Olympic hockey for the first time in 1998 in Nagano, which allowed Barbara and I to take a vacation to Miami Beach during the league's break in the schedule. I was expecting a similar break in February 2002 when the NHL paused its season so players could take part in the Salt Lake City Olympic Games. I was in New Orleans (the site of that year's Super Bowl) in late January 2002 hosting a College Football All-Star Challenge show that aired on FOX later that week. We taped the show at Zephyrs Stadium, the minor league ballpark located next to the Saints facility in Metairie, Louisiana. After wrapping up the taping, I headed to my rental car in the stadium parking lot for the short drive to the airport. I received an urgent voicemail asking if I would be interested in calling Olympic hockey for NBC. It turns out Mike "Doc" Emrick's dog was diagnosed with cancer, and Doc did not want to leave his wife Joyce home alone for more than two weeks. Doc and Gary Thorne were scheduled to be the two hockey play-by-play callers for men's and women's ice hockey in Salt Lake. Fortunately, Doc and I were represented by the same agency, so the wheels were put in motion with the folks at NBC before the word spread. I was in shock when I learned of the opportunity. I needed permission from the bosses at FOX in order to work for another network—even for only a short span. I am so grateful that David Hill and Ed Goren immediately gave their blessing and I flew home from New Orleans on cloud nine.

I had about a week to learn a multitude of men's and women's hockey rosters before flying to Salt Lake City. I was familiar with all of the NHL players who would be representing their countries, but several of the other men's teams were filled with non-NHLers. I had watched some of the women's games in 1998 but really had to cram to learn about the rules, history, and most of the players who would take part in Salt Lake. Interestingly, a year or two earlier, I played in a charity hockey game at Madison Square Garden along with several members of the gold medal-winning 1998 U.S. women's team, including captain Cammi Granato. I even scored a goal against netminder Sara Tueting, who was between the pipes when the United States defeated Canada to win gold in Nagano, Japan.

I recall watching Super Bowl XXXVI between the New England Patriots and St. Louis Rams (Tom Brady's first title) in my home office with one eye on the television and another on my computer screen while doing my Olympic prep work. Upon arriving in Salt Lake, I received an invitation from NBC Sports president Dick Ebersol's office to attend the Opening Ceremonies as a thank you for coming on board at the last minute. I turned it down because I felt I was still behind in my preparation and didn't want to give up five or six hours the night before my first games the next day: Belarus vs. Ukraine and Austria vs. Latvia. In hindsight, I probably should have gone! I worked 23 games in 12 days along with color analysts Joe Micheletti (men's and women's hockey) and Lisa Brown-Miller (women's hockey), who had played on the 1998 U.S. team. The hockey broadcast crew stayed at a La Quinta Inn on the side of a highway about 15 minutes from downtown Salt Lake. (And you thought the Olympics were glamorous!) It was a short drive from our hotel to the main hockey arena called The E Center. But while I called a few games there, most of the matches on my schedule were played at The Peaks near the BYU campus, so we all made the daily 45-minute van trip to Provo, Utah.

One of the United States women's games we called was against China. As you can imagine, it took some time to learn the pronunciations of the names on the China roster. As Micheletti, Miller, and I watched warmups from our broadcast perch, we were handed a pronunciation guide about 20 minutes before the start of the game. Fortunately, from a broadcast perspective, the U.S. dominated the game, and its opponents barely touched the puck. Hence, I got away with not mentioning too many of the names on the China roster— aside from the goaltender, Guo Hong, nicknamed "The Great Wall," who made several spectacular saves in a 12–1 loss. "The Great Wall" faced 71 shots and received praise from us throughout the game for her performance. Micheletti, Miller, and I called the women's gold medal game between the United States and Canada a week later. That 3–2 Canada victory gave the Canadians a dose of revenge following the United States' triumph in Nagano. We also announced the women's bronze medal game.

Four years later I called 16 men's and women's games in Torino, Italy, while spending countless hours going over notes and pronunciations with Emrick, who returned as the lead Olympic play-by-play voice for the 2006 Games. A.J. Mleczko, who won gold in 1998 and silver in 2002 as a member of the United States women's team, joined me in the booth for the first time in Torino. She is a terrific broadcaster and wonderful person, and we have gone on to work a total of five Winter Olympics (as well as many NHL games) together.

The most memorable moment of the 2010 Olympics in Vancouver actually occurred during a game I wasn't working. After calling 20 men's and women's games (including both bronze medal contests), I attended the men's gold medal game between the United States and Canada. With my media credential, I was able to sit in the broadcast area behind Emrick and Olczyk, who were calling the game. I'll never forget how quiet it was in the arena after Zach Parise tied the game for the United States with 25 seconds remaining in regulation and how loud it was when the building exploded after Sidney Crosby scored the Golden Goal in overtime on Canadian soil.

During one of the women's hockey games I called in Vancouver at the secondary hockey rink on the campus of the University of British Columbia, I smashed one of my fingers in between the concrete blocks Mleczko and I were sitting on in our broadcast booth. I held my hand in a bucket of ice during the remainder of the game, and a doctor drained the blood from underneath my fingernail later that night to alleviate the pain. I was prone to injury again a few years later prior to a New York Rangers game in Philadelphia. After I exited my car in the Wells Fargo Center parking lot on a frigid evening, my lip cracked, and I couldn't stop the bleeding. Fortunately, longtime Rangers medical trainer Jim Ramsay came to the rescue. Outside the team locker room, Rammer applied a paste that did the trick.

I was always intrigued to visit Russia someday and finally received the opportunity in 2014 when I traveled to Sochi for the Winter Olympics. I took an NBC charter flight direct to Sochi. Our hotel was just minutes from the Black Sea and a short walk from the Olympic Park, which housed many of the sporting venues. During my two weeks in Sochi—and especially while inside the park—it felt and looked like Disneyland. We could have been anywhere in the world. The only times I felt like I was in Russia were when we had a few group dinners at a restaurant a few blocks from the hotel and during a three-hour layover at the Moscow Airport during my trip home. The weather was great during most of our time in Sochi. It was as high as 60 degrees some days in February! One day, I even rolled up my jeans and wandered into the Black Sea. Following one of my broadcasts, I walked to the other hockey arena to watch the latter portion of the U.S.–Russia matchup; I arrived just in time to witness the shootout in which T.J. Oshie scored four goals on six attempts. I was at the mic for 18 games in Sochi, including the women's bronze medal game.

As part of my preparation prior to the Sochi Olympics, I spent about 15 minutes with Mats Zuccarello in the locker room following a Rangers practice. He was about to represent Norway in his second Olympic games (he was signed as a free agent by the Blueshirts following an excellent showing at the 2010 Vancouver Olympics). There wasn't much information available about his Norwegian teammates, most of whom did not play in the NHL. "Zuc" graciously looked at my roster sheet and shared anecdotes about most of the players on the squad. I was able to weave the information seamlessly into the broadcasts as if I had covered the team for years.

I was asked by NBC to work track and field, a sport I had never called before, at the 2016 Summer Olympics in Rio de Janeiro, Brazil. I grew up around ball and puck sports, but any time I've been called upon to learn a new sport, I have embraced the challenge. I purchased as many books on track and field as I could find, watched videos of events from previous Olympics, and worked a few meets for NBC prior to the Summer Games, including the Olympic Trials in Eugene, Oregon. It was a bit of a whirlwind studying the various events in both the track and field genres, but it was a lot of fun. Fortunately, I had a tremendous partner in Tim Hutchings, who represented Great Britain at the 1984 Olympic Games.

Less than two years later, I was on the A crew for the 2018 Winter Games in Pyeongchang, South Korea, and called 19 games. Similar to my experience in Sochi, the hockey crew stayed in a very nice hotel. Unfortunately, the NHL did not send its players to Pyeongchang. The United States entry—coached by Tony Granato—consisted of some former NHL pros, minor leaguers, and three college players. The gold medal match was a terrific game won by the "Olympic Athletes from Russia," who had to compete as a team unaffiliated with its home country, against Germany on an overtime goal scored by Kirill Kaprizov, who won the 2020–21 Calder Trophy as NHL Rookie of the Year with the Minnesota Wild. We called the men's bronze medal game—a 6–4 Canada victory over the Czech Republic—as well.

On the women's side, the U.S. and Canada were once again on a collision course to the gold medal game. In a sense the women's tournament benefitted from the NHL players not participating in Pyeongchang because they had a bigger piece of the spotlight. The two North American countries skated for gold in 1998, 2002, 2010, and 2014. Canada won the previous four gold medals in women's Olympic hockey, including in 2006 after Sweden upset the United States in the semifinal round. I called the gold medal game live on NBC (late at night in the Eastern time zone) with Mleczko and Pierre McGuire (who was at ice level between the benches). The tension in the arena was palpable. Canada took a 2–1 lead into the third period and was less than seven minutes from a fifth consecutive gold medal when Monique Lamoureux-Morando tied the game. After a tense, scoreless 20-minute over-time (my heart was beating even harder than during the Brooks interview 27 years earlier), her twin sister Jocelyn Lamoureux-Davidson scored to give the U.S. a 3–2 lead in the sixth round of the shootout. Goaltender Maddie Rooney then stopped Canadian superstar Meghan Agosta. "The United States wins gold in Pyeongchang!" I exclaimed as pandemonium took place on the ice. It is one of my favorite and most memorable calls of my entire career.

Blue gloves and sticks flew in the air, as the American women celebrated. Throughout the game, Mleczko was part of a group text chain with all of her 1998 teammates; they could not have been happier for their 2018 counterparts who duplicated their Olympic gold medal. This game immediately moved toward the top of my list of memorable games I have called throughout my career. Although I am impartial when broadcasting network games, there was definitely a different, emotional feeling while at the mic when my home country won a gold medal. At one point during the celebration, I even sensed my voice cracking a bit.

The 2020 Tokyo Games were pushed back a full year due to the pandemic and took place in the summer of 2021. I was assigned to another new sport for me—volleyball (both beach and indoor). Due to health and safety protocols, the majority of the NBC commentators did not travel overseas; we called the events off monitors from the network's studios in Stamford, Connecticut. Similar to my experiences with horse racing two decades earlier and track and field in 2016, I purchased *Volleyball for Dummies* and several other publications. I arranged a meeting with the longtime volleyball coach at our local high school, Beth Powell, who was a godsend. She educated me on the rules, as well as the strategy and lingo of her sport during our 90-minute cram session. It was much easier to identify the participants during the beach volleyball matches; there were just two per side as opposed to six indoors. The points were usually shorter than during indoor volleyball, and the matches ended much quicker. My analyst, Amy Gant, a former All-American at BYU, was a tremendous resource as well and taught me so much about the sport during our time together. Due to the 13-hour time difference between Tokyo and the eastern time zone in the U.S., we were on a reverse schedule for two weeks. Most of the matches we called were in the middle of the night and/or very early in the morning. Fortunately, the NBC cafeteria was open 24/7; I once found myself eating a cheesesteak at 9:00 AM because I had already been up for 12 hours. During the Tokyo Games, I also called two United States baseball games against Israel and South Korea.

Seven months later I was back in Stamford to call 16 Olympic men's and women's hockey games (including both gold and bronze medal games). It was my sixth consecutive Winter Olympics, though this time I was announcing the games off monitors and not in person. Similar to the previous summer, we called many games late at night or early in the morning due to the time difference between Connecticut and Beijing, China. Calling games off monitors became an even bigger challenge when certain countries' jersey color combinations blended together. For example, Canada wore black uniforms with red numbers and vice versa; it was very tough to see the numbers, but we managed.

An added bonus during the Olympics I called from Stamford in the summer of 2021 and February 2022 was the fact that I saw my daughter Amanda almost every day. She worked overnight hours as a digital producer/editor, so I was able to stop by her work area before and after my games. It was so special to work within a couple hundred feet of each other and share daily meals in the cafeteria. During the Beijing Games, she was often assigned to compile highlight packages of the same hockey games that I was calling.

# 11
## MEMORABLE GAMES

From 1994 to 2006, my good friend since our college days at NYU, Eric Mirlis, was my primary statistician on NFL telecasts. He asked me to pen the foreword for his 2007 book, *Being There*, a compilation of 100 professionals from the world of sports media discussing the best sporting events they ever witnessed firsthand. My top five (in no particular order) at the time were:

- New York Yankees pitcher Ron Guidry's 18-strikeout game against the California Angels on June 17, 1978
- The 1992 Summer Olympics in Barcelona, for which I had a front-row seat as an NBC statistician for all eight games played by the Dream Team
- Game Seven of the 1994 Stanley Cup Final between the New York Rangers and Vancouver Canucks
- Cal Ripken Jr.'s record-breaking 2,131$^{st}$ consecutive game, which occurred at Camden Yards on September 6, 1995
- Game Seven of both the 2003 and 2004 American League Championship Series between the Yankees and Boston Red Sox

For honorable mention, I included Roy Jones getting robbed of a medal at the 1988 Seoul Olympics, the "Jeffrey Maier" Game at Yankee Stadium in October of 1996, and Terrell Owens stomping on the Cowboys star at Texas Stadium in September of 2000.

Three years after Mirl's book was published, I was on hand for Sidney Crosby's golden goal for Canada at the 2010 Winter Olympics in Vancouver. I have attended four Super Bowls, which all deserve merit. I was in the stands for the first three—Super Bowl XXIII (January 22, 1989) at Joe Robbie Stadium won by the San Francisco 49ers against the Cincinnati Bengals, Super Bowl XXXI (January 26, 1997) at the Louisiana Superdome won by the Green Bay Packers against the New England Patriots (Brett Favre running around the field celebrating with his helmet off is forever etched in my memory), and Super Bowl XXXIV (January 30, 2000) at the Georgia Dome won by the St. Louis Rams against the Tennessee Titans. I called Super Bowl XLVI (February 5, 2012) at Lucas Oil Stadium for the international feed. In that game the New York Giants bested Tom Brady and the New England Patriots.

I could certainly include any of the Stanley Cup-clinching games, gold-medal hockey games, and NFL playoff games that I have called on my greatest game list as well. Aside from the thousands of games in a variety of sports that I have worked as part of my regular gigs through the years, there are many other memorable events that I have either worked or attended.

At the age of nine, I witnessed the Stanley Cup being presented for the first time when I accompanied my father on a road trip to Boston, where the Montreal Canadiens completed a four-game sweep against the Boston Bruins on a Jacques Lemaire overtime goal. Just more than a year later—on December 23, 1978—I was in the stands at Nassau Coliseum when the New York Islanders' Bryan Trottier scored five goals in a game against the New York Rangers. I didn't know that Trottier had scored five until I read the newspaper the next day because one of them was originally credited to a teammate, then changed by the official scorers well after the game had ended. Trottier also set an NHL record with six points in one period. I called the game more than 42 years later when Mika Zibanejad tied Trottier's record by becoming the second player in league history with six points in one period.

Through the end of the 2021–22 season, there have been 59,994 regular season games played all time. There were exactly two instances in which one player scored six points in a single period, and I was in the building for both. So was Dave Maloney, who was on the ice for the 9–4 Rangers loss the night Trottier scored five. He also called the Zibanejad six-point period on radio. So was Larry Brooks, who covered both games for the

*New York Post.* We may have been the only three! I attended the game when Mikko Leinonen of the Rangers set an NHL playoff record with six assists in a playoff game against the Philadelphia Flyers in 1982 (matched by Wayne Gretzky five years later). Perhaps six is my lucky number. Aside from attending Trottier's five-goal masterpiece, I have called two other games in which a player scored five goals: Marian Gaborik (for the Minnesota Wild against the Rangers) in 2007 and Zibanejad (at Madison Square Garden against the Washington Capitals) in March 2020—one week prior to the pandemic shutdown.

I attended Game Two of the 1990 Stanley Cup Final (with my brother Brian) between the Bruins and Edmonton Oilers the day after my graduation from NYU. The trip was a present from my parents. Jari Kurri's hat trick sparked the Oilers to a 2–0 series lead.

In March of 2004, I was asked to call the Women's Hockey Frozen Four for CSTV (College Sports Television Network) in Providence, Rhode Island. Minnesota, Harvard, Dartmouth, and St. Lawrence were the participants. I was familiar with several of the players whose games I had called during the 2002 Winter Olympics. My partners were Ellen Weinberg-Hughes (in the booth) and my close friend Dave Starman (rink-side). Weinberg-Hughes was a three-sport star at the University of New Hampshire (and a member of the UNH Athletic Hall of Fame) who played for the United States national hockey team in the early 1990s.

We had first met more a decade earlier after being introduced by a mutual friend. As we settled in for the broadcast, Weinberg-Hughes told me about her three young boys: four-year-old Quinn, two-year-old Jack, and six-month old Luke. Quinn and Jack, of course, have become NHL stars, and Luke was a 2021 first-round pick (fourth overall) by the New Jersey Devils. I kept in touch with Ellen through the years and have followed her sons' careers closely. I have gotten to know each of the boys. They are all polite and well-mannered and clearly have been raised very well by their parents. Ellen, husband Jim, and Luke attended a Detroit Lions–New York Giants game that I was calling in October 2019. I brought them to the field for photos prior to the game.

Luke (then 16) marveled at being so close to Eli Manning as he was warming up. Just more than three years later, during an off day in the Detroit area, I was in the stands watching Luke and the Michigan Wolverines beat Ohio State at Yost Arena.

In 2017 and 2018, I called BIG3 basketball games for FOX in Tulsa and Toronto. It was exciting for all of us to not only meet the league's cofounder, Ice Cube, but also to be included on email chains with him prior to the broadcasts. He even performed a few songs for the crowd between games in Tulsa.

I was on hand for the first game at Giants Stadium (1976), the last game at Baltimore's Memorial Stadium (1991), the first game at Camden Yards (1992), the first game at Montreal's Molson (now Bell) Centre (1996), the last game at Busch Stadium (2005), and the first regular-season game at MetLife Stadium (2009).

It has always been a valuable tune-up to work a team's local preseason television package in order to get reps prior to the regular season. I was hired to work Rams preseason games alongside Kellen Winslow Sr. in 1997. The next season, it was the New York Jets on WPIX Channel 11 with Hall of Famer Joe Namath. From 1998 to 2003, I partnered with Todd Blackledge, Ron Jaworski, and Mike Mayock on Philadelphia Eagles exhibition telecasts. In 2004 I was part of the first-ever crew hired by NFL Network to handle three preseason games with boothmates Dan Fouts and Terrell Davis. Since 2009 I have called Washington Redskins/Commanders preseason games—usually with Joe Theismann.

For several years I was invited as a guest lecturer at the NFL Broadcast Boot Camp held at the NFL Films campus in Mount Laurel, New Jersey. The league would identify 20 current or recently retired players who showed an interest in entering the world of broadcasting to attend week-long sessions. They would learn about all aspects of the business from media executives, producers, directors, play-by-play broadcasters, color analysts, and studio hosts. I would spend one day annually at the camp, speaking first in front of four separate groups of five about what goes into my job as a play-by-play announcer. I would then broadcast one quarter of a game off a monitor with five of the attendees. Among my pupils were Nate Burleson, Tim Hasselbeck, and Dan Orlovsky, who have all gone on to enjoy terrific careers in television, and Kevin O'Connell, who was named head coach of the Minnesota Vikings prior to the 2022 season. I immediately identified that all four would have bright futures following their playing careers.

I first called a boxing card in the early 1990s on radio. My analyst was former NBA head coach and referee (and Baltimore radio personality) Charley Eckman, who was quite a character. I then called the Golden Gloves at MSG in 2010. I was asked to call several BKB (bare-knuckle boxing) events by DirectTV. A few years later, I called several PBC (Premier Boxing Champions) cards for NBC—both in person and off monitors in the Connecticut studio. My color analyst for two of these shows was the great "Sugar" Ray Leonard, including one in Montreal, the same city where he won a gold medal at the 1976 Summer Olympics. I was then asked to call bouts on the *PBC on FOX* series (2018–2019) alongside former heavyweight champion Lennox Lewis and trainer Joe Goossen. We called several championship fights at venues including AT&T Stadium in Dallas, Barclays Center in Brooklyn, and various hotels in Las Vegas. The most memorable was the Manny Pacquaio–Keith Thurman showdown in Vegas in July 2019. Former champions Shawn Porter and Deontay Wilder joined us as guest analysts on some of the shows, and Ray "Boom Boom" Mancini was a regular on the pregame and post-fight shows.

One sport I have never covered is fencing. However, in March 2014, I attended a collegiate fencing tournament. It was the first time I have ever stepped foot on the campus of Ohio State University. I arrived in Columbus, Ohio, with the Rangers on a weekday afternoon and noticed a bunch of folks in the hotel lobby wearing warmup suits representing various colleges and universities. Coincidentally, I ran into my second cousin Michael Aufrichtig, who was wearing a Columbia University fencing jacket. Our grandfathers were brothers, and I had only met my cousin a few times previously. I was aware that he was Columbia's head coach and was on the coaching staff of the

2012 U.S. Olympic team. He was kind enough to invite Maloney and me to attend the matches the next day and spent time with us explaining the intricacies of his sport. I put some of the knowledge to good use when I attended a fencing match with my family at the 2016 Rio Games. Perhaps I will be asked to call the sport in the future.

I called a game between the Las Vegas Raiders and New England Patriots in December 2022, which ended unlike any other sporting event in my lifetime. With the game tied at 24 and seemingly headed for overtime, the Patriots ran one final play from scrimmage (with three seconds remaining in regulation) from their 45 yard-line. Running back Rhamondre Stevenson ran for 23 yards to the Raiders' 32 yard-line and then lateraled the ball to teammate Jakobi Meyers, a wide receiver. Meyers then tried to lateral it to another Patriots player, but it was caught in the air by Chandler Jones of the Raiders, who returned it 48 yards for an improbable game-winning touchdown. After Stevenson flipped the ball back to Meyers, I exclaimed, "the Stanford band is nowhere in sight," a line I had used previously, referring to the famous play in a 1982 game between Stanford and Cal. Seconds later my partner Jonathan Vilma and I were stunned as we watched the play develop.

Vilma screamed, "Oh no! Oh wow!"

I used the terms "unbelievable" and "incredible" followed by "Have you ever seen an ending like that?" This is another example of why sports is the best reality TV.

# 12
## IN UNIFORM

realized at a young age that I was not going to be a professional athlete. However, I have enjoyed several brushes with greatness on the ice, court, and field. I spent countless hours playing basketball and roller hockey on my driveway as a youngster. We had both a 6' hoop, which was great for dunking, and a regulation 10' basket. I always pretended I was playing for the New York Knicks or New York Rangers. I played Little League baseball in Port Washington, Long Island, and once registered for the youth football program but quit during the first session because the helmet was too small and very uncomfortable. (I had an oversized head—even back then.)

I took tennis lessons for many years at the prestigious Port Washington Tennis Academy, where Queens native John McEnroe perfected his craft just a few years prior. I once arrived at my assigned court a few minutes early for my lesson, and Martina Navratilova was running through drills with basketball star Nancy Lieberman. From the ages of eight through 13, I spent most Saturdays at Twin Rinks, our local ice rink. My friends and I would attend a public skating session in the afternoon followed by an intramural hockey scrimmage. Weeks after my 12th birthday, the U.S. Olympic hockey team won gold in Lake Placid—The Miracle on Ice—and there was an immediate boon in the number of young boys and girls who started playing ice hockey in the United States over the next few years.

I played for the club hockey team during my high school years. Most of our games were played in an old airplane hangar at Nassau Community College/Mitchel Field—just across the street from the home of the New York Islanders. We practiced one weeknight every week—starting around 10:00 PM—and would play one game each weekend. Lou DiLeo, who played in the Dodgers system in the 1950s, was the father of my best friend in elementary school, Dale. Lou usually drove us to practice, and Dale and his brothers, Kenny and Anthony, all played on the team. Our best player was Scott Wood. He was a senior when I was a freshman and went on to play for St. John's University before becoming a police officer in Port Washington. Another high school teammate, Ruth Rosenthal, taught a young boy on Long Island how to skate a few years later. That boy, Matt Gilroy, won the Hobey Baker Award as college hockey's top player in 2009 before signing with the Rangers. He played in more than 200 NHL games and was a member of the 2018 U.S. Olympic team.

My club hockey career continued in college for four more years. We played several games at Nassau Coliseum and Brendan Byrne Arena, homes of the Islanders and New Jersey Devils. Playing at actual NHL arenas was a huge thrill for all of us. I learned many years later that an opponent in one of our games against Hofstra University in 1989 was Jon Cooper. He has gone on to great success as head coach of the Tampa Bay Lightning.

During the 2015 NHL postseason, Joe Micheletti and I were in Montreal to call a game between the Montreal Canadiens and Tampa Bay Lightning. Following the Lightning's morning skate, we were standing toward the back of the horde of reporters when Coach Cooper, whom I had never met, motioned toward me that he wanted to speak. For a moment I wondered if I had said anything on a broadcast that may have upset him. "Did you play hockey for NYU?" he asked me.

I was aware that Cooper attended Hofstra and played lacrosse but did not know that he played club hockey. I was astonished that Cooper recalled that we had played against each other. It turns out one of his college buddies was aware that I played for NYU and told Coop that he should mention it if we ever met. We have since become good friends. Cooper has brought his son to my broadcast booth at Raymond James Stadium on a couple of occasions during Tampa Bay Buccaneers games. He joined Rondé Barber and me for a few meals at Donatello's Restaurant in Tampa, and I was honored to call the game on NBC when Cooper and the Lightning won their second consecutive Stanley Cup on July 7, 2021. We have both come a long way since playing club hockey against each other in front of fewer than a hundred fans back in the late 1980s.

I enjoyed playing in pick-up games at Sky Rink late on Monday nights throughout my collegiate years. Those games were set up by John Dellapina. Then a *New York Daily News* sportswriter, he became the vice president of communications for the NHL. Many other media numbers took part, including goaltender Frank Brown, a *Daily News* hockey columnist who also went on to work for the NHL for many years and is a member of the Hockey Hall of Fame; writers Colin Stephenson and EJ Hradek; and Dave Starman, my former partner who is now the preeminent analyst in the world of college hockey. Other celebrities from the world of sports and entertainment would occasionally join us on the ice at Sky Rink, including actors Tim Robbins and DB Sweeney, boxer Donny Lalonde, and NHL linesman Pat Dapuzzo.

Many of the media members from the Sky Rink Monday night games took part in U.S. vs. Canada media hockey games—usually heated affairs—in the days leading up to various NHL All-Star Games. I played in the media games at Montreal Forum (1993) and Madison Square Garden (1994), scoring a goal in both games, and in Boston (1996) at a local college rink.

During my early years broadcasting Rangers games, I was fortunate to participate in the Christopher Reeve Foundation charity hockey games at Madison Square Garden in front of 10,000 fans, including Christopher and his wife, Dana. The rosters included celebrities such as Denis Leary, Kiefer Sutherland, Robbins, Boomer Esiason, McEnroe, as well as media members, including ESPN's Steve Levy and MSG's John Giannone.

With all Rangers players in attendance in 1999, I scored a goal on Garden ice...and was congratulated after the game by none other than Wayne Gretzky. In the final Reeve game (in 2002), the entire Rangers team joined us; half played on the white team, and half played on the blue. I started the game as the left wing on a line with center Mark Messier and New York Giants wide receiver Amani Toomer at right wing. I lined up for the opening faceoff opposite Eric Lindros, the right wing on the opposing squad. Lindros had suffered numerous concussions by that point of his career. Although I was wearing a full cage, my chin strap was hanging down from one side of my helmet. Lindros noticed this, reached over, and snapped it in place. I will never forget the symbolism of that moment. It was surreal playing with—and against—the Rangers squad...in the middle of the regular season. I continued to play men's league hockey on a team called the Brewers at the Ice House in Hackensack, New Jersey, over the next decade with a great group of guys.

I enjoyed some other memorable athletic moments. Due to my father's personal relationships, professional athletes would occasionally visit our house. Dale DiLeo and I once played 2-on-1 basketball against Phil Jackson. I remember passing the ball to DiLeo through the legs of the future Hall of Fame coach. I shot orange street hockey balls against then-Devils goaltender Chico Resch, who visited our house during the 1982–83 NHL season and strapped on *my* goalie equipment. My mother even beat Julius Erving in a game of H-O-R-S-E at his Long Island home one day. I'm pretty sure Dr. J wasn't allowed to dunk in that game!

During the summers of 1987 and 1988, I ventured to the Concord Hotel in New York's Catskill Mountains (only a few miles from my camp), where NHL stars converged for one week each summer. In exchange for free meals and access to the golf course and pool, the players would put on a hockey clinic for hotel guests and then allow the guests to skate in a pick-up game with them. Rich Ackerman and I skated on a line with Luc Robitaille, and the group on the ice prior to us played with Mario Lemieux.

During the 1993 NBA Finals in Chicago, Jerry Coleman and I joined a pick-up game on a hotel basketball court with NBC personnel. At one point, the two of us found ourselves on a 3-on-1 with Earvin "Magic" Johnson, who was working as an NBC analyst during the series. Magic fed me for a layup, and yes, it went in! Later in the game, Coleman set up Magic for a basket. The Hall of Famer pointed at him as a thank you for the assist—just as we had seen thousands of times on television.

I played in two "Boomer and Carton"/WFAN charity softball games at Yankee Stadium—one in 2011, the other in 2015. In the first game, I reached first base on a base hit up the middle off pitcher—and former star center fielder—Bernie Williams. My teammates that day included Ralph Macchio (of *The Karate Kid* fame) and Rangers superstar Brian Leetch. I had the surreal opportunity to ice skate at Yankee Stadium in 2014 during the same week the Rangers played two outdoor games in the Bronx.

Speaking of Esiason and his charities, I once nearly broke my hand catching a pass from him at a practice the week of one of his high school charity games. Our entire *NFL on FOX* crew, including Daryl Johnston and Tony Siragusa, once played a touch football game in a park in Green Bay, Wisconsin. Years later, our crew did the same along with Barber at the Buccaneers' indoor practice facility, and I caught a touchdown pass off a deflection.

At a FOX Sports football preseason seminar, I gained a reputation as a quality Ping-Pong player. I defeated two former NFL quarterbacks, Joey Harrington and Heisman Trophy winner Matt Leinart, who were then FOX college football analysts. Leinart's serve was tremendous; however, I still pulled out the victory. At a subsequent FOX baseball seminar, matchmaker Eric Karros, the Los Angeles Dodgers' all-time home run leader and a frequent partner of mine on FOX Saturday baseball games, had heard about my Ping-Pong prowess. So he set up a showdown between lead FOX analyst John Smoltz (who would be inducted into the Baseball Hall of Fame in Cooperstown a year later) and me. According to Smoltz, he only lost one table tennis match during his entire pro baseball career, and that was to a Detroit Tigers minor leaguer. I felt it was a moral victory when I scored 15 points in the first game (a 21–15 loss) in front of a crowd, including Hall of Famer and FOX studio analyst Frank Thomas and Karros, who was filming it on his phone. Smoltz beat me pretty handily in two subsequent games. My Ping-Pong performances top my other accomplishments against a major leaguer. During a Wiffle Ball event in the streets of Minneapolis in 2018, I got a base hit (I use the term loosely) off Minnesota Twins closer Fernando Rodney.

During the 2018 FOX football seminar, I wound up across the court from four-time Super Bowl champion Terry Bradshaw in a doubles tennis match. Bradshaw was my broadcast partner a decade earlier at the Sugar Bowl. As you probably can tell from watching Bradshaw on *FOX NFL Sunday* for the past 29 years, he is quite the character. At a younger age, Bradshaw was probably a terrific player; you could tell that. By this point, he had gone through multiple knee surgeries, and I felt bad when I accidentally placed a few drop shots well out of Bradshaw's reach. In December of the next year, our football crew spent a few hours having fun on the ice at the Green Bay Curling Club, and it became quite competitive.

I attended SmashFest, a charity Ping-Pong tournament in Toronto involving NHL players, in the summer of 2022. I was invited by former Rangers player Dominic Moore, who founded the event a decade earlier. During the doubles competition, NHL players and broadcasters were paired with fans, and my partner, who was one of the sponsors, and I recorded a victory against Hockey Hall of Famer Doug Gilmour. Unfortunately, in the singles bracket, I was on the wrong end of the score against two-time Stanley Cup champion Craig Adams.

# 13

**PANDEMIC**

E arly in 2020, we all started to hear about the Coronavirus, but nobody had any idea about the kind of impact it would have worldwide within months. Amanda flew to Australia in late December 2019 for a semester abroad. In early February she traveled to Vietnam, Thailand, and Singapore with friends and sent us photos of many passengers on her flights wearing surgical masks. She then purchased a mask and wore it on subsequent flights.

When I traveled with the New York Rangers to Dallas on Monday, March 9, rumors started to circulate about the NHL potentially postponing games. At the morning skate at American Airlines Center the next day, the media contingent was told we could not go into the locker room (a common practice for decades). A media interview room was set up, and the coaches and players, who were brought in, sat behind a table a safe distance away from the reporters and broadcasters. Barbara gave me Clorox To Go Packs and Purell hand sanitizer to bring on the trip and she suggested that I wipe down the headset in the broadcast booth.

After flying with the team to Denver following the game, it was the same drill the next morning and at the game. Then…a shock. As I was setting up in the radio booth at Ball Arena and waiting for warmups to begin, I glanced up at the television monitor and noticed a report about the suspension of the Utah Jazz game. A few minutes later, I received an email from the NBA public relations department about game cancellations and a pause to their season. Simultaneously, Amanda texted a photo of herself climbing the side of a building in Gold Coast, Australia, a complete 180 from what was taking place thousands of miles away.

Everybody in the press box was wondering if the NHL would follow suit. The Rangers were scheduled to fly to Phoenix after their game, but I was going to stay in Denver and fly to Miami the next morning for a New York Knicks telecast on Friday, March 13, before heading west to Arizona for Saturday's Rangers–Arizona Coyotes matchup. Once the NBA canceled its season, I found myself in a dilemma. I would fly with the Rangers, but I had left my luggage at the hotel. I paid a member of the TV production crew to go to the hotel, pack my suitcase, and bring it back to the arena so I could head out with the team after the game. My bag arrived during the second period; soon thereafter, we were told we would stay in Denver after the game while waiting for the NHL to make a determination the next morning. So, it was back to the hotel and my room to unpack once again.

The next morning our MSG radio/TV group milled around the hotel lobby along with head coach David Quinn and some other Rangers staff members waiting to hear our destination. We filled two buses and headed to the airport. The NHL Board of Governors were scheduled to hold a meeting in the late morning. Even after the entire team and traveling party boarded the plane, we did not know if we would be heading west to Arizona or back home to New York. We all refreshed our Twitter feeds constantly. Finally, the press release arrived announcing that the NHL would be pausing its season as well. We all assumed it would be a short, two-to-three-week break, and then things would be back to normal. Little did we know. I sat in my usual seat against the window on the right side in the back row of the plane. Sam Rosen occupied the aisle seat to my left. Joe Micheletti and John Giannone were on the left side across the way. Dave Maloney sat a few rows in front of us. While flying we found out that Major League Baseball paused its season as well. At one point, Rosen blurted out, "What are we going to do for entertainment?"

Upon arriving home, we started to work on a plan to bring Amanda back. COVID-19 hadn't shut down Australia yet, and she would have done anything to stay, but we were concerned about the borders closing and flights selling out quickly. During the early days of the pandemic, gloves were much more common than masks. When I picked Amanda up at Newark Airport on March 20, one of the only other people waiting at the baggage claim area was my friend and fellow sportscaster Ian Eagle, whose daughter Erin—like Amanda, a Syracuse University student—was on the same flight. I have a photo of Ian and me standing with their luggage while socially distanced from each other and I am wearing blue surgical gloves.

I was home for 146 straight days and nights—sleeping in my own bed—from March 12, 2020, until I left for the Edmonton bubble on August 5. This was by far the longest stretch I had been home without traveling during my entire professional life. It was quality time with the family that I had never experienced. During the craziest portions of my schedule prior to the pandemic, I would frequently be away for four or five nights at a time. Amanda was 20 years old at the time; Sydney was 17. Being alone with their parents was probably not the way they wanted to spend more than four months, but they both handled it like champs. We had dinner as a family every night; I would announce how many straight days it had been (example: "Dinner No. 14"). They quickly started making fun of me for this. I started referring to Barbara as "master chef" because her cooking was excellent. With not much to do aside from cleaning and organizing my home office, I rode the Peloton bike and took long walks daily. It paid off! I lost 37 pounds from early January through the end of July.

The first few weeks at home were surreal. For my entire adult life, there was always that next event to prepare for and look forward to. During September in normal times, I could look ahead at the next six months and know where I would be just about every hour of every day because the schedule is laid out for the NFL and NHL seasons, Knicks games, etc.

The NHL announced it would return to action in two playoff bubbles—in Toronto and Edmonton—in early August. A few weeks before that, the Rangers held a summer minicamp. It was great to be able to attend practice sessions at the MSG Training Center in Greenburgh, New York. We all had to wear masks, have our temperature taken upon entering, and then stood in marked spots 8' apart from one another. There would not be any interaction with players or coaches. Press conferences took place via Zoom, a video platform most of us never had heard of prior to the pandemic.

Team broadcasters did not travel to the bubbles, so Maloney and I called the Rangers games against the Carolina Hurricanes in the qualifying round off a monitor from the ESPN Radio studios in Manhattan. (I also called several games played in Edmonton off a monitor from the NBC studios in Stamford, Connecticut, while the Rangers were still alive.) I was asked by NBC to head to the Edmonton bubble as soon as my Rangers duties concluded, so I had to take three COVID tests during the series just in case the Rangers lost. Sure enough, the Rangers were swept by the Hurricanes. The series ended on August 4, and I was on a flight to Edmonton (through Toronto) the next day.

I had not been on an airplane in nearly five months—since that Rangers charter home from Denver on March 12. Things were certainly different! The airports were pretty empty. The seat next to mine was left open. I wore a mask and goggles on the flights. Upon arriving in Edmonton, I was transported directly to the Delta Hotel a few blocks from Rogers Place (the Edmonton Oilers' home arena). After checking into my room, I began a four-day quarantine, which was required for all media members entering the bubble. To make me feel at home, Barbara and the girls snuck family photos into my luggage, which I taped onto the hotel room mirror. A nurse came to my room each day to perform a COVID test. I ordered room service for all meals, which were left outside my door. It was strange to not be allowed to leave my hotel room. Meanwhile, I could see the arena out my window! One saving grace: there were four or five hockey games on TV every day—from late morning through early evening—played both in Toronto and across the street. I got all my prep work done for the first round and spent a lot of time reading and on FaceTime with family and friends. When I was finally released from quarantine, I immediately walked to the arena and attended a game between the St. Louis Blues and Dallas Stars. It was surreal; I was one of the only "fans" in the arena. I sat about 20 rows up—next to our broadcast location—and could hear many of the conversations taking place on the ice amongst players, coaches, and officials.

Beginning the next day, it was full steam ahead. I called multiple games almost every day—most of them with Pierre McGuire at ice level. During the first round, Eddie Olczyk worked several games with us from his home in Chicago. I was in the booth, McGuire was a couple of hundred feet away from me, Olczyk was 2,000 miles away, and our producer was in Stamford! But we made it work, and hopefully the viewers at home didn't notice the difference from typical telecasts when we are all in the same building. Olczyk and Brian Boucher joined us in Edmonton for the later rounds. On two occasions during the first round, I called *three* games in one day. McGuire and I called both Western Conference second-round series: Vancouver Canucks vs. Vegas Golden Knights and Colorado Avalanche vs. Dallas Stars, including two Game Sevens in the same day.

There were some wild games as well. In Game Six of the first round against the Calgary Flames, the Stars became the first team in NHL playoff history to trail by three goals, then take a four-goal lead. In Game Four of the second round, the Avalanche, playing against the Stars, were the first team in postseason history to lead a game by two goals in the third period, fall behind, and then restore their two-goal lead. I called 17 of the 22 Western Conference games played in the first round and every game in the second round. For a hockey broadcaster, it was heaven. I was in the bubble for 37 days and loved every minute. It was so quiet in the building that one of the game officials told me he could actually hear some of my play-by-play calls while on the ice during games.

The two hotels and the arena were surrounded by a 10' fence. We couldn't leave the bubble, and nobody could enter from the outside. We were all tested for COVID every single day. On even-numbered days, we received a Q-tip up the nose, which wasn't bad. On odd-numbered days, we had a throat swab, which was pretty annoying. To kill time—and get a tiny bit of exercise—I played Ping-Pong almost every day. My usual partner was statistician Ryan Moir. Some days we played for over an hour, and all were highly competitive matches. NHL referee Chris Rooney joined us on occasion. During the Western Conference Final, I challenged Boucher; unfortunately, the floor was slippery, and Bouch pulled his quad muscle. Do you think we might have chided him about it during that night's telecast? It was a great Ping-Pong matchup until he got hurt; it was tied at 13.

The NHL set up a bus schedule for anyone inside the bubble who wanted to get some exercise at Commonwealth Stadium, the longtime home of the Edmonton Elks franchise. The bus would go directly from inside the fence at the hotel and then straight down the loading dock at the stadium. Security kept a close eye at both ends because those entering the stadium were still considered "in the bubble." During the one day I took advantage of this perk, I walked a few laps around the football field, threw a frisbee, kicked a soccer ball, and attempted to kick a few field goals. I finally connected from 15 yards out; I guess a career as a placekicker is not in the cards. It was nice to get out in the fresh air aside from the small courtyard outside Rogers Place (others called it the "Jail Yard"), where there were a few food trucks set up, tables for eating lunch, a basketball hoop, cornhole, etc. I enjoyed spending time there. I never would have expected to sit for a haircut on the main concourse of a hockey arena, but that was the case toward the end of my stay in the bubble. The NHL hired a few stylists for players, coaches, staff members, and even broadcasters, and they set up shop at Rogers Place.

The NHL did a terrific job with sound effects in the building during play, as well as music and goal songs from every team's home arena. It added to the ambience for the small number of us in the building and the viewers at home (and helped raise my energy level during broadcasts). Kudos to NHL chief content officer Steve Mayer and his entire staff!

I called the first three games of the Western Conference Final between Dallas and Vegas before I was scheduled to leave Edmonton and travel to Detroit on Friday, September 11, for the start of the NFL regular season. I received a phone call from a FOX Sports executive earlier that week. He mentioned that one of the *NFL on NBC* production crew members, who had been in the NHL's Toronto bubble, was not allowed into the television compound at Arrowhead Stadium a few days prior to the Thursday season opener between the Kansas City Chiefs and Houston Texans.

Apparently, the NFL was requiring all media and broadcast workers to fill out a health and safety questionnaire, which included a question asking if the individual had been out of the country during the past 14 days. This clause was initially put in place to discourage players and team personnel from leaving the country close to the start of training camp. FOX petitioned with the NFL to try and allow me to work the Detroit Lions–Chicago Bears game (and New York Jets–San Francisco 49ers the next week) considering I had taken COVID tests for 37 consecutive days in the bubble and I would be traveling from arguably the safest location in North America. I flew on Friday morning from Edmonton to Toronto to Detroit (and even participated on a Zoom call with Lions quarterback Matthew Stafford from the airport in Toronto). While I was about to board the connection to Detroit, I received word that the NFL would not budge. Rules were rules. After landing in Detroit, I rechecked my luggage onto a flight to New York and headed home. FOX recruited the legendary Dick Stockton to fill in for me in Detroit. Jonathan Vilma thought our production crew was playing a prank on him. But in reality, his first two FOX NFL broadcasts would *not* be with his new partner. It was weird to think that Vilma and I had not yet met since receiving the news that we would be paired together. The annual *NFL on FOX* seminar, which took place in recent years at the Terranea Resort in Rancho Palos Verdes, California, was instead held virtually due to the pandemic, and we called one half of a practice game together via Zoom. I did my portion from my Edmonton hotel room.

Brandon Gaudin pinch hit for me the next Sunday on the Jets–49ers telecast. While serving my two-week break before I was allowed back in NFL stadiums, I called the 2020 Stanley Cup Final with Micheletti on Westwood One Radio—albeit off monitors from NBC in Stamford.

In September of 2020, Sydney began her senior year at Northern Valley Regional High School in Demarest, New Jersey. Because she played on the tennis team, I received notices via email from the school's athletic department. Due to health and safety protocols, only immediate family members would be allowed to attend sporting events at NVD. The school made arrangements for certain games to be live-streamed, including home football games. I asked the school's longtime athletic director, Greg Butler, if he could use a volunteer announcer for one of the games. He immediately took me up on my offer. I prepared like it was an NFL game: I attended practices, spoke with coaches, and Sydney helped me with pronunciations. On November 12 I was at the mic for a Thursday evening game against rival Dumont High School. A former NVD student (who was attending Harvard Law School at the time), named Eli Nachmany provided excellent color commentary. The home team enjoyed its best offensive output of the season in a 46–22 victory.

During normal times, I spend basically the entire weekend (Friday morning through Sunday night) with my production crew throughout the football season. We usually fly into the home city on Friday morning and go straight to practice and production meetings with players and coaches. We have dinner together on Friday night, then spend most of the day Saturday together. On Saturdays we typically have lunch, sit around a hotel conference room getting our work done while watching college football games, head to the visiting team hotel in the late afternoon for meetings, and then have a production meeting of our own on Saturday night.

In November of 2019, I called a hockey game the day after Thanksgiving. Our football crew set up a conference call with Miami Dolphins players and coaches that day. About an hour prior to the opening faceoff, I dialed in to chat with quarterback (and Harvard graduate) Ryan Fitzpatrick. It was pretty quiet in our broadcast booth for a moment...until loud music started blaring from the public-address system. I scrambled to find the only quiet spot in the TD Garden press box—inside the men's room—where I proceeded to ask questions and somehow take notes while standing near the sink. Once in a while, improvisation is required.

During the 2020 NFL season, however, things were much different. All of the team meetings took place via Zoom since the teams did not allow visitors in their facilities due to health and safety protocols. We did not have group meals, so most of us arrived in the city on Saturday morning or early afternoon. Instead of taking taxis, Ubers, or car services, we all rented our own cars to drive to and from the hotel, airport, and stadium. The only benefit to having no fans or a limited number of fans in the stadium: there was no traffic heading to the airport after the games. Similar to my time in the hockey bubble in Edmonton, it was surreal calling games in empty stadiums while socially distanced (anywhere from 8' to 15' away) from Vilma. During broadcasts we normally rely heavily on non-verbal communication (hand signals, touching each other's arm or shoulder). I give Vilma a lot of credit for navigating his way through his first full season in the broadcast booth under difficult circumstances.

When hockey and basketball finally got back underway (in late December 2020/January 2021), similar challenges and protocols were instituted. I even set up my own personal bubble within my house in order to keep both me and my family as safe as possible. For all Rangers home games and Knicks home games played at Madison Square Garden from the start of the season until April (when most people were vaccinated), anybody entering the building (broadcasters, media, security, staff etc.) was given a COVID-19 test in the Hulu Theater approximately three to four hours before the start of the game. A Q-tip was placed up our nose, and then we would sit in an assigned, socially-distanced seat and wait for the results approximately 45 minutes later. Once the test came back negative, we were then given a bracelet and allowed to enter the building. The broadcast crew would then congregate (masked and socially distanced, of course) in a couple of suites to kill time in the empty building. We would eat dinner, take part in Zoom interviews with coaches, and finish our game prep.

For Rangers games, Maloney and I would call the action from our usual booth on the Chase Bridge, but a plastic partition separated us. For Knicks

TV games, I called the games with Walt "Clyde" Frazier from a platform about 20 rows off the court with partitions in between the statistician, Frazier, the stage manager, and me. There were plastic panels in front of us as well. Late in the regular season, MSG (and most other NHL and NBA arenas) began to allow fans back in. When there were 2,000 fans in the building for Rangers games, it sounded like 10,000 (after we were so used to the silence of the empty arena).

Throughout the 2020–21 season, I called Rangers away games (on radio) from the ESPN Radio studios in Manhattan and Knicks away games (on TV) from the MSG Networks studios across the street from Madison Square Garden. I also called some *NHL on NBC* games from empty arenas in various cities and others off the monitors in Stamford. I even worked two New Jersey Devils telecasts for MSG Networks—while Steve Cangialosi recovered from COVID-19—alongside Ken Daneyko. We called these games off monitors from the Devils TV booth at Prudential Center in Newark. One was played at MSG; the other was in Boston. I must have brought them good luck because the Devils won both games.

By not traveling, I was available to work even more games than usual. During the 2021 NHL playoffs, I called 25 playoff games for NBCSN and NBC—some in the first round from Stamford and then the others on-site. Things were back to normal inside the venues during the second round when I worked the Vegas–Colorado series with Olczyk and Boucher; the arenas in both cities were filled to capacity. It was similar during the Eastern Conference Final between the Tampa Bay Lightning and New York Islanders, including the final three games played at Nassau Coliseum. Then, it was on to the Stanley Cup Final and the second straight championship for the Lightning.

During the start of the 2021–22 NHL and NBA seasons, testing was no longer required prior to home games at MSG. However, it was necessary when traveling on charter flights with the teams. In December of 2021, I called a Knicks game in Toronto with Frazier. We sat shoulder to shoulder at the court-side press table at Scotiabank Arena for close to three hours without masks. Though masks were required for those around us, broadcasting is one of the only professions in which it would be nearly impossible to work while wearing one. Less than two days later, I received word that Frazier had tested positive. Unlike the previous year, a close contact getting infected no longer required you to quarantine if vaccinated. Even though I tested negative, it was recommended that I test five-to-seven days later. As long as I didn't have any symptoms at that point, all was clear.

As the calendar turned to 2022, things started to get back to normal. The MSG Networks television crew traveled for the majority of Knicks road games. We still called most Rangers away games on radio from the New York studio (off monitors) during the regular season, then were on-site for playoff games in Pittsburgh, Raleigh, and Tampa. In 2022–23 the Rangers radio crew was back on the road for all but a select number of games.

# 14
## PAYING IT FORWARD

Throughout my professional career, I have enjoyed speaking at various sports broadcasting camps, usually filled with high school and college-aged students, some even younger. I have been a guest lecturer every summer for the last two decades at Hofstra University at a program founded by the late Ed Ingles, a longtime New York radio sportscaster and terrific man. For many years Jeremy Treatman, a Philadelphia native who called Kobe Bryant's high school games, invited me to the New Jersey chapter of his "Play by Play Sports Broadcasting Camps." I've also made numerous trips to the Ian Eagle/Bruce Beck Sportscasting Camp at the Yogi Berra Museum on the Montclair State University campus; a camp run by Brooklyn Nets broadcaster Tim Capstraw and Seton Hall radio voice Dave Popkin; and the broadcasting program at Brookwood Camp in Glen Spey, New York, owned by longtime NFL quarterback Jay Fiedler and his brother, Scott.

I always enjoy speaking to the campers about my life in broadcasting. I try to entertain them with many of the stories I have included in this book and answer whatever questions they might have. All of these programs provide them with such great insights (as well as a head start) into the various on-air positions, as well as behind-the-scenes aspects of the business. The kids interact with guest speakers from the world of broadcasting and gain practical experience as well by handling play-by-play, reporting on sports, and refining their interviewing skills. I wish similar camps and programs existed when I was a high school student.

I have also done countless interviews through the years with high school and college students on their radio shows and podcasts. I remember how excited I was when I was their age to have the opportunity to speak with professionals and enhance my interviewing skills, so I always try to return the favor. I initially met Ed Cohen (New York Knicks radio), Brendan Burke (New York Islanders TV/TNT), and Steve Gelbs (New York Mets TV) while they were college students. They all sent me samples of their work. Hopefully, I provided advice and support, which helped them advance in their careers.

I learned at a young age that research and preparation are the most important aspects of my job. Although I often feel like I am, a sportscaster can never be overprepared. You never know what subject might come up during a broadcast, what curveball you may be thrown, or what question you might be asked by your color analyst. A strong play-by-play broadcaster probably uses only 5 to 10 percent of the information he or she has accumulated leading up to a broadcast.

During a typical NFL week—this may shock some people—I prepare between 30 to 40 hours for a single game. During football season it's similar to what coaches go through, though their hours are truly crazy. If I'm not sleeping, eating, spending time with my family, or working another game, I'm preparing for that Sunday's game. From Monday through Thursday, I am on my own—either at home or traveling for another event. Early in the week, our crew exchanges emails, texts, and Zoom calls (something we've added in recent years). I have a checklist that I go through for every game.

That starts with watching each team's previous game and reviewing my prior game. When I started with FOX in 1994, this couldn't be done until Wednesday, when we received VHS copies of the games from the network. In the early 2000s, it became DVDs, which arrived on Tuesdays. I also started to record games at home on DirecTV and could begin viewing those on Monday. These days NFL+ (formerly NFL Game Pass) offers access to watch game replays on any device, which has made it a lot easier when traveling. Back in the day when on the road, I would occasionally rent a VCR in my hotel room, usually wheeled in on a big cart. Times have certainly changed as technology has evolved. I saved all of the tapes and DVDs of my games from the first 20 years at FOX—until they stopped sending them in that fashion due to the advances in technology—in what I refer to as my personal tape vault. Visitors to my house are shocked to see my collection of VHS tapes, DVDs, newspapers, magazines, team media guides, game programs, and charts from my broadcasts. Fortunately, many teams now print their guides digitally, so the volume of publications entering the house has declined in recent years. I refer to myself as an "organized hoarder." If I am on the road and need information from one of the charts, I, for example, can call Barbara and explain: "It's in the second drawer from the top in the file cabinet to the left of my desk…in the third folder from the right."

I prepare charts for every broadcast. (I've included some examples of these in the appendix of this book.) All play-by-play broadcasters have their own system regarding charts or spotting boards, depending on the sport. My football and basketball charts have a similar look to what my father used throughout his career. I still do most of my charts by hand. I have always felt that I remember and memorize information a lot quicker if I write it. I use different colors to correspond with those associated with a particular team.

I am very particular as far as the type of ballpoint pens that I use. I loved the feel and texture (and the blue ink) of the writing instruments left in guest rooms at Ritz-Carlton hotels during the late 1990s/early 2000s. I used to take a few extras off the housekeeping carts in the hallway. (Some people steal hotel robes; I took pens.) Barbara and the girls surprised me by ordering 200 similar pens online with my name inscribed on the side after the Ritz changed to a thinner model. Fortunately, they have lasted for years. I often share the pens with friends and colleagues. Guy Gadowsky signed his contract to coach the Penn State hockey team in 2011 with a Kenny Albert pen thanks to an assist from Ben Bouma. John Tortorella once filled out the official form, listing which players would take part in a shootout, with one of my pens after it was tossed to him by radio producer Frank Moretti, who was standing near the New York Rangers bench. (One of the trainers was screaming for a pen.)

My football charts evolve throughout the week. I start by inputting every player's name, along with their uniform number, height, weight, college, and number of years in the league. I then add statistics and various other notes in each player's box. These days, some broadcasters farm out the charts to services who do the work for them. If I was a network executive, I would not hire anyone who does not prepare his or her own charts; it's like cheating on a test. If the person who prepares your chart makes a mistake and you recite that note on the air, it's on you. I'm certainly all for gathering information from as many different resources as possible, but my advice to young sportscasters is prepare your own charts!

Aspiring broadcasters should read, read, read! Knowledge is power. We had four newspapers delivered to our house daily during my childhood. I devoured each and every one of them. I continued reading multiple newspapers throughout college and to this day I still have four papers delivered daily. I always have enjoyed reading out-of-town newspapers while traveling. I also subscribe to the same publications on my iPad to read when I'm away. I definitely spend more money than needed, but it's essential in order to do my job properly. When I'm out of town, I can read the *New York Post*, *New York Daily News*, *The New York Times*, *The Bergen Record*, and *USA TODAY* (in newspaper form on my iPad). But when I'm home, I love sitting in the backyard reading an *actual* newspaper. If you surf a paper's website, you only click on articles you're interested in. By reading the actual publication, you see everything. I also read numerous articles online from various websites and via social media (usually for hours every day), but I feel I miss certain things if I don't read a newspaper. I am constantly reading clips from the cities of whatever teams I will be broadcasting in a given week. I also pore through press releases and statistics provided by the teams, the NFL, and the FOX research department. Our crew could be assigned to a game in Week 15, for example, involving two teams we haven't yet seen. It is our responsibility to review and catch up on the entire season because the rabid fans tuning in have probably watched every game their favorite team has played. The announcers must sound like they have as well.

It is very important to study and learn the history of whatever sports you may wind up covering. I enjoy dropping various historical nuggets into my broadcasts. One of my favorite sports trivia questions: who is the only person to win an NBA championship as a player *and* coach in a Super Bowl? The answer: Bud Grant, who won a title as a member of the 1950 Minneapolis Lakers and was later head coach of the Minnesota Vikings and reached four Super Bowls. Another is the fact that Hall of Fame pitcher Tom Glavine was selected in the fourth round of the 1984 NHL Draft by the Los Angeles Kings—ahead of hockey Hall of Famers Brett Hull (Calgary Flames, sixth round) and Luc Robitaille (Los Angeles, ninth round).

I am a stickler for keeping up with the rules in all of the sports that I cover; they get more complicated every year. I pride myself on reading the rule books prior to every season. Broadcasters have been aided significantly in recent years with the addition of rules analysts such as Mike Pereira and Dean Blandino, who are tremendous assets to NFL on FOX telecasts, and hockey's Don Koharski and Stephane Auger, who were hired by Turner in 2021. Despite the assistance from Pereira, Blandino, Koharski, and Auger, I try to know the rules as well as the officials. I also try to keep the viewers informed on game management situations toward the end of games—how many timeouts remain in basketball or football or when the losing team can potentially get the ball back in the final moments of an NFL game. Al Michaels, Mike Tirico, Joe Buck, Mike Breen, and Ian Eagle—just to name a few—do a fabulous job in these areas as well.

One of the biggest changes since I began my professional career has been the advancements in technology. When I started calling NFL games in 1994, I received daily clips via fax and relied heavily on reading weekly publications such as *The Sporting News* and *Pro Football Weekly*. During the Internet revolution in the mid-to-late 1990s, information became available at a much quicker pace. Social media (especially Twitter) has become essential for gathering news immediately, but I don't take any shortcuts. Reading newspapers (via whichever method you choose) is still essential. I enjoy posting photos and videos from stadiums and arenas around North America (and the world) on Twitter (@KennyAlbert) and Instagram (@kennyalbert1) to help promote the broadcasts.

Occasionally, I receive tweets from fans accusing me of saying something on a telecast when I'm not even working. I have been mistaken for Kevin

Harlan (of CBS and TNT) on many occasions…even by my kids when they have quickly walked past the TV and heard his voice. When the girls were young, if my father and I were working games simultaneously on different channels, Barbara would click back and forth and ask the kids, "Daddy or Grandpa?" "Guess the announcer" was part of the fun and games in the Albert household.

On Friday morning I usually fly to the city where our Sunday football game will be played. I meet up with my analyst, sideline reporter, producer, and director at the home team's practice facility. We watch practice and then head inside for sit-down meetings with four or five players and coaches. The interview subjects are usually the head coach, one or both coordinators, the quarterback, and a defensive player. We occasionally add an additional player on either side of the ball. These meetings originated back in the 1980s; John Madden was one of the first NFL analysts to meet with players. Prior to that, only the team's public relations director (and on occasion the head coach) would get together with the broadcast crew.

These meetings can last anywhere from five minutes to a half hour. They are mandated as part of the various networks' contracts with the league and have become part of the weekly routine for coaches and key players. Some enjoy the meetings more than others; some share more information than others. My analyst leads the way with questions, and then I will chime in. The analyst looks for key points relating to strategy and X's and O's that will assist in explaining and describing what is happening on the field to the viewers on Sunday. For the most part, my questions have to do with personal stories that I try to integrate into our broadcasts. One example: toward the end of Eli Manning's playing career, he would occasionally face an opposing starting quarterback who was a teenage camper at the Manning Passing Academy, an annual summer camp for quarterbacks run by Eli, Peyton, and their dad, Archie. I would ask both Eli and the young quarterback on the other side what they remembered about their time together, which would make for a fun anecdote on the air.

Through the years we learned how to navigate through meetings with various coaches. Many could be intimidating to young broadcasters (Buddy

Ryan, Bill Parcells, Tom Coughlin…just to name a few). We figured out pretty quickly that Bill Belichick did not enjoy sharing much information about his current team. However, once you get him going on historical subjects (the 1986 New York Giants, Lawrence Taylor, Navy football), he will sit and tell stories for 45 minutes. Jeff Fisher, the longtime Tennessee Titans and St. Louis Rams head coach, often shared with us trick plays on special teams that he had up his sleeve. He trusted us to keep the information to ourselves and wanted us to be prepared. Sure enough, on at least two occasions, his teams pulled off the exact plays (on special teams) that he had described to us. During meetings with New Orleans Saints coach Sean Payton, he would run down his team's entire roster and share a piece of information about each and every player. During my first FOX season, Tampa Bay Buccaneers coach Sam Wyche told us that he would start *two* quarterbacks in the game the next day. We thought he was pulling our leg. Sure enough, for the first offensive play of the game, rookie Trent Dilfer was under center, and Craig Erickson was split out as a receiver in an attempt to deceive the San Francisco 49ers. The San Francisco defenders weren't fooled, and the Bucs lost four yards on the play. Most offensive and defensive coordinators are very helpful and willing to share information during production meetings. Many realize that if they are referenced during broadcasts, it can help enhance their career path.

With health and safety protocols in place during the COVID pandemic, most of our NFL meetings during the 2020 and 2021 seasons took place via Zoom. In October of 2021, on a pleasant autumn afternoon, I decided to take part in the video calls with the Green Bay Packers from my backyard. Aaron Rodgers asked if the trees behind me were real or if I was using a "green screen" (used in the TV world to drop images into the background). Later that season, prior to a Buffalo Bills game, I was in my home office (with a circa-1990s NHL All-Star jersey hanging behind me). When offensive coordinator Brian Daboll logged on to his computer for our virtual meeting, he immediately noticed the jersey and asked, "Campbell or Wales Conference?" Daboll, who was hired as head coach by the Giants months later, showed impressive hockey knowledge (and attended several Rangers playoff games in the spring of 2022). Those conference monikers went away in 1993, but he was a huge fan of the sport while growing up in the Buffalo area.

My preparation for hockey, basketball, and baseball games is similar, though not as time consuming as football because the teams play so many games throughout each week, and there are fewer players to study. In addition, I work so many Rangers and Knicks games that I know those teams like the back of my hand. Preparation for nationally-televised hockey and baseball games—involving teams I am not as familiar with—take more time. Similar to football, I have a checklist that I go through for every broadcast: watch past games; read everything I can get my hands on involving both teams; prepare charts; study media guides, press releases, and statistics; attend practices and press conferences, etc.

Historically, hockey broadcasters gather information at practices and morning skates on gameday. Schmoozing with the announcers from other teams and networks is valuable. So is time spent in the locker room chatting with players and coaches. One of my favorite stories that I relayed on the air during a hockey telecast took place during a Pittsburgh Penguins–Columbus Blue Jackets playoff series. I learned through my research that Sidney Crosby and Columbus defenseman Jack Johnson had been high school teammates at Shattuck St. Mary's in Minnesota. I asked both of them about their relationship following a morning skate. It turns out that not only were they hockey teammates, but also baseball teammates as well, and they took classes together. As one of them relayed to me (and the other verified the story): Crosby and Johnson were sitting toward the back of the classroom one day; instead of taking notes on their laptops, they were watching hockey highlights. Much to their chagrin, they were called out by their teacher at the front of the room. Crosby and Johnson were perplexed as to how they were caught, considering they were watching without volume. It turns out there was a window behind them, and the reflection of the hockey videos from their computers was visible to the teacher. It made for a funny story during the telecast. By the way, I will always have a soft spot for Crosby. He was kind enough to record a short video for my daughter Sydney's Bat Mitzvah video montage—even after a loss in St. Louis—from one Sidney to another Sydney. He even played along with our theme and referred to my Syd as his "favorite Albert."

There are vast differences between radio and television from a play-by-play standpoint. On radio you have to describe everything that takes place on the ice, court, or field. Because the viewers can see the action, the play-by-play broadcaster on television doesn't have to say as much and can leave more time for the color analyst to speak. In addition, on radio the score and time (or inning) must be mentioned a lot more frequently than on television because it cannot be seen on the screen (thanks to FOX Sports chairman David Hill, who invented the perpetual FOX Box prior to the 1994 NFL season). In my opinion, beginning a career in radio is invaluable; radio is where young broadcasters learn the fundamentals and build a foundation. Chuck D of Public Enemy even credits listening to hockey games on the radio during his childhood as a big influence on his rhythm, cadence, flow, and voice inflections. The play-by-play broadcaster has many roles. The first is obvious: calling the play and also weaving in anecdotes, statistics, historical information, rules explanations, stories from meetings with players and coaches, while also serving as somewhat of a traffic cop.

When I get asked the most difficult sport to broadcast, most people expect me to answer hockey. To me, it is actually the easiest of the four major sports, but perhaps that's because I have been doing hockey on a consistent basis longer than the others. Hockey and basketball play-by-play are similar, though hockey moves at a much quicker pace. The hockey puck is in action for the entire 60 minutes during a game; the basketball is in action for the entire 48 minutes. The play-by-play broadcaster during a hockey or hoops game (in particular on radio) is calling the action for most of the actual game time. Football is the most rhythmic. It's one play followed by 20 to 35 seconds until the next play. Lather, rinse, repeat. The play-by-play announcer sets up the play (example: first and 10 from the 25-yard line), calls the play, recaps the play (four-yard run by Barber...second and 6). Then, the analyst explains the why and how. Baseball to me is the most challenging; the ball is only in play for between eight and 12 minutes during a typical nine-inning game. For more than two decades, I worked between 15 and 20 baseball games per season for FOX (or various FOX cable networks). I would prepare like I would for an NFL game, though it didn't take as many hours. The big difference between the two sports: football teams play only once a week, while the baseball teams play five or six games during the week leading up to my game. I give a lot of credit to baseball team broadcasters who call up to 162 games per season. That's a lot of time to fill!

I also inform the students about the challenges in preparing for sports that I'm not as comfortable with like soccer, lacrosse, track and field, boxing, and beach and indoor volleyball. The only sport that I worked—only once— that I really didn't fully grasp was college wrestling. I once called the ACC Championship for Home Team Sports in Chapel Hill, North Carolina. Despite hours upon hours of studying (including speaking on the phone with Olympic gold medalist Jeff Blatnick), I felt somewhat helpless during the telecast. Fortunately, I had a terrific color analyst (a former college wrestler) who carried me on his back that night.

Hockey is the only sport I go back and forth between local and national broadcasts. Almost all of the football and baseball broadcasts I have worked have been on television (with only a few exceptions). I am often asked what teams I "root" for in the various sports. Although I cheered for both New York football and baseball teams as a youngster, as a professional broadcaster I am neutral. I always root for a close game, as well as a flawless broadcast. I also root for people; I have close friends amongst the front office, coaching, and public relations staffs in all four pro sports. But I never let those personal relationships impact my calls.

When calling Rangers or Knicks games for MSG (either on TV or radio), my analysts and I realize that most of our viewers/listeners are fans of the team. Those of us on the crew certainly want the Rangers and Knicks to have great success, but we don't outwardly root on the air. Their success benefits our broadcasts and ratings, the interest in the teams, etc. And the deeper they go in the postseason, the more games we work. Some of my greatest memories from calling Rangers games since 1995 have been their deep playoff runs. We spend hours preparing for the opposing teams as well and give credit when they do something worthy of praise.

When I call a Rangers game on national television, I often remind myself that I have to sound just as excited when the opposing team scores. Some fans on the other side will probably never hear it that way because they associate me with the Rangers. But objective viewers will realize that I am calling the game straight down the middle. Similarly, Mike Emrick called multiple Stanley Cup Final series involving the New Jersey Devils while he also worked the team's games on local cable. Buck was the voice of the St. Louis Cardinals for many years and called their playoff and World Series games on FOX.

I try not to worry about comments on social media during or following broadcasts, but many make their way back to me from family members and friends. During national broadcasts—no matter the sport—some fans think I am a jinx to their team. It's funny. Fans never give announcers credit when their team wins; it's only blame after losses. I am never reluctant to mention a "no-hitter" or "shutout" during the course of broadcast, though some fans think that's a jinx, too. If someone tunes in mid-game and I don't reference that the pitcher has not allowed a hit, I am not doing my job; that viewer or listener may change the channel. Certain fans may find this hard to believe, but an announcer's words have *zero* effect on what takes place on the ice, field, or court. The likes of Michaels, Buck, and Bob Costas have told stories about receiving hundreds of letters filled with criticism from *both* fanbases following a World Series.

When I first work with a particular analyst, researching their career is a big part of it. When paired with Walt "Clyde" Frazier, a percentage of our viewers were avid fans of his during the Knicks' championship runs in 1970 and 1973. So we incorporate some of those stories into the broadcasts. The play-by-play man has many roles. The first is obvious: calling the play. We also weave in anecdotes, statistics, historical information, rules explanations, and stories from meetings with players and coaches, while also serving as a traffic cop. Helping to set up my analyst is a huge part of my job. I have been fortunate in that I have gotten along with—and clicked with—just about all of the partners I have worked with. You develop a rhythm and flow with your partners on a consistent basis and learn each other's cadence and tendencies from years of working together.

A radio or television broadcast is a team effort. The listener or viewer only hears the announcers, but there are countless others involved in each and every broadcast. I emphasize that there are so many other positions essential to getting a sporting event on the air. I suggest that students get as much experience as possible—even if not in their exact area of interest. During a typical NFL regular-season game on FOX, there are approximately 75 people working on the crew aside from the announcers, including producer, director, associate director, graphics, camera folks, replay operators, statisticians, spotters, etc. There are wonderful opportunities for students at many colleges to get hands-on experience both on-air and behind the scenes with the ACC Network, Big Ten Network, etc., as well as in athletic departments, school radio, and school television stations.

Pronouncing names correctly is as important as anything else I do during a broadcast. Every player has family and friends watching their games; mispronouncing a name should never happen. Most teams include a written pronunciation guide within their media guide and/or press releases. If I'm still not sure, I check with either a team broadcaster, public relations official, or—if possible—the player. When defenseman Boris Mironov was traded to the Rangers in 2003, he insisted that his name was pronounced MEER-uh-noff despite the fact that his brother Dmitri, who had spent nine seasons in the NHL, went by meer-ON-off. I recall Pavel Bure laughing in the locker room after practice one day when asked about his fellow countrymen from the same parents pronouncing their last name differently than one another. During a production meeting for a Giants game, we chatted with offensive lineman Rich Seubert. I had heard his name pronounced two different ways by broadcasters through the years: SOY-bert and SIGH-bert. I asked him which was correct;

he said that he didn't care. I then inquired how his mother pronounced their surname, and he said SOY-bert. So, that's what we went with.

During John Tavares' nine seasons with the Islanders, the team's broadcasters always pronounced his last name as "tuh-VAIR-ess." After he signed with his hometown Toronto Maple Leafs in 2018, Canadian broadcasters started saying "tuh-VAR-ess." Prior to an NBC telecast at Madison Square Garden, I wandered down to the locker room area and found the center working on his sticks with a blowtorch. I stopped and asked him, "When you introduce yourself to someone, what do you say?" He chuckled and said, "John tuh-VAIR-ess." I asked him to repeat it. Same thing. A few seasons later, the Maple Leafs distributed a video on social media, in which all of their players pronounced their names. Wouldn't you know it…now he says "tuh-VAR-ess"! A similar story involved Brad Marchand. I've always been told by Boston Bruins radio broadcasters Dave Goucher and Judd Sirott that when recording promos for their radio station, the player himself always said "mar-SHAND" with the last syllable rhyming with "hand." However, others in the Boston market refer to him as Brad "mar-SHOND."

But oftentimes what you *don't* say is actually more important than what you do say. I learned the art of laying out (shutting up) early in my career by watching various other broadcasters who mastered allowing the sights and sounds to tell the story after a big call. Vin Scully and Buck were perfect examples of that. Following my call of the Jose Bautista home run in the 2015 American League Division Series—"Bautista with a drive…deep left field… no doubt about it!"—I remained quiet for 12 seconds before my partner Harold Reynolds stepped in to describe the replays.

In Game Seven of the first round of the 2022 Stanley Cup playoffs, Artemi Panarin scored the overtime goal to send the Rangers into a second-round matchup with the Carolina Hurricanes (after trailing 3–1 in the series). I was calling the game on TNT from the Chase Bridge at Madison Square Garden. The crowd was as loud as I had ever heard at the World's Most Famous Arena after Panarin's shot got through the pads of goaltender Tristan Jarry. I was brief: "Panarin...right wing circle...he shoots...he scores!" Then I let the ambience of the game take over.

In his May 19, 2022, column for the *New York Post*, Phil Mushnick praised my approach. "Albert's application of modesty, situation awareness, and common sense to have said nothing, allowing live TV to fulfill its promise and purpose as a visual medium...he allowed the cameras and crowd microphones to take over. Over the next one minute and 58 seconds, he said nothing. He allowed the delirious and the disappointed to speak for themselves. No attempt by Albert to put his signature to the scene. No attempt to scream over the natural sights and sounds. No attempt to intrude. He didn't say a word. Great call."

If Panarin had scored the goal on the road, it would have been a much different story. The arena would have been silent; there would not have been many crowd shots for the director to show aside from dejected fans. I would have spoken much sooner. You have to let the situation and elements dictate what comes out of your mouth—or doesn't. If I was on the radio, that call would have had required wall-to-wall description.

Many of my colleagues make light of the fact that I don't curse...period. Well, there's a reason. If I avoid cursing in everyday life, then I won't do it during a broadcast. Good habits lead to even better habits. My parents didn't curse while I was growing up, so my father probably had a similar philosophy. I rarely drink alcohol; I have never liked the taste. It makes me the perfect designated driver. I also hate coffee, which some people find hard to fathom given my schedule of frequent early-morning flights followed by games at night. I do love Diet Coke however! I only drink tea when I have a sore throat.

Prior to a Rangers broadcast in Montreal (the season finale in April 2003), I enjoyed two of the legendary hot dogs in the press room. The *chien chauds* have been devoured by media, coaches, executives, players, and scouts at Canadiens home games for decades. There is something special about the way they're grilled. For some reason, on this particular night, they did not agree with me. With about seven minutes left in the game, my stomach started churning. Fortunately, I was able to remain in the booth until the final buzzer. Ever since that night, I have adjusted my pregame eating habits before broadcasts…but still enjoy a *chien chaud* whenever I'm in Montreal!

Following the Montreal incident, lunch is usually my biggest meal of the day when scheduled to work a game at night. Then, I usually eat either a light snack before the game or during halftime/intermissions. At most arenas and stadiums, there is usually a meal offered to the working press prior to the game. The Tampa Bay Buccaneers always have a terrific spread in their press box consisting of deli sandwiches, as well as carving stations. The Dallas Cowboys have been known to provide a sushi platter at halftime to the network broadcasters. In addition to the pregame meal in the press room at ice level, the Chicago Blackhawks offer a hot, catered meal in their press box after the second period. At baseball games I have sampled Dodger Dogs, Fenway Franks, and items from Shake Shack at Citi Field. You can usually count on me enjoying a soft pretzel between periods of hockey games at Madison Square Garden and in Philadelphia.

I am a creature of habit when it comes to meals on non-work days. I will only eat my steak well done. I can't stand the taste or smell of eggs, tomatoes, and mushrooms. I'm usually up for a Caesar salad and turkey club (hold the tomato). Pizza, sushi, or a well-done cheeseburger are among my staples.

There are certain restaurants on my personal list of favorites in various cities around the country. I was introduced to Moby Dick House of Kebab, a Persian/Mediterranean chain in the Washington, D.C., area, in the early 1990s by my friend, David Steinberg (now the CEO of Zeta Global). My order is always the same: the Combo II platter, which is one Koobideh beef kebab and one grilled chicken kebab served over rice. I have enjoyed lunch at various Moby Dick locations during my more than a hundred excursions to our nation's capital since I moved back to New York in 1995. Every bite still tastes just as good as during my first ever trip.

Aside from my home arena, Madison Square Garden, I have always enjoyed calling games at historic venues such as Yankee Stadium, Fenway Park, Wrigley Field, Lambeau Field, Soldier Field, and Los Angeles Memorial Coliseum. During my early years in the NHL, I was fortunate to call one game at Boston

Garden and a few at the Montreal Forum and Maple Leaf Gardens. I never worked a game at Chicago Stadium but attended one Chicago Blackhawks and several Chicago Bulls games there. I judge most arenas and stadiums by the location of the broadcast booth and its proximity to the field/ice/court. The booth at Sun Devil Stadium in Tempe, Arizona, where I called many Arizona Cardinals games between 1994 and 2005 (prior to their move to Glendale), was probably the highest I've ever called a game from. The players looked like ants scurrying around the field. We were pretty high up at the "Big Sombrero," the former home of the Buccaneers, and the Liberty Bowl in Memphis, where I called a Giants–Tennessee Oilers game in 1997.

Most network television booths in the current NFL stadiums are in prime locations—at or near the 50-yard line at varying heights. The booth at Allegiant Stadium in Las Vegas (home of the Raiders) might be bigger than most Manhattan apartments. In baseball the booths at PNC Park in Pittsburgh and Nationals Park in Washington, D.C., are way up near the top of the respective ballparks, though the Nats set us up much lower—on suite level—during the 2016 National League Division Series. These days most hockey booths are in the upper press box. My favorites are the overhang broadcast facilities in Montreal and the Chase Bridge at MSG; those allow for the best views of the ice. The new buildings in Detroit and Seattle have similar setups to Montreal, though at a bit of a different angle. In some hockey arenas, there is a lower booth made available to the network broadcast crew, which I always appreciate. The upper press box/broadcast booths at Nassau Coliseum, the former longtime home of the Islanders, was lower than most others due to the fact that it was a smaller building. I always enjoyed the atmosphere there. For decades all NBA broadcasters (television and radio) were located at a court-side table. Most teams then realized they could enhance their revenues by selling tickets in those locations, and radio broadcasters became the first victims and moved to higher areas. Television announcers still call the games from the first row at approximately half of the NBA arenas. Others have moved to the second row or in some cases about 20 rows off the floor. I have always loved calling basketball games from court-side seats because the game unfolds right in front of you, you can feel the intensity, and you occasionally receive personal explanations from the officials. At Madison Square Garden, the television broadcast location is on the opposite side of the court from the team benches, so we are never obstructed by coaches.

Sitting court-side, however, can be a disadvantage at times. Coaches often roam the sidelines and could block an announcer's view of half the court. The first time I experienced this was when I filled in on a Washington Bullets radio broadcast in 1994 for Charlie Slowes, who missed the game for the birth of his son. Bullets head coach Wes Unseld—the 1969 NBA Most Valuable Player and a 6'7", 250-pound man—stood directly in front of me for most of the game. The next year, Slowes showed me a Calbert Cheaney basketball card. Ironically, my face was clearly in the background while wearing the radio headset. Slowes joked that he was jealous that the photo was taken during the *one* game he missed.

Wayne Gretzky and Brett Favre are two of my favorite interview subjects. They are both such down-to-earth, regular people. If you were in a room alone with them, you would never get the feeling they are among the best in their fields historically by the way they act. I would include Peyton and Eli Manning in their category as well. Peyton seemed to have a photographic memory. In production meetings he would bring up a play from the past and would recall the opponent, at what point in the game it took place, and the result of the play. Los Angeles Rams head coach Sean McVay has the same ability to recall specific plays in precise detail.

The last 55 years have been a blast. From spending the first 10 weeks of my life in a hospital incubator following my premature birth…to a global pandemic…and thousands of sporting events in between, I am very fortunate to say I would not have done much differently and am so grateful to have had all of my experiences—both in and out of arenas, stadiums, and ballparks. The stories are endless. Hopefully, I gave you an inside look into the hectic (but incredible) life of a sportscaster. I have lived a charmed life with a front-row seat to sports history. And I look forward to writing a sequel after another couple of decades in the broadcast booth.

# Appendix I: My Charts

Green Bay Packers 42, Seattle Seahawks 20—NFC
Divisional Playoffs, January 12, 2008

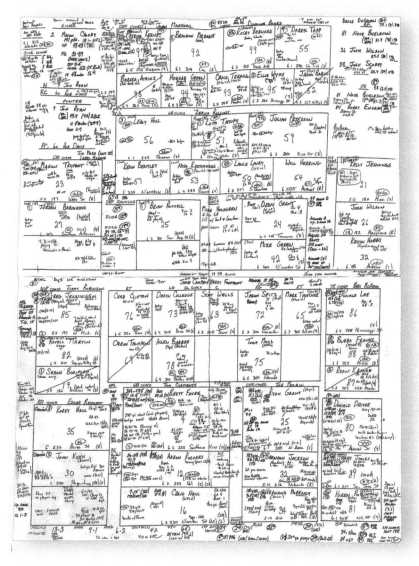

## Toronto Blue Jays 6, Texas Rangers 3—Game Five, American League Division Series, October 14, 2015

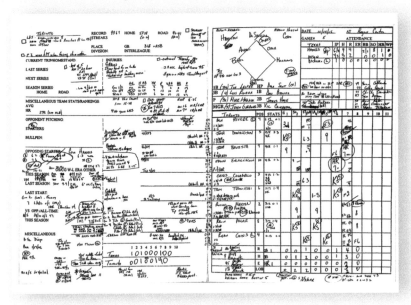

## Tampa Bay Lightning 5, Montreal Canadiens 1— Game One, Stanley Cup Final, June 28, 2021

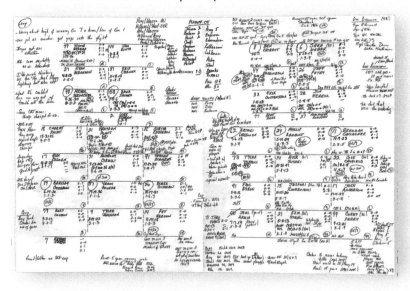

# New York Knicks 128, New Orleans Pelicans 106— February 25, 2023

NEW YORK KNICKS

Madison Square Garden (19,763)

Tom Thibodeau

| # | Player | Ht/Wt | College | |
|---|--------|-------|---------|---|
| 30 | Julius Randle | 6'8", 250 | Kentucky | 9th |
| 9 | RJ Barrett | 6'6", 214 | Duke | 4th |
| 23 | Mitchell Robinson | 7'0", 240 | Western Kentucky | 5th |
| 6 | Quentin Grimes | 6'4", 210 | Houston | 2nd |
| 11 | Jalen Brunson | 6'1", 190 | Villanova | 5th |
| 1 | Obi Toppin | 6'9", 220 | Dayton | 3rd |
| 3 | Josh Hart | 6'5, 215 | Villanova | 6th |
| 5 | Immanuel Quickley | 6'3", 190 | Kentucky | 3rd |
| 45 | Jericho Sims | 6'9", 250 | Texas | 2nd |
| 55 | Isaiah Hartenstein | 7'0", 250 | | 5th |
| 2 | Miles McBride | 6'2", 195 | West Virginia | 2nd |
| 13 | Evan Fournier | 6'6", 205 | | 11th |
| 4 | Derrick Rose | 6'3", 200 | Memphis | 15th |

253

# Appendix II: My Analysts

## Football

Troy Aikman, Barry Alvarez, Brian Baldinger, Rondé Barber, Tiki Barber, Anthony Becht, Todd Blackledge, Tony Boselli, Terry Bradshaw, Aaron Brooks, Erik Coleman, Charles Davis, Terrell Davis, Dan Fouts, Tim Green, Ron Jaworski, Jimmy Johnson, Daryl Johnston, Sean Jones, James Lofton, Howie Long, John Lynch, Marty Lyons, Bill Maas, Mike Mayock, Matt Millen, Anthony Muñoz, Joe Namath, Greg Olsen, Ron Pitts, Mike Quick, John Riggins, Matt Robinson, Tim Ryan, Tony Siragusa, Michael Strahan, Joe Theismann, Gino Toretta, Jonathan Vilma, Rick "Doc" Walker, Kellen Winslow Sr.

## Hockey

Colby Armstrong, Martin Biron, Blake Bolden, Brian Boucher, Andy Brickley, Lisa Brown-Miller, Anson Carter, Colby Cohen, Kendall Coyne-Schofield, Terry Crisp, Ken Daneyko, John Davidson, Kevin Dineen, Darren Eliot, Brian Engblom, Mike Farrell, Patrick Flatley, Jim Fox, Rod Gilbert, Gary Green, Wayne Gretzky, Brian Hayward, Shane Hnidy, Billy Jaffe, Keith Jones, Monique Lamoureux-Morando, Craig Laughlin, Josh Lewin, Dave Maloney, Pierre McGuire, Peter McNab, Sal Messina, Joe Micheletti, Mike Milbury, A.J. Mleczko, Dominic Moore, Brian Mullen, Bobby Nystrom, Eddie Olczyk, Darren Pang, Denis Potvin, Rob Ray, Daryl Reaugh, Mickey Redmond, Jeremy Roenick, Sherry Ross, Mike Rupp, Bryce Salvador, Patrick Sharp, Craig Simpson, Shawn Simpson, Neil Smith, Dave Starman, Pete Stemkowski, Tim Taylor, Gene Ubriaco, Ellen Weinberg-Hughes

## Basketball

John Andariese, Jack Armstrong, Rolando Blackman, George Blaney, Brendan Brown, Doris Burke, John Celestand, Phil Chenier, Glenn Consor, Matt Doherty, Patrick Ewing, Walt "Clyde" Frazier, Terry Gannon, Tate George, Kevin Grevey, Alan Hahn, Jim Jackson, Mark Jackson, Bernard King, Bernadette McGlade, Mary Murphy, Tom Nissalke, Meghan Pattyson, Dom Perno, Ron Perry, Mark Plansky, Mike Quick, Bill Raftery, Mike Rice, Wally Szczerbiak, Dickey Simpkins, Dave Sims, Jim Spanarkel, Earl Strom, Dick Tarrant, Kelly Tripucka, Bucky Waters, Bob Wenzel, Gary Williams

## Baseball

Rod Allen, Larry Andersen, Bert Blyleven, Bob Brenly, Ken Brett, Sean Casey, Rick Cerone, Gary Cohen, Ed Coleman, David Cone, Ron Darling, Cliff Floyd, Ray Fosse, George Frazier, Joe Girardi, Mark Grace, Tom Grieve, Mark Gubicza, Keith Hernandez, Al Hrabosky, Rex Hudler, Tommy Hutton, Darrin Jackson, Jay Johnstone, Jim Kaat, Eric Karros, Kevin Kennedy, Mike Krukow, Duane Kuiper, Mark Langston, John Lowenstein, Fred Lynn, Steve Lyons, Joe Magrane, Rick Manning, Leo Mazzone, Tim McCarver, Jessica Mendoza, Kevin Millar, Paul Molitor, Jose Mota, Bobby Murcer, C.J. Nitkowski, Steve Palermo, Jim Palmer, A.J. Pierzynski, Lou Piniella, Jerry Remy, Harold Reynolds, Bill Ripken, F.P. Santangelo, John Smoltz, Jeff Torborg, Tom Verducci, Suzyn Waldman, Bob Walk, Chris Welsh, Mitch Williams, Dontrelle Willis

## Boxing

Kathy Burke, Steve Cunningham, Charley Eckman, Corey Erdmann, Steve Farhood, B.J. Flores, Robert Garcia, Joe Goossen, Daniel Jacobs, "Sugar" Ray Leonard, Lennox Lewis, Mark Kriegel, Ray "Boom Boom" Mancini, Mike Marchionte, James "Buddy" McGirt, Tony Paige, Shawn Porter, Kenny Rice, Deontay Wilder

## Horse Racing
Caton Bredar, Ron Ellis, Suzy Kolber, Jay Privman

## Lacrosse
Willie Scroggs

## Soccer
George Kennedy, Tony Meola

## Track And Field
Ato Bolden, Trey Hardee, Todd Harris, Tim Hutchings, Lewis Johnson, Craig Masback, Adam Nelson, Sanya-Richards Ross

## Volleyball
Amy Gant

# SIDELINE REPORTERS, GUEST HOSTS, ETC.
## FOOTBALL
Marv Albert, Dean Blandino, Byron Boston, James Brown, Sherree Burruss, Charley Casserly, Jimmy Cavallo, Walt Coleman, Lindsay Czarniak, Toi Cook, Boomer Esiason, Irving Fryar, Jay Glazer, Jen Hale, Jack Ham, Ken Harvey, Lou Holder, D.J. Johnson, Dan Jiggetts, Curt Menefee, Hugh Millen, Marisa Miller, Chris Myers, Laura Okmin, Pam Oliver, Megan Olivi, Logan Paulsen, Mike Pereira, Kristina Pink, Clinton Portis, Antwan Randle-El, Beasley Reece, Carl Reuter, Sid Rosenberg, Peter Schrager, Brad Sham, Mike Silver, Holly Sonders, Dave Spadaro, Shannon Spake, Pat Summerall, Charissa Thompson, Amy van Dyken, Sara Walsh, Jeanne Zelasko

## HOCKEY

Marv Albert, Glenn Anderson, Stephanie Auger, Barry Beck, Jennifer Botterill, Rob Carlin, Bill Clement, Tarik El-Bashir, Mike Emrick, Ray Ferraro, Steve Gelbs, John Giannone, Michelle Gingras, Steve Goldstein, Dan Graca, Ron Greschner, Bob Harwood, Shannon Hogan, Nabil Karim, Don Koharski, Al Koken, Nick Kypreos, Don LaGreca, Jocelyne Lamoureux-Davidson, Jim Lampley, Barry Landers, Aly Lozoff, Liam McHugh, Brad Meier, Meghan Mikkelson, Pat O'Keefe, C.J. Papa, Bill Patrick, Jean Potvin, Leila Rahimi, Jackie Redmond, Jeff Rimer, Sam Rosen, Angela Ruggiero, Gary Stein, Kevin Stevens, Kathryn Tappen, Erica Wachter

## BASKETBALL

Rachel Bonetta, Tina Cervasio, Kevin Frazier, Gene Golda, Rebecca Haarlow, Batt Johnson, Michael Kay, Jill Martin, Bill Pidto, Michael Rapaport, Al Trautwig

## BASEBALL

Bret Boone, Thom Brennaman, Joe Buck, Tom Davis, Mike Flanagan, Al Leiter, Curt Menefee, J.P. Morosi, Chris Rose, Ken Rosenthal

## BOXING

Kate Abdo, Heidi Androl, Dave Briggs, Jenn Brown, Felix DeJesus

# Appendix III: My Favorites

## Favorite Restaurants

A La Familia (Pittsburgh)

Bada Bing (Buffalo)

Bern's (Tampa)

BOA Steakhouse (Los Angeles)

Cheesecake Factory

Del Frisco's

Dimora (Norwood, New Jersey)

Donatello's (Tampa)

Gibson's (Chicago)

Ike's (Minneapolis)

Martin's BBQ (Nashville)

Metropolitan Grille (Seattle)

Moby Dick House of Kebab (Washington, D.C.)

Nobu

Prime 112 (South Beach, Florida)

River Palm (Edgewater, New Jersey)

Rudy's (Closter, New Jersey)

Sabatino's (Baltimore)

St. Elmo's (Indianapolis)

The St. Paul Grill (St. Paul, Minnesota)

State Street Brats (Madison, Wisconsin)

## Favorite Stadiums

AT&T Stadium (Arlington, Texas)

Bell Centre (Montreal, Canada)

Fenway Park (Boston)

Lambeau Field (Green Bay, Wisconsin)

Madison Square Garden (New York)

T-Mobile Arena (Las Vegas)

U.S. Bank Stadium (Minneapolis)

Wembley Stadium (London, England)

Wrigley Field (Chicago)

Yankee Stadium (Bronx, New York)

# Appendix IV:
# NHL Game Sevens Called

1994 Canucks 2 at Rangers 3—NHL Radio (SCF)

2009 Rangers 1 at Capitals 2—radio

2012 Senators 1 at Rangers 2—radio

2012 Capitals 1 at Rangers 2—radio

2013 Rangers 5 at Capitals 0—radio

2014 Flyers 1 at Rangers 2—radio

2014 Rangers 2 at Penguins 1—radio

2014 Kings 5 at Blackhawks 4 (OT)—NBCSN

2015 Capitals 1 at Rangers 2 (OT)—radio

2015 Lightning 2 at Rangers 0—radio

2018 Jets 5 at Predators 1—NBCSN

2019 Maple Leafs 1 at Bruins 5—NHL Radio

2019 Hurricanes 4 at Capitals 3 (2 OT)—NBCSN

2019 Stars 1 at Blues 2 (2 OT)—NBCSN

2019 Blues 4 at Bruins 1—NHL Radio (SCF)

2020 Stars 5, Avalanche 4 (OT)—NBCSN

Golden Knights 3, Canucks 0—NBCSN

(Same day in Edmonton bubble)

2021 Islanders 0 at Lightning 1—NBCSN

2022 Lightning 2 at Maple Leafs 1—TNT

2022 Penguins 3 at Rangers 4 (OT)—TNT

# Acknowledgments

**W**riting this autobiography has been a labor of love. I never thought I would have the time but then received the impetus from my family during the pandemic when I started writing several chapters. I took advantage of the time during cross-country plane trips once I started traveling again, then made the final push during the summer of 2022. I can't thank Barbara, Amanda, and Sydney enough for their input. They spent countless hours reading, writing, and editing. This book would not have been possible without their love and support!

Thank you to my book agent, Andrew Blauner (Blauner Books), my agent Lou Oppenheim, and the good folks at Triumph Books (shoutout to editor Jeff Fedotin) for collaborating on this project. And to Michael Rappaport of the New York Rangers communications department and public relations whiz Sammy Steinlight for their assistance along the way.

There are so many people who were instrumental in my hiring and have continued to support me over the past three-plus decades:

*Port Washington News*—Amy Pett

Cox Cable—Roy Menton

Staten Island Stallions—Evan Pickman

NHL—John Halligan, Stu Hackel

New York Islanders—Arthur Adler

WEVD Radio—Joel Blumberg, Tom Bird

WFAN Radio—Joel Hollander, Mark Chernoff, Eric Spitz, Howie Rose

Baltimore Skipjacks—Joyce and Tom Ebright, Alan Rakvin, Jim Riggs

WTOP Radio—Pat Anastasi

Home Team Sports—Jody Shapiro, Bill Brown, Bill Bell

Washington Capitals—Dick Patrick, Lew Strudler, David Poile

FOX Sports—David Hill, Ed Goren, George Krieger, Larry Jones, Bill Brown, Eric Shanks, Doug Sellars, John Entz, Jacob Ullman, Brad Zager, Mark Silverman

NHL Radio/Westwood One—Gregg Baldinger, Howard Deneroff

MSG Networks—Joe Cohen, Mike McCarthy, Marty Brooks, Pete Silverman, Leon Schweir, Lydia Murphy-Stephans, Laurie Orlando, Mike Bair, Dan Ronayne, Andrea Greenberg, Jeff Filippi, Kevin Meininger

Madison Square Garden—James Dolan, Dave Checketts, Bob Gutkowski

New York Rangers—Neil Smith, Glen Sather, Jeff Gorton, John Davidson, Chris Drury

New York Knicks—Donnie Walsh, Glen Grunwald, Steve Mills, Phil Jackson, Scott Perry, Leon Rose

ESPN+—Mike Moore

FOX Sports Net/FX—Bill Borson, Larry Meyers

NBC (Olympics/NHL)—Dick Ebersol, Mark Lazarus, Sam Flood, Jim Bell, Molly Solomon, Becky Chatman, Elyse Noonan, John McGuinness

OLN/Versus—Mike Baker

Washington Commanders—Daniel Snyder, Larry Michael, Julie Donaldson

DirecTV—Chris Long

Warner Media/TNT—Jeff Zucker, Lenny Daniels, Craig Barry, Scooter Vertino, Tara August, Michele Zarzaca, John O'Connor, Luis Silberwasser, Nate Smeltz

There are numerous others who have helped along the way. Alan Sanders and Lou Oppenheim have been my only agents during this entire journey. Thanks to both for their tremendous work, as well as the late Arthur Kaminsky, Michael Glantz, and Steve Rosner (also my neighbor and frequent tennis opponent).

Thank you to all of the members of the production and technical crews through the years; you are all the lifeblood of the broadcasts. A special salute to Tony Siragusa's sideline producer, the late Lou Tribuiani!

Along with all of the individuals mentioned throughout this book, big shoutouts to so many others whom I've been lucky enough to either work with or cross paths with: Joseph Abboud, Scott Ahrens, Mark Askin, Pete Abitante, Glenn Adamo, John Arnone, Betsy Aronin, Steve Baldwin, Joe Band, Matt Banovic, Jeanie Baumgartner, Steve Becker, Mike Behan, Peter Beilin, Dan Bell, Bruce Bennett, Michael A. Berger, Jim Bernard, Win Bernfeld, Bryan Biederman, Jonathan Biles, Gary Bettman, Darren Blake, Pat Boller, Zack Bolno, Chris Botta, Mike Bovino, Judy Boyd, Derek Boyko, Joe Browne, Frank Buonomo, Eric Burak, Rich Burg, Kathy Burke, Mike Burks, Eddie Caggianelli, Neil Canell, Rick Carpiniello, Alex Case, Andy Cavanaugh, Rick Cerrone, Matt Celli, Myles Chefetz, John Cirillo, Rich Claffey, Jay Clark, Blair Cofield, Colby Cohen, Mark Cole, Scott Cooper, Mickey Corcoran, Lou Corletto, Aaron Cummins, Gord Cutler, Dennis D'Agostino, Maureen Daley, Mark Dalton, Bill Daly, Skylar Darel, Chris DeLauro, Janis Delson, Lou D'Ermilio, Chirag Devaskar, Ricky Diamond, Kenny Dichter, Anthony DiGiovanni, Jerry Dineen, Jackie DiPiazza, Jackie Dixon, Roland Dratch, Mike Eaby, Damian Echevarrieta, Mike Eldridge, Megan Englehart, Dr. Joe Esposito, Nate Ewell, Patti Fallick, Cayden Feifer, Brian Fergensen, Wayne Fidelman, Zac Fields, Brian Finkelstein, Dave Fischer, Joel Fisher, Mike Folga, Marc Forest, Daren Foster, Anthony Fucilli, Nick Gagliano, Larry Gaines, Eric Gelfand, Shawn Gerchicoff, Larry Getlan, Anthony Goenaga, Dr. Ron Goldenberg, Ivan Gottesfeld, Bruce Gould, Reg Grant, Dr. Ed Greaney, Bobby Green, Harvey Greene, Jerry Grossman, Ernie Grunfeld, Bobby Hacker, Dave Hagen, Noah Hanstedt, Jordan Harrison, Artie Hecht, Pat Hanlon, Lindsay Hayes, Ricky Henne, Jack Hicks, Roger Hinds, Dr. Bryan Ho, Major Howe, Tom Huet, Cathie Hunt, Rob Hyland, Robby Incmikoski, Gary Jeffries, "Beets" Johnson, Jim Johnson, Dan Kagan, Larry Kahn, George Kalinsky, Jeff Kamis, Rick Kamps, Dan Kaufman, Harold Kaufman, Howard Katz, Marcy Kempner, Rabbi David-Seth Kirshner, Kari

Kloster, Rob Koch, Colleen Kolibas, John Kollmansperger, Greg Kwizak, Bob Lalwani, Lou Lamoriello, Matt Langer, Derek Lapinski, Jon Ledecky, Todd Levy, "Woody" Leydig, Bruce Lifrieri, Matt Lipp, Matt Loughran, Michael Maisel, Chris Majkowski, Joel Mandelbaum, Paul Marmaro, Acacio Marques, Leeanne Marks, Kevin Marotta, Lynn Marschke, Dave Martella, Mike Martinez, Jamie Mathews, Dick Maxwell, Steve Mayer, Bernadette McDonald, Kevin McDonald, Brendan McIntyre, Tom Meberg, Millie Melendez, Jeff Mitchell, Frank Moretti, Jeff Morin, Bill Murillo, Bruce Murray, David Newman, Gary Nicholas, Drew Nieporent, Tracy Nieporent, Ryan Nissan, Cody Novak, Chris Ober, Fran O'Connell, Jim Oettinger, Scott O'Neil, Marty Orner, Tony Osso, Dave Paladino, Jeff Pearl, Mark Piazza, Joe Pinto, Allyne Price, Ed Quinlan, Jim Ramsay, Bill Richards, Mitch Riggin, Betsy Riley, Fred Robinson, Mike Roig, Cindy Ronzoni, John Rosasco, Lon Rosen, Dr. Ritchard Rosen, Andy Rosenberg, Dr. Alan Ross, Mitch Rubenstein, Mark Ruberg, Steve Russ, Dan Sabreen, Doug Safchik, Dr. Don Salomon, Ray Santiago, Kevin Saylors, Dan Schoenberg, Andrew Schwartz, Gregg Schwartz, Jon Schwartz, Jeff Schwartzenberg, Jennifer Schwartzenberg, Greg Scoppettone, Ben Segelbaum, Sarah Servetnick, Seth Shaifer, John Shannon, Doug Shearer, Jack Simmons, Ryan Sirgiovanni, Robert Slawsby, Karlie Smith, Becky Solomon, Keith Soutar, Jody Sowa, Gary Spitalnik, Mike Steavpack, Jerry Steinberg, Gary Steinman, David Stern, Rob Stern, James Stuart, Jonathan Supranowitz, Brooks Thomas, Dino Ticinelli, Ray Tipton, Chuck Torres, Jim Townsend, Anthony Triano, Dominic Tringali, George Veras, Jason Vogel, Paul Wagner, Yvonne Wagoner, John Warner, Barry Watkins, Jeremy Watkins, Jerry Weinstein, Brian Wendth, Joe Wheeler, Dan Weine, Joe Williams, Geordie Wimmer, Jacob Wisniewski, Vince Wladika, Rich Wolff, Stan Wong, Gilbert Zepeda, Mark Zguro, Jim Zrake

# About the Author

Kenny Albert, a three-time National Sports Emmy Award finalist, is the only play-by-play broadcaster currently calling all four major sports in North America. He is the lead play-by-play voice of the *NHL on TNT.* The 2023 season marks Albert's 30th year broadcasting NFL games on FOX (including five NFC divisional playoff games); he has worked Major League Baseball games on various FOX networks for the past 27 years. Albert is entering his 28th season as the radio voice of the New York Rangers and also calls New York Knicks games on MSG Networks. He has called men's and women's ice hockey at the last six Winter Olympics for NBC, as well as track and field, volleyball, and baseball at the 2016 and 2020 Summer Games. Albert has called 10 Stanley Cup Final series (two on TV, eight on radio) in addition to television calls of postseason baseball and basketball, the Sugar Bowl, Orange Bowl, Cotton Bowl, NFL Pro Bowl, the international feed of Super Bowl XLVI, and the World Baseball Classic. He has also been behind the mic for Premier Boxing Champions on both NBC and FOX. Albert began his professional career as the radio voice of the American Hockey League's Baltimore Skipjacks followed by three seasons calling Washington Capitals games on Home Team Sports. He graduated from New York University in 1990 with a degree in journalism. Albert resides in northern New Jersey with his wife, Barbara, and daughters, Amanda and Sydney.